MOTOCROSS
OFF-ROAD MOTORCYCLE
PERFORMANCE
HANDBOOK

ERIC GORR

MBI Publishing Company

First published in 1996 by MBI Publishing Company, PO Box 1, 729 Prospect Avenue, Osceola, WI 54020-0001 USA.

MBI Publishing Company books are also available at discounts in bulk quantity for industrial or sales-promotional use. For details write to Special Sales Manager at Motorbooks International Wholesalers & Distributors, 729 Prospect Avenue, PO Box 1, Osceola, WI 54020-0001 USA.

Library of Congress Cataloging-in-Publication Data

Gorr, Eric
   Off-road motorcycle performance handbook / Eric Gorr.
      p. cm.
   Includes index.
   ISBN 0-7603-0244-8
   (pbk. : alk. paper)
   1. Trail bikes—Maintenance and repair. 2. Trial bikes—
Performance. I. Title.
   TL441.G67 1996   96-8850
   629.227'5—dc20

On the front cover: Team Kawasaki mechanics work on Damon Huffman's factory KX125. *Joe Bonnello*

On the back cover: Mechanic Skip Norfolk has tuned for some of the best riders of the past two decades, including four-time Supercross champ Jeremy McGrath. Riders like McGrath, Ricky Johnson, and Jeff Stanton could win on any brand, but the dominance displayed by Team Honda can come only under the tutelage of an ace mechanic and tuner like Norfolk. *Joe Bonnello*

Printed in the United States of America

CONTENTS

ACKNOWLEDGMENTS

Many people from companies involved in the motorcycle industry helped me with the preparation of this book. A book as comprehensive as this one takes years to develop, especially when you consider that it covers 170 models of Japanese dirt bikes spanning an 11-year period. Here are some of the people who gave me the benefit of their experience so I could pass it on to you.

For the first two chapters of this book, Dave Antolak of TUF Racing gave me the use of his motorcycle shop, racing team, and mail-order business. That was very helpful for getting photos of used bikes and compiling information on the costs of repairs and on mail-order services. Dave also supplied the Factory Concept stickers used to demonstrate how to fit radiator and tank graphics in chapter two.

Scott Swinehart of Race Tools provided me with samples of special tools to use for sections on tools, handlebar fitting, and suspension rebuilding. Scott's knowledge of Bridgestone tires is also featured in chapter five.

Chapter three features advice from several people. George Quay of Pro Action provided spring charts, definitions of terms, and the benefit of half a lifetime worth of suspension repair and tuning knowledge. Rick Johnson of Too Tech Racing contributed an excellent section on suspension forces. Jeremy Wilke of MX Tech provided a sample of his shock-revalving specs for a Yamaha YZ250 used in combination with a DeVol link. Ted DeVol from DeVol Racing gave me helpful insight into the design of aftermarket linkage systems. Mark Hammond of MH Racing in England made available his excellent workshop and expertise during the preparation of the shock-rebuilding section.

Chapter four features the expertise of many people. Jim Richards from JR Electronics supplied me with an Optak for the carb tuning section. Richard Rohrich of U.S. Robotics has given me technical support on personal computers since they were first put on the market in 1982. Rich also provided expertise on the subjects of flow-bench testing, fuel, and four-stroke engines. Tom Turner of TSR and Curt Leaverton of VP Engineering provided me with PC design programs for two- and four-stroke engines, plus hours of telephone support and engineering consultation. Steve Johnson of Wiseco Piston Company and Geoff Slater of Langcourt helped me with many different top-end engineering projects related to overboring and electroplating of cylinders. H. Sean Hilbert of Red Cedar Engineering contributed some material for the piston section and supplied me with one of his excellent crankshaft-rebuilding tools for the crankshaft section. Sean also provided the drawings of the two-stroke engine for the basic two-stroke tuning section.

For help on chapter nine I'd like to thank the following people: Scott Swinehart from Bridgestone, Frank Stacy of Dunlop, and Ludo Boniard of Braking. Thanks also to Jeff Fredette for demonstrating his techniques for studding tires for those brave enough to bear the winter cold.

Chapter ten features the expertise of the following people: Fred Bramblett and Scott Summers of Summers Honda Racing for help on the XRs, Pete Dennison of A-Loop Racing for his help on the RMX, and Jeff Fredette of Fredette Racing Products for help on the KDX models.

Thanks to Joe Bonnello for the excellent cover photo. Thanks to off-road racer Troy Bradshaw, who patiently taught me how to be an emphatic listener and an organized race mechanic while we traveled the country in search of cheesy trophies and small cash purses. Thanks to my editor Lee Klancher for putting up with my constant delays and cryptic e-mail files.

Thanks to all the magazine editors that have supported my work over the years, including Charlie Morey, Tom Webb, Ken Faught, Fran Kuhn, and Karel Kramer from *Dirt Rider*, Mike Greenough, Roddy Brooks and Sean Nicholson, and Peter Donaldson from *Dirt Bike Rider*, and Davey Coombs from *Racer*.

Also, thanks to you, the reader, for choosing this book.

Most of all I'd like to thank my dad, John, for bringing home mechanical junk for me to disassemble and learn from, and my mom for helping me prepare the manuscript for this book. Finally, thanks to Geoff Pierremont of Biker's Choice, the best motorcycle mechanic and teacher in the world.

American Donny Schmidt aboard his world championship-winning 1993 Chesterfield Yamaha YZ250. Schmidt won the 250cc world championship in 1992 and 1993. After returning to his home in Minnesota, Schmidt passed away unexpectedly due to illness in 1996.

INTRODUCTION

The image is still fresh in my mind after 30 years. The scene of dirt bikes racing around a scrambles course. The smell of the nitro fuel additives made my eyes burn tears of excitement. The deep bass sound of the open-megaphone four-stroke singles poked at my eardrums and pounded on my chest.

The riders were decorated with mud, some more than others. They all had something in common, a big smile! Maybe you have one of those smiles, too. I certainly do because I like to ride dirt bikes. They are such a unique machine, an extension of our physical abilities, letting us live out our dreams by becoming one with the bike.

The better the bike performs, the easier it is to meld with your bike. Whether that means faster lap times or just a better experience on the trail, that is what this book is all about. By raising your awareness of how to get in touch with your bike's performance, you can learn to fix little problems before they rear their ugly heads and become catastrophic. Learning how your bike works, and gaining a basic understanding of how to tune the engine and suspension to complement your riding demands, will enhance your dirt riding experience. Whether you are flying through the air, climbing an impossible hill, or just exploring the wilderness with your friends, dirt bikes are the most fun when they run right.

With each component of the motorcycle, I used my years of experience as a race mechanic, tuner, and "Ask Dr. Dirt" of *Dirt Rider* magazine to show you what the shop manual doesn't tell you. I'll show you how to keep your stock bike performing its best, lending inside tips and techniques on everything from exhaust valves and changing fork oil to choosing tires and setting up your suspension. I'll also tell you how to modify your bike and create anything from a grunty torque beast for Supercross or enduro to a top-end monster capable of gobbling straights on motocross or desert courses.

The book is designed for readers with a wide range of mechanical skill levels. Tasks like suspension setup, jetting, and gearing are important for the rider to understand well, and I cover these things thoroughly. I'll also take you step-by-step through tasks like top-end rebuilding, brake repair, linkage maintenance, and so on. You might find that as you gain confidence and try more, you will grow as a mechanic. The great thing about

that is the more you do yourself, the more time you have to spend riding your bike!

Of course, there are always things that need to be sent out. Porting is a good example of a job best left to the pros (although I'll show you a few tricks if you want to give it a shot). Suspension revalving is another thing the novice tuner is better off avoiding. For this situation, I've provided some guidelines on choosing a tuner as well as a comprehensive resource guide listing tuners and shops from the United States and Europe. With this ammunition, you'll be well armed to make good choices on performance work.

You'll also benefit from my 16 years of being bombarded by questions about dirt bikes. Every day my mailbox is stuffed with mail generated by my column in *Dirt Rider* and *Dirt Bike Rider*, my tuning business, and from guys I've gotten to know over the years. For each section of the book, I've chosen the most common questions and compiled them into a list of frequently asked questions (FAQs). When you have a problem, you probably aren't the first one, and the answer may be in the FAQs!

The place to begin your search for a faster bike is the first chapter, Getting Started. In this chapter, I'll explain some basic techniques, help you evaluate and purchase a used bike, and discussion the types of tools needed to do the job right. More important, though, I'll explain how to spend your money wisely and choose which components to upgrade when, depending on your budget and performance needs.

The second chapter, Basic Maintenance, covers all the things you need to do to your bike after a hard day's ride. Experienced riders and mechanics can learn from this chapter, too, because there are tips that are obvious but often overlooked. Performing simple maintenance at scheduled intervals is one of the simplest and most effective ways to keep your bike performing its best.

The third chapter, Suspension and Chassis, lends insight into the process of rebuilding and tuning suspension components. This includes a section on video suspension tuning, which I believe is the best way to tune today's off-road motorcycles. If you are considering work as a home-based dirt bike mechanic, the section on shock and fork rebuilding will be especially beneficial. I'll give you tips that take dealership mechan-

ics years to learn through trial-and-error experiences. I'll also give you some guidelines on figuring out what kind of suspension work would benefit your riding style and how to find and tell someone to do it.

Chapters five, six, and seven cover both two- and four-stroke engines. The chapters' subsections offer more information than any magazine article or a factory service manual. All the information presented comes from racking my brain for hours trying to solve a fluke mechanical problem. Sometimes these experiences can help you figure out the root cause of a persistent mechanical problem.

The ninth chapter, Wheels, Tires, and Brakes, covers basic maintenance and gives you tips to help select the proper tires and tire pressure for different conditions and brake pad material. There are even tips on how to stud tires for winter riding.

The tenth chapter, Tuning Tips for Specific Motorcycles, includes specific tuning information for most Japanese dirt bikes built from 1985 to 1996. The typical problems for each model are listed, as well as ways to fix those problems. I've also recommended some of the modifications that will give you the most for your money on that particular model. This information will come in handy when searching for a used bike or when budgeting for improvements.

This is the first motorcycle book to be supported interactively through the Internet. As you read this book, you may have questions; write them down. I offer a free service of answering tech questions through Internet e-mail. I also accept regular posted letters, but e-mail is much faster and efficient. E-mail is easy to use, and many public libraries offer free or low-cost e-mail accounts. You can reach me at egorr@interaccess.com.

You may find it helpful to keep a journal along with this book to write down questions and file copies of the answers. Recording race day data and suspension settings can also help you get your bike set up properly and, ultimately, get around the track or through the woods faster.

The information presented in this book assumes that you know the limitations of your mechanical abilities. If you lack the specialized knowledge or tools needed to do the job right, then have the sense to trust the work to a qualified technician. Remember, it costs twice as much to fix it the second time!

GETTING STARTED

The road to better performance is paved with pitfalls. Simply throwing money at your bike won't make it faster. Even if it does, it might become so hard to ride that you go slower despite the fact that your bike is faster. The key to performance mods is starting with the biggest problem areas, which may turn out to be swingarm and steering head bearings rather than engine or suspension work. Once you have your bike working the way it should, you can start to intelligently improve the systems that need the most help. In this way, you'll spend less money and get the results you're after.

The place to start is evaluating your bike (this is the same process you go through if you're buying a used bike). Check all the basic systems and figure out what needs help. Then take an inventory of your checkbook and decide how much more you can spend. Now you can map out a path to better performance.

In order to make your bike perform better, you need a clear understanding of what it's doing well and where it needs help. Certainly, you'll have some basic ideas already: "It needs more low end to get a better drive out of corners," or "It seems to need more top end because I'm getting passed on long straights and uphills." In order to get more specific, though, you should start a log and keep notes on your bike. When you notice a

problem, make a note of it. When something is working well, write that down. Keep track of when you service and replace things or if you inspect a component. Use the suspension data log (see chapter three) to track what suspension settings you're using and how the suspension works in different conditions. After a while, you'll find you have a very specific idea of what works and what doesn't on your bike.

Also, you can keep track of questions that arise and forward them to me. This is the first book in off-road motorcycling that offers you a reader service for answering your questions on dirt bike repair and tuning. Refer to the appendix for ways to contact me with your questions.

Where to Spend Your Money

Perhaps you've looked over the latest models of dirt bikes and decided that those bikes aren't that much better than the bike you're riding. And maybe you're in the market to upgrade your current bike to be competitive with the new bikes. If you are considering investing in rebuilding services or performance mods, then use this section as a guide to determining a budget and priority list of upgrades. The most important thing to remember is to focus your resources on improving the mechanical condition of

your bike before spending your money on the "wants." A new pipe won't make up for the horsepower you lose to a worn top end and a suspension revalving can't cure the instability found with shot steering head or swingarm bearings. Aftermarket accessories such as radiator and tank graphics, seat covers, and colored plastic are one of the biggest temptations and they won't do you any good if the engine is ready to fall apart!

In order to evaluate the condition of your bike, you have to be very objective. Most guys tend to deny certain mechanical problems exist because they don't want to deal with fixing the problem. Make a list of the maintenance tasks that you've been avoiding. Then think about the hidden problems that your bike might have. Review the sections of this book that describe how to inspect and evaluate components such as the crankshaft, transmission, brakes, shock, and so on. In the end, your list should be tiered, starting with maintenance tasks, followed by performance mods, and ending with cosmetic changes.

If you are considering some performance mods for your bike, you've got to ask yourself questions about your riding demands. Are you having problems keeping up with lesser-skilled riders because your bike doesn't handle right? If so then you should browse chapter three—in particular, the section on revalving. That chapter also contains a suspension troubleshooting guide that helps you determine what changes will be needed to the forks and/or shock.

Regarding engine mods, you also have to ask yourself what type of riding demands do you have. Consider things like powerband choices, fuel economy, the type of fuel, the altitude where you ride, noise restrictions, and engine longevity. Chapter four contains key information on how changes to engine components affect the powerband. Also, check out the model-specific tuning tips in chapter six for recommendations on the best value mods for your dirt bike.

Every region of the country has dealers who specialize in dirt bikes. They have to take in trades in order to sell new bikes. Dealers such as these are good places to buy your first bike. TUF Racing in America takes trades on used dirt bikes. They have a large selection and mail-order ship new and used bikes all over the world.

Evaluating Dirt Bikes

Whether you are figuring out what to do to modify your own machine or buying a used bike, the best way to start is to use the following simple tests to evaluate the bike. Here is a list of the major components of a dirt bike and some tips on evaluating and estimating the cost of repairs. Use chapter six's sections on model-specific tuning tips to help you focus on the characteristic mechanical problems of the model you are looking to buy. Those sections have subsections on flaws, fixes, and best value mods. The section on mods can help you evaluate the aftermarket accessories on the bike. Some aftermarket products really give performance value, but others can actually cause mechanical failures.

Spark Plug

A spark plug is a record of the engine's condition. Large globules of aluminum melted to the plug denote that the piston is disintegrating because of a crankcase air leak. A glazed finish on the plug denotes sand that passed through the air filter and has probably ruined the engine. Heavy carbon build-up denotes a leaking crankshaft seal on the clutch side. A bike with this problem will have white smoke billowing out the exhaust pipe and oil oozing from the exhaust manifold.

Compression Test

The correct way to perform a compression test is to thread the gauge into the spark plug hole, hold the throttle wide open, hold the kill button on, and kick the engine over until the gauge needle peaks. An 80, 125, 200, or 500cc bike should have 150–190 psi. A 250cc bike should have 170–230 psi (these numbers are for sea level). If the compression gauge reading is far below these numbers, the top end will need to be rebuilt. Prices for this vary based on the condition of the cylinder bore. Modern plated cylinders cost $200 to electroplate, while steel-lined cylinders cost $40 to bore. Piston kits and gasket sets range from $50 to $100.

Crankshaft

Remove the flywheel cover and look for rust or corrosion on the flywheel. That indicates that water either entered the side cover or condensation was allowed to occur. Look for an oily residue below the flywheel. This denotes a crankshaft seal leak. A new seal only costs about $5 and can be replaced externally except on KX 80s, 250s, and 500s. On those bikes, the cases must be split, which can be very expensive. To check the main bearings, grasp the flywheel and try to move it

back and forth and up and down. If you feel any movement, the engine's lower end needs to be rebuilt. Normal service intervals for lower ends are once per season on 60cc to 125cc engines and every two to three years on 200cc to 500cc engines. That is assuming that the owner serviced the air filter regularly and always mixed oil in the fuel. The average cost to have a motorcycle shop rebuild the lower end is $300 to 500.

Air Filter

You can tell a lot about how a guy maintains his bike just by looking at the air filter. If he neglects the filter, he probably never works on the rest of the bike. Check the filter for tears that could have allowed dirt to enter the engine.

Frame

Lay the bike on its side and inspect the underside of the frame. Look for smashed frame tubes, a cracked shock clevis (common on YZs), and bent link bars. Smashed frame tubes and broken motor mounts look expensive to fix, but a good fabricator can splice in a new tube or weld a mount if you strip the entire frame down. Frame repairs range from $50 to $200. New frames cost from $500 to $800.

Suspension Components

Check the rear shock for oil leaks. If the seal is leaking, then the gas bladder may be punctured. The average cost of rebuilding a shock is $150 for parts and service. Look closely at the shock shaft. If the chrome has peeled, has deep scratches, or is blue from overheating, then the shaft will need to be replaced or re-plated. The average cost of this is $150 more than standard rebuilding.

Hold the front brake and compress the forks. Does oil ooze out of the seals? Are the forks difficult to compress? Check the fork tubes and the aluminum sliders for rock dents. Rock dents in the tubes can be incredibly expensive to repair. Each of the four fork tubes can retail for as much as $300!

Coolant System

Remove the radiator cap and check the fluid level. A low level means the system has a leak. If the

Although this bike looks tough, the crankshaft and suspension components were in good shape and the damage was mostly cosmetic. With solid components to start with, a bike like this can be purchased cheap ($400 in this case) and made competitive at the amateur level.

color of the coolant is brown, the head gasket may be leaking internally. That means combustion pressure has leaked into the coolant system. The worst-case scenario is when the leak has caused erosion on the top edge of the cylinder. That costs $300 to repair and new cylinders cost from $300 to $850. If the color of the coolant is gray and foaming, that indicates that the water pump seal is blown. The blown seal allows transmission oil to mix with the coolant. Check the radiators for crash damage. Radiators can be welded or sealed with epoxy when minor damage occurs. Check the side of the cylinder head where the head stay is mounted. Look for white or green residue of leaking coolant. This is common on older CR250s and all KXs. This indicates that the head gasket is leaking externally. Cylinder head surfacing costs about $50 and a gasket or O-ring set is about $25. The common cause of external leaks is excessive forces transferring from the top shock mount through the head stay brackets. Check the rear-suspension linkage on a bike with an external leak, chances are the bearings are seized or worn.

Swingarm and Linkage

Sit on the bike and bounce up and down to compress and rebound the rear suspension. Do you hear a screeching noise? Is the rear suspension seized in an extended or compressed position? This would indicate that the bearings, bushings, and seals need to be replaced because they weren't greased. The cost of this repair could vary greatly. The average cost of just the bearing parts is $125.

Grasp the linkage with your hand and try to move it back and forth to feel for freeplay. If the linkage is bent or the bearings have disintegrated and elongated the mounting holes, then the linkage will need to be replaced. The average cost of the linkage is $100 without any bearing parts.

Wheels and Brakes

Put the bike on a stand and grasp each wheel with your hands. Try to move the wheel from side to side with the axle held stationary. If you feel any movement, then the wheel bearings are worn out. This could cost as little as $30 for new bearings, or the hub could be damaged from riding the bike with the bad bearings. Hubs cost about $180 each. Check the surface of the brake discs for deep scratches or signs of overheating. Discs can be resurfaced for as little as $25. Bent front discs on enduro bikes are common. New discs cost about $130. All brake pads have wear-indicator lines scribed into the sides of the pad for quick visual checking. If you can't see the lines, then the pads need to be replaced. Average cost is $30 per set.

Drivetrain

The drivetrain consists of the clutch, transmission, chain, and sprockets. The trans oil can give clues to mechanical problems. Dip a strip of white paper in the trans oil. If the oil sample is gray and bubbly, then the water pump seal is blown, and the coolant has polluted the trans oil. You can confirm this problem by test riding the bike. The clutch action will be prone to slipping when loaded and dragging when engaged.

The chain and sprockets can be visually checked for wear. The chain can be checked by putting the bike on a stand so you can rotate the wheel and check the chain slack at several different points. If the slack varies greatly, then the chain is worn out. The average cost of replacing the chain and sprockets is $115.

The cost to replace the waterpump shaft, seals, and bearings is about $90 and labor is about 1.5 hours.

Tips on Test Riding

Clutch

Pull in the clutch lever and put the bike in first gear. Rev the engine. Does the bike creep forward? If so, then the clutch basket may need to be replaced. When you rev the engine does the clutch slip? If so, then the plates and springs may need to be replaced. That can cost between $55 and $90. The price of clutch baskets varies from $150 to $350.

Throttle Response

Ride the bike in second gear at 1/4 throttle. Snap open the throttle quickly. Does the bike bog or die completely? If so, then the engine may have a problem as simple as a clogged pilot jet or a major problem such as a crankcase air leak.

Transmission

Ride the bike in third gear. Accelerate while gently applying the rear brake. Does the clutch slip? Does the transmission pop out of gear? Third gear is the most abused gear in the transmission. If the transmission pops out of gear, the shift forks may be bent or the engagement dogs on the gears may be worn. This is a common problem on RM250s and KX500s. Repair costs range from $300 to $550 if a motorcycle shop performs the repairs.

Brakes

Apply the brakes separately. Does the lever or pedal pulsate as you apply the brake? This means that the disc is bent or warped and needs to be replaced. Does the front brake have a spongy feeling? If so, then the problem could be as simple as trapped air in the system or as major as a worn master cylinder. Check the brake line for leakage. Even if the guy cleaned the leak, brake fluid will damage the plastic cover on the brake hose.

Crankshaft

Put the transmission in neutral. Rev the engine and let off the throttle. Does the bike make a loud, shuddering vibration? Do you feel the vibration transfer through the foot pegs and handlebars? If so, then the engine's lower end may need to be rebuilt.

Once you've been through the bike, you can calculate how much it will cost to bring the bike back to tip-top condition. At this point, you can decide whether or not it's worth fixing your bike or begin to budget. If you are looking at a used bike, you can determine how much you are willing to pay for the bike (see section on buying a used bike later in this chapter).

Shopping for Rebuilding and Tuning Services

The popularity of mail-order engine rebuilding and tuning services has increased in recent years. Most people who live in rural areas don't have any dirt bike shops near them. Buying by mail order offers them access to experts.

The tasks of rebuilding dirt bike components such as shocks, engines, and forks is fairly complex for the average franchised-dealership mechanic. Sometimes you need to look to specialists. There are companies that specialize in crank rebuilding; porting; cylinder boring, sleeving, and electroplating; suspension; and wheels. There are several specialists in each category so you'll have plenty to choose from nationwide. Read on for some tips on evaluating the best specialists to suit your needs and budget.

If you have already read chapter three's section on suspension-component rebuilding, then you know how difficult and tedious suspension servicing can be. The average cost of $60 to perform basic service to a set of forks or a shock doesn't seem very expensive. Buyer beware: Not all suspension technicians do the same quality work. Technicians aren't regulated by the manufacturers, and it doesn't take a big investment in tools to get started in suspension servicing. As a

consequence, the motorcycle industry is glutted with suspension-service companies. How can you choose a suspension technician that you can trust? Here are some tips on screening technicians in order to find the best one to suit your ongoing suspension servicing needs.

Bike Evaluation Chart

Use the following chart to make notes as you evaluate a bike, either your own for your modification plan or a bike you are considering buying. Note if each system is OK, and refer to the text for more specific information on each test.

Spark Plug Condition?
Compression Test: psi
Crankshaft (engine revs smoothly?)
    Oil under flywheel cover?
    Main bearings tight?
Air filter condition?
Frame Condition
    Frame tubes?
    Motor mounts?
    Shock mount?
    Linkage mount?
Suspension
    Rear shock oil leaks?
    Rear shock shaft OK?
    Front fork seals?
    Front fork tubes?
Coolant System
    Fluid level?
    Fluid clear-green color?
    Radiators straight?
    Radiators leaking?
Swingarm and Linkage
    Suspension compresses
        smoothly and silently?
    Rear linkage tight?
Wheels and Brakes
    Hubs tight?
    Brake discs smooth?
    Brake pads fresh?
Drivetrain
    Transmission oil clean?
    Chain and sprockets fresh?

Test Ride
Throttle response smooth?
Transmission OK?
Brakes smooth and positive?
Crankshaft balanced?

Approximate Costs to Repair

Note: These costs are average for a Japanese full-size bike. You may find you pay a bit more or less for your particular model, especially if you have a European bike (more) or a mini. Still, this should give you a ballpark figure to use when estimating repair costs or evaluating a used bike. Note that the labor is listed in times. Call your local shop to get an hourly rate, and you can figure costs.

Component	Parts	Labor (hours)
Rebuild top end	$100–150	2.0
Rebuild bottom end	$100–150	4.0
New exhaust pipe	$125–300	0.3
Carburetor rebuild	$25–35	0.5
New radiator	$80–200	0.8
New chain & sprockets	$80–150	1.5
Replace Fork seal	$20–30	1.0
Install new fork tubes	$200–300	1.0
Rear shock rebuild	$125–150	2.0
New rear shock	$400–650	1.0
Replace brake pads (per caliper)	$20–25	0.3
Brake rotors	$150	0.6
New hubs	$150–300	-
New spoke sets (per wheel)	$90	-
Replace and true wheel		1.3
New tires	$50–100	0.3

The plastic, graphics, and the seat cover were replaced and the dents were blown out of the pipe. Normal wear and tear parts were replaced and the engine and suspension fluids were changed. Total investment was $1,000. If you are budgeting, you may have some money left over to start improving the performance.

Screening Tips for Rebuilding and Tuning Services

1. Make a list of at least five potential service companies, preferably a mixture of local and national mail-order companies.

2. Determine what range of services the technicians offer—suspension oil changing, seal and bushing replacement, shaft chroming, and revalving; engine cylinder repair, crank rebuilding, porting, electrical, and carbs.

3. Make a survey list of prices for services and ask what is included. Examples: labor, oil, parts, or cleaning supplies. Inquire about a complete breakdown of the costs. Some companies charge extra for rush service, and some charge excessive shipping and handling fees.

4. Ask about technical support. Some companies provide free support materials in the form of booklets and videos; other companies direct technical phone calls to a toll 900 number. These are things that must be considered when comparing costs for services.

5. Ask about turnaround times on ser-

vices. Consider the time it takes to ship your package there and back.

6. Ask what information you need to supply with your parts. The most important things are your name, address, city, postal code, telephone number, and the best time to call you.

Additional Information

In order for a technician to do a proper job, he may need information about your riding demands and the condition of your bike. If the suspension is being revalved, copy and complete the suspension data log in this chapter. The more information you can provide to your suspension technician, the better he can tune your suspension components.

Pricing Methods

The last thing you should be concerned with is the price. A reputable technician will charge a fair price for high-quality work. Don't make the mistake of rating technicians by price. Oftentimes, novice technicians will set high prices because it takes them longer to do a job than an expert. Some companies set their prices based on volume. In the

motorcycle business there is absolutely no connection between price and quality. Prices for mail-order services vary based on factors such as the average price published in magazines. If a company spends a lot of money on race teams and support programs, their prices are bound to be a little higher.

Packaging Parts for Mail-Order Service

If you've made the decision to send your engine or suspension components to a mail-order company, then you will need to package the parts carefully. Here is a checklist of how to package your parts for mail-order service:

1. Start by getting a strong cardboard box that is about 1.5 times larger than the part you are sending.

2. Leave the engine or suspension component assembled, especially engine parts. Those parts are heavy, and if they bump up against one another they could get damaged. If you are sending a shock, don't bother removing the shock spring. The difference in shipping weight doesn't reflect much in the shipping price. If the shock has a remote reservoir, don't loosen the banjo bolt that connects the hose to the reservoir. The suspension technician won't know where to position the hose when he tightens it to complete his work.

3. Center the part in the box and tightly pack crumbled newspaper around the part. Styrofoam peanuts don't offer good impact resistance, and they are difficult to pick out of the part. If you are sending a cylinder, make sure you protect the sleeve that protrudes out of the bottom of the cylinder. I recommend using a four-inch PVC cap fitting to protect the sleeve. Those are available from any hardware store, located in the plumbing department.

4. Put a letter in the box with your name and address information. You will need to include your telephone number and the best time to call, just in case the technician has any specific questions about your parts.

5. Ship the box by UPS and insure the package for the retail value of the parts. Insurance is cheap, at about 30 cents per $100.

Special Packaging for Engines and Forks

If you are sending a set of forks for service, you will need a special box. A box that is rectangular and 40 inches long. Look to your local auto parts dealers. Ask for a box used to package parts such as mufflers, suspension control arms, and torsion bars. Even if you have to pay $10 for a used box, it's still worth it if the box prevents the forks from being damaged in transit.

If you are sending an entire engine, put it in a plastic milk crate first, then into a cardboard box. Always drain the engine fluids. It is illegal to knowingly send flammable liquids through the mail without the proper labels.

Personal Suspension Tuners

When your suspension is tuned properly, it will make you a more competitive racer and your bike safer to ride. I recommend that you find a suspension technician with whom you can develop a long-term working relationship. Everyone has questions on suspension tuning. Once you develop a rapport with a technician by purchasing his services, you can then ask his advice on tuning. Take care not to abuse this privilege! Suspension tuners spend a lot of time developing their proprietary knowledge without pay. You may think they charge a lot of money for revalving, but consider this: When you call to ask a basic question, he has to stop working to answer your free question.

Most technicians work on commission, so they are only earning money when working, not talking! Try not to waste their time by asking questions that are already answered in this book. Let this book educate you so you can ask important advice from your tuner. To get the most benefit from your tuning questions, keep a logbook of all the current settings. A good tuner will need settings data before he can make an informed suggestion as to how to fix a tuning problem. The best type of information that you can provide to a suspension tuner is a videotape of you riding your bike on the sections of terrain where handling problems occur. Refer to the section on video suspension tuning in chapter three.

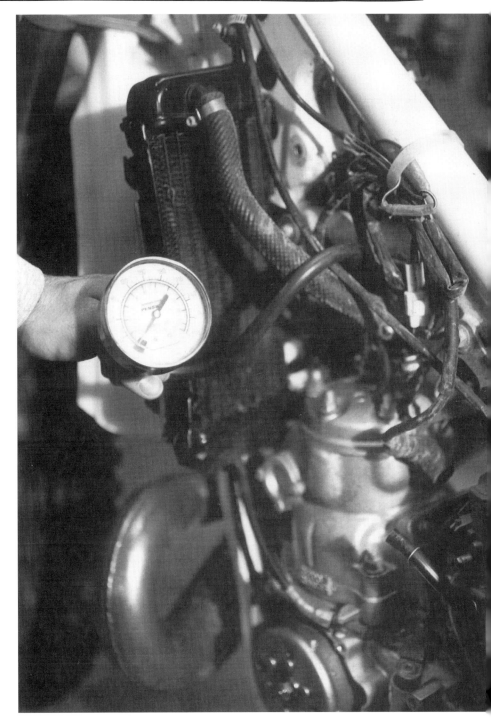

Take a compression tester with you when you evaluate a used bike. A compression test will give you an indication of top end wear and will help you gain a bargaining advantage.

◆ My First Dirt Bike

Finally, after years of pain and suffering, I recently found my way to purchase a used bike. It's a 1984 RM250 and it seems to be in pretty good shape (it looks better than a lot of 1990s bikes I saw). Now that I actually have a bike, I have a few questions that I would like to ask you.

Question One: When I rode the bike before I decided to buy it, the bike would not idle. Otherwise, the bike rode great. The guy I bought the bike from said that this was typical for a 1984 RM250.

Could you please give me some guidance on this? It sounds like it could be the jetting, but I am not sure.

Answer: Many dirt bikes have carbs without idle circuits. I don't remember if that carb was like that. Is there a screw mounted horizontally on the left side of the carb? If the jetting is too lean or the carb jets are partially plugged, then that would cause the dying problem when the throttle is closed.

Question Two: The bike has never had a top-end job or had the air filter replaced. How soon should I have these things done?

Answer: As soon as possible! Especially the air filter. You should take apart the air box and seal the flange and box with weather-strip adhesive.

Question Three: The bike also has a very stiff clutch. Is this a characteristic of the 1984 RM250, or can something be done to smooth out the clutch action?

Answer: Try lubricating the cable. Also take apart the clutch and check the condition of the plates. The old oil that was in the bike while it was stored is causing a chemical reaction with the aluminum to form sulfuric acid. The acid may make the clutch plates and inner hub fuse together, making the clutch lever hard to pull in. If you clean the clutch hubs and plates with degreaser, that will probably solve the problem.

Good luck with your new bike and don't hurt yourself working on it!

Buying a Used Dirt Bike

Buying a used dirt bike can be very risky because the most expensive components to repair are the ones that are most difficult to examine. First, use the section earlier in this chapter on evaluating a used bike. It gives you a guide to examining a used dirt bike and estimating the cost of repairs, so you can gain bargaining leverage with the seller.

Rats and Race Bikes

Bikes that are trail-ridden usually have more time on them than race bikes. Used race bikes purchased from expert riders are normally well maintained and have relatively little running time. Expert riders usually have several sponsors so their bikes may have extra accessories such as suspension or engine modifications, stiffer springs, good tires and brakes, or a special pipe. Don't be afraid of race bikes; they can be a good bargain.

"Rats" are bikes that have been crashed and abused. Normally they will have loads of serious mechanical problems. If you are mechanically confident, you can do well to repair and resell these bikes. Normally you can buy these types of bikes very cheap. Sometimes franchised motorcycle dealers will have dirt bikes that were abandoned by their owners because the repair estimate was too expensive. In most cases the dealer just wants to get rid of the bikes because they take up space in the service department.

Where to Find Used Dirt Bikes

There are three main places to look for used dirt bikes: motorcycle shops, riding areas, and newspapers. Here is how each rates in time spent versus the value of the deal.

Few franchised dealers take trades on dirt bikes. However, there are independent motorcycle shops who service, buy, and sell used dirt bikes. These are good places to buy your first dirt bike from because the shop owner will know some maintenance history on the bike. Another reason is you will need to know people who can answer your questions and supply you with reliable parts and services. Sometimes you can meet other enthusiasts at dirt bike shops and get leads on new places to ride.

Race tracks and riding areas are also good places to find used bikes, especially in the summer. In the heat of the summer, dirt bike riders tend to slack off riding and switch to water sports. Some riders get injured and desperately need to sell their bikes. Others may want to sell their bike in order to buy a new bike when they are released in August. Often times, riders will show their bike at the race track. You can also ask racers if they know of anyone who wants to sell their bike. July and August are the best months to find deals on used bikes from private parties.

The newspapers can be real lame places to look for dirt bikes. In the Chicago area there is a popular consumer newspaper where many people advertise their bikes. This newspaper only charges for the ads if you sell your merchandise. Shopping for bikes in that paper can be frustrating because the advertisers either put a ridiculous asking price on the bike, or they have already sold the bike and are dodging the accounts-payable people from the newspaper. The best newspapers for used bikes, in America and England are *Cycle News* and *Motorcycle News*. Their classified advertisers tend to be serious enthusiasts who price their bikes and parts to sell.

Bargaining Tips

If you find a bike that you like but it needs some obvious repairs, make a list of the parts or outside service needed to do the repairs. Check with dirt bike salvage companies, mail-order parts specialists, or your local dealer for the cost of replacement parts. Go back to the owner of the bike and explain to him the nature of the mechanical problems and the cost of repairs. He may not know about the bike's problems or how much they will cost to repair. Don't try to intimidate or harass the guy into lowering the price. Honesty is the best way to negotiate the price of a used bike.

Buyer Beware!

If you are looking for a 1980s model Japanese or Italian dirt bike, consider that the price of OEM Japanese parts increases over time, and because of the acquisition of Husqvarna by Cagiva, some parts for those bikes aren't even available anymore.

Motorcycle are built with parts from several small subcontractors and assembled by a motorcycle manufacturer. The manufacturers try to order all the parts for the bikes and parts stock, up front. If the manufacturer runs out of stock, they have to order a new batch of parts from the subcontractor. Each subcontractor has a minimum order for a parts run, so individual parts orders may accumulate for months before they are fulfilled. Small parts runs mean that the individual part's price will be higher. Generally speaking, parts for older bikes are more expensive than parts for new bikes. Example; A cylinder for a 1986 CR250 is over $100 more expensive than a 1996 cylinder.

When Cagiva bought-out Husqvarna in the early 1980s, the OEM-parts-manufacturing network of subcontractors had to be revised. All the blueprints and specs on the parts had to go through a bidding system in Italy before the contracts could be awarded to the small manufacturing firms. There are some models of Huskys that you can't even get parts for. For replacement parts, you would have to look to salvage companies. If you have one of these bikes sitting in a shed broken down and waiting for a part, then your bike is worth more in pieces than together.

Selecting the Right Tools

If you've made the commitment to spend more time working on your bike, you will need the right tools and workbench setup. This section is a guide to the different types of tools needed to maintain a dirt bike and rebuild the engine or the suspension components. Having the right tools can make a tough job less frustrating and save you money in labor.

Tool Lists

Here are lists of tools for different types of maintenance applications. You could spend a fortune on good tools or buy a bunch of cheap tools that wear out fast. Then, there is the rip-off factor to consider. If you have expensive tools, people will borrow them and conveniently forget to return them.

I believe in buying cheap tools for the items such as T-handles, wrenches, and screwdrivers. Craftsman (Sears) makes good-quality tools for a low price and you can get free replacements if the tools break. Harbor Freight company sells T-handle sets for under $10. Eventually, the socket corners will become rounded but overall they are a good bargain.

Light Maintenance

There are only about five different sizes of bolts on Japanese dirt bikes, so you don't need a lot of tools to do light maintenance. Here is a list of the basic tools that you need in your tool collection:

1. Special wrenches: spark plug, spoke, rear-axle, and carb main jet wrenches
2. Combination wrenches in sizes of 8–19mms
3. T-handles in sizes of 8–14mms
4. Screwdrivers: one wide and one narrow flat-blade (10 and 3mms wide) and a #2 and a #3 Phillips driver
5. Allen-wrench combination set (2.5, 4, 5, and 6mms)
6. Miscellaneous tools: feeler gauge, air-pressure gauge, measuring tape, cable-lubing tool, chain brush, pliers, and plastic mallet

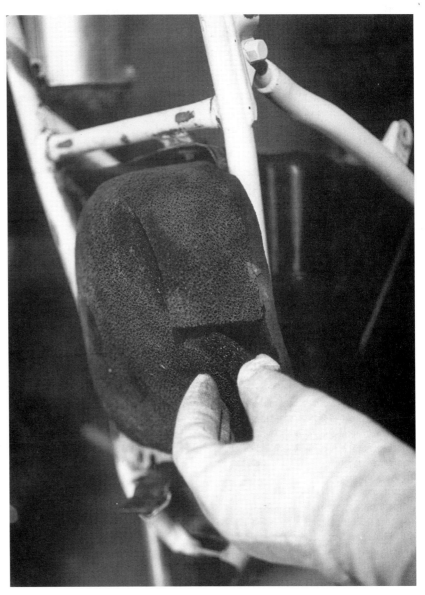

Check the condition of the air filter. If it's torn, you can assume the least you'll have to do is rebuild the top end and take $300 off the asking price!

When evaluating a bike, the bottom end is one of the key factors. Grasp the flywheel with your hand and try to lift it up and down and back and forth. If you feel any movement, the crank bearings are worn.

Intensive Maintenance

These are the tools you will need to do intensive maintenance on Japanese dirt bikes. Include all the tools listed in the light-maintenance list plus the following:

1. 3/8-inch ratchet wrench and sockets in six-point shallow socket sizes of 8, 10, 12, 14, 17, 19, 22, 24, 27, 30, and 32mms; and Allen sockets in sizes of 2.5, 4, 5, 6, 8, and 10mms
2. Combination wrenches in sizes of 22, 24, 27, and 32mms
3. Needle-nose and channel lock pliers, side cutters, chain clamp, and tweezers
4. Hand-powered, electric, or pneumatic impact driver
5. Torque wrench, 3/8-inch
6. Ball-peen hammer
7. Rat tail, big flat file, and triangular files; set of needle files; and a thread file
8. Large- and small-diameter round punches and a 1/4-inch-wide flat chisel
9. Parts washer
10. Miscellaneous tools: flywheel puller, chain breaker, magnet, flashlight, and propane torch

Engine Rebuilding

These are the tools you will need to rebuild a two-stroke engine. Include the tools from the light- and intensive-maintenance lists. You may also need some special tools that are brand and model specific, such as case splitters, flywheel pullers, or blind-side bearing removers.

1. Bearing and seal driver set
2. V-block and dial indicator
3. Machinist's square
4. Crankcase-splitting tool
5. Stud remover
6. Flywheel puller
7. Dial caliper
8. 10-ton Press

Suspension Rebuilding

These are the tools you will need to rebuild Showa and Kayaba forks and shocks:

1. Scribe set
2. Oil level setting tool
3. Nitrogen tank
4. Pressure regulator
5. Bladder cap remover
6. Allen socket, 14mm
7. Vise
8. Cartridge wrenches
9. Seal drivers
10. Bleeder rods
11. Digital caliper

This is an example of how a motorcycle crate can be adapted into a mobile workbench. The air compressor and tank are mounted in the bottom right corner with shelves and storage bins above. The bench top is plywood and a vise is mounted to the top corner where the steel frame of the crate is strongest. A three-gallon parts washer is mounted in the bench top. There is still enough room left over for a power washer, welder, or spare parts storage.

How to Build a Mobile Workbench

It's difficult to work on your bike when you don't have the tools. Reserving a small place in your garage, shed, or basement is too permanent for most people. What you need is a mobile workbench that you can move around to whatever place suits you best. On sunny days you don't want to be stuck in a dingy basement working on your bike, and what do you do when you go to the races? Move all your tools around like a gypsy? Here is an inexpensive solution to the problem of organizing your tools and workshop.

Think about the things you need for a workshop. You need a solid bench, a vise, a parts washer, and a safe place to store your tools and parts. I designed a mobile workbench that I could use in my shop or put into my van for use at the

races. I started with a steel motorcycle crate that I picked from the garbage at a local motorcycle shop. These types of crates are ideal because they are fastened together with bolts and are very sturdy. Next, I bolted wheels to the bottom so I could pack a lot of weight in it and still move it around easily.

Then I increased the rigidity and made it more secure by bolting sides and a bench top to the crate. I bought a stainless steel sink from a building supply store so I could rebuild engines or suspension components in it without making a mess. Then I positioned a large vise over the sink so I could hold the engine or suspension in place while I worked on it. The next thing I needed was a parts washer. I mounted a three-gallon mini parts (Harbor Freight or Enco) under one basin of the sink. Once you clean parts you need to

blow them dry with air, so I bought a 1/2-horsepower electric compressor and linked it to a five-gallon air tank for storage. This little unit makes enough pressure and has enough volume to pop the bead on tires. There was so much space left in the motorcycle crate that I added storage shelves and bins, and still had enough room to mount a tool box. Because I had some expensive tools housed in the crate, I made it secure by adding flip up sides with hasps so I could fit a lock. The sides of my mobile workbench were so large and blank that I just had to fill them up with stickers from my friends' businesses. So there you have it! Next time you are scrounging through your messy garage looking for a 10mm T-handle, or you just had your tool box stolen from a race track, think about this simple inexpensive mobile workbench.

BASIC MAINTENANCE

The best way to extract maximum performance from your bike is to maintain it well. It's just that simple. Maintenance is generally economical and doesn't require a ton of time. It can, however, make the difference between the front and back of the pack or a great ride and being left stranded in the woods.

This chapter covers the myriad maintenance tasks that you will need to perform to your bike on a frequent basis. In addition to explaining simple maintenance tasks and enabling you to diagnose and repair common problems, this section is packed with tips and techniques not found in factory service manuals or even the off-road magazines. At the end of nearly every section there is a subsection titled "Frequently Asked Questions." These FAQs will help you expand your mechanical experience by learning from others.

Air Intake System Maintenance

The air intake system comprises the air box, boot, air filter, and box drain. A cheap piece of foam and a thin barrier of oil—the filter—is all that protects the expensive engine parts from disintegrating into a pile of melted metal, so if you don't learn the basic maintenance practices for air filters fast, you won't be riding for very long! I remember when I was a service manager at a motorcycle dealership and a guy brought in his kid's bike. The bike was only two weeks old, yet the engine seized because dirt had passed through the filter. This man was outraged and argued that his car went 30,000 miles before it needed a new air filter. Air filter maintenance doesn't seem obvious until your engine chokes to a grinding halt, but by then it's about $500 too late!

Clean and Inspect

Every time you clean a filter you need to check the seams for tears. Some filters are sewn together, and others are bonded together with adhesives. Filters don't last forever. Over time the seams will split. Professional racing teams only use a filter for a moto. That may be extreme, but the point is to replace the filter after about 20 cleanings.

The best way to clean a filter is with detergent and water. I recommend mixing equal parts of water and Simple Green, a biodegradable detergent made by Gunk that is sold at most hardware and auto parts stores. Let the filter soak for five minutes and then work it with your hands. If you have sensitive skin, wear a pair of rubber gloves to protect your hands. Squeeze and expand the filter several times until all the particles of dirt have come off the filter. Rinse the filter with running water. Dry the filter by squeezing it and allowing it to air dry. The remaining moisture will be displaced when you oil the filter.

Oil and Grease

The filter must have a special oil for the foam and grease for the mounting surface. Filter oil is blended with chemicals that keep the oil diluted, so it pours and spreads throughout the filter. These chemicals evaporate quickly in the open air, allowing the filter oil to become very tacky. Don't be tempted to use substitutes for filter oil. Filter oil is available from most motorcycle shops. Apply the oil evenly and sparingly across both the inner and outer surfaces of the filter, and squeeze the filter several times, adding oil periodically until the filter foam is lightly saturated with oil.

Apply a thin layer of grease to the flange mounting surface to help prevent leakage at the mounting surface. I recommend Bel Ray waterproof grease.

Making It Easy

Nobody likes to clean and oil air filters, but there are a couple of things you can do to make air filter maintenance easier. If you can extend the time between cleaning and do three filters at one time, you'll save yourself time, so I recommend that you buy two spare filters. Apply oil to the filters and store them in Zip-Lock plastic bags. Then, if you have to service the filter at the race track or riding area, you don't have to clean it, just replace it with one of the pre-oiled spares. Disposable rubber gloves (the thin kind used in laboratories) are useful for keeping the goo off your hands when changing filters between motos. The gloves come in boxes, typically of 100 and are not especially expensive. You can find them at pharmacies or in the paint department of hardware stores.

Filter covers can extend the service interval of air filters. There are two types of filter covers: a cloth sock cover for the filter and a plastic cover for the top of the air box. These things shield the filter from dust and mud. Some people think that the plastic air-box covers choke off the air flow to the air box and hinder performance, that's not true; the covers are designed to reduce intake noise. When you remove the cover, the bike makes more noise, and you think it has more power. Leave the plastic cover on the air box. It will save you from cleaning the filter so often.

The Air Box and Boot

It's easy to overlook the air boot and box when you don't even want to clean the filter, but consider this: A small leak at the air boot or box flange can allow dirt to bypass the filter and go directly into the engine. Here are some tips to consider when servicing the filter:

1. After you remove the filter, look into the air boot from the filter side. Look for dirt that indicates a leak. Sometimes, the chain roller will wear through the boot, or sticks and rocks could puncture it.
2. Never aim the power-washing wand directly at the boot-to-box flange. There is sealant at that junction, but the high-pressure detergent can easily penetrate the flange and blow-out the sealant. It is advisable to power-wash the air box from the top. Twin-Air makes special air-boot covers so you can block off the boot and wash the box. This serves to flush the drain located on the bottom of the box.
3. Seal the flange-to-box junction with weather-strip adhesive only. Never use silicone sealer because it is fuel soluble.

Spark Plug Basics

Spark plugs must operate within a fairly narrow temperature range. At idle, a spark plug must run as hot as possible so it doesn't cold-foul, which occurs at about 800 degrees Fahrenheit. At full throttle, a spark plug must dissipate the heat quickly so it doesn't exceed 1,800 degrees Fahrenheit, where pre-ignition occurs. Consequently, spark plugs are often cursed by many riders as they sit stranded on the side of a trail, trying to clean the oily goo off the plug. This section will tell you how a plug problem can be a sign of a more serious mechanical problem.

Common Problems

Modern dirt bikes have come a long ways from the days when a pocketful of spark plugs was necessary for even a short ride. Some bikes even had two plugs in the head so you could switch when one fouled! Today, if your bike is tuned properly, a spark plug can last an entire season. Even so, two-stroke engines do occasionally foul plugs. If you do have chronic troubles, here are a few places to look.

Cold Fouling

This occurs when the bike and engine are still cool. On the extreme, cold fouling occurs when the plug's electrode temperature falls below 800 degrees Fahrenheit. At this point, carbon deposits accumulate on the insulator (the ceramic part of spark plug that holds the center wire), and because the voltage will travel the path of least resistance, these deposits act as a path for the voltage to follow to ground rather than arcing across to the plug's electrode. Keep in mind that it is more difficult to fire a spark plug under compression pressure rather than at atmospheric pressure, so just because a plug fires in the open air doesn't mean it will work inside the engine.

Melted Plug

When you find a plug that has been melted or is coated with globules of melted metal, something is seriously wrong. Combustion pre-ignition occurs when the spark plug or anything in the combustion chamber reaches a temperature over 1,800 degrees Fahrenheit. At this point, the hot-spot could ignite unburned mixture gases before the spark occurs. Hot-spots can be caused by everything from too-lean jetting, air leaks, lack of cooling, lack of lubrication, or a sharp burr in the head.

▶ Ground Arm Melts

Question: My bike frequently melts the ground electrode of the spark plug. The engine is running great right before it shuts off. Do you think my ignition is too hot? I put an aftermarket booster wire on the ignition coil that produces 150,000 volts.

Answer: The carb jetting may be slightly lean. That would raise the spark plug temperature, causing the ground arm to melt off. Check the old plug. Look at the stub of the ground arm. Is the stub end rounded, as if it had melted? You may be using a spark plug with a funky ground arm design that can't take the heat and pressure that a modern two-stroke engine produces.

Regarding the question of the hot spark, the amount of voltage needed to jump the spark plug's gap is proportionate to the pressure in the cylinder and the size of the gap. Electricity will jump the gap with the minimum required voltage. Aftermarket voltage boosters don't deliver high voltage to the plug on each engine revolution, so you don't have to worry about the spark being "too hot."

▶ Engine Loads Up and Wet-Fouls Plug

Question: I have a problem with my 1995 YZ250. Every time I start it up after it has sat for a while it will load up and bog, causing the spark plug to wet foul. Once I have cleaned it out, it runs like a top. I've checked the carb jets and have the recommended 48 pilot and the stock main jet. I have everything to spec, and I have the mixture at 40:1 with Yamalube.

Answer: Do you ever leave the fuel valve on? It sounds as if fuel is getting into the crankcases. That's why the plug fouls only when you start it. Check the fuel tank's valve by turning it off, unplugging the hose from the carb, and routing the hose to drain into a catch-tank. Check it after 10 hours to see if there is any fuel leakage. If there is fuel, then you need to replace the fuel valve.

Heat Ranges

A plug's heat range of operating temperatures is largely determined by the length of the insulator nose. Colder range plugs have a short heat flow path, which results in a rapid rate of heat transfer. The shorter insulator has a smaller surface area for absorbing combustion heat. Conversely, hotter range plug designs have a longer insulator nose and greater surface area to absorb the heat from combustion. It is most important to install a spark plug of the heat range specified by the manufacturer, as a starting point. When tuning racing engines, it is not uncommon to go up or down three heat ranges of plugs to optimize performance. For example, when your jetting is slightly rich but not enough to require a jet change, you could select a plug one range hotter to achieve the target exhaust-gas temperature. Each step in heat range will effect a 50 degree Fahrenheit change in the exhaust-gas temperature.

Types of Spark Plugs

Fine-Wire Plugs

Fine-wire electrodes provide easier starts and reduced cold fouling, partly because they require slightly less voltage to fire the plug, compared to standard-size electrode center wire. This is because the fine wires are made of precious-metal alloy, which are excellent conductors of voltage. Fine-wire spark plugs produce a more direct and confined spark that is better for igniting the air-fuel mixture.

Projected-Insulator Plugs

Projected insulator refers to the extension of the insulator beyond the end of the shell. This design can only be used if there is sufficient clearance to the piston crown at top dead center (TDC). The advantage of this design is that it benefits from the cooling effect of the incoming fuel charge at high rpm, which provides some pre-ignition protection. At low rpm when cold fouling occurs, the insulator is more exposed to combustion. This helps to burn off deposits on the insulator that can cause cold fouling. Projected-insulator plugs can be used on any 200cc to 500cc dirt bike. These types of plugs cannot be used on 125cc engines with shal-

Only use filter oil on air filters. Some filter oils are detergent soluble. That makes the filters easy to clean, and the filter oil is biodegradable. Use weather-strip adhesive to seal the flange of the air boot that fits into the air box. Never use silicone sealer because it is fuel soluble.

low-domed combustion chambers or ones with flat-top pistons. These engines do not have enough clearance between the piston and head, and the plug would be contacted by the piston.

Resistor Plugs

Nonresistor spark plugs give off excessive electromagnetic interference (EMI). This can interfere with radio communications. That is the primary reason why the manufacturers recommend resistor spark plugs. In North America, engine manufacturers must install resistor plugs in new engines because many people in rural areas depend on CB radios for their communication needs. In Canada, it's actually a law that you must use resistor plugs in your off-road vehicle.

The resistor in the plug demands higher voltage to jump the gap. On older bikes, where components of the ignition system are deteriorating, resistor plugs might foul more often than non-resistor plugs or run rough because the ignition system cannot produce enough voltage to jump the gap. I don't recommend using resistor plugs because they are overpriced and offer no advantage in performance.

Spark Plugs with Gimmicks

There are many different types of plugs on the market featuring every possible gimmick. Some manufacturers make ridiculous claims for their plugs, such as resistance to fouling, more power, or better fuel economy. There is an old saying, "Paper accepts all ink in advertising and litigation." That is certainly true with spark plug ads. The sad truth is that if an engine isn't tuned properly, an expensive plug will foul just as fast as a cheap plug. The best spark plug design is one with a precious-metal electrode and ground arm, shaped to a fine point, and a core sealing ring that resists high pressure. Unfortunately, no such plug exists. However, there are plugs with precious-metal electrodes and excellent core designs. Forget about the funky ground-arm shapes because the spark is going to jump from the electrode to the ground arm at the point of least resistance, so these specialized ground-arm shapes offer no real advantage. Worse, the shapes of some ground arms can actually make susceptible to breaking off. Forget the gimmicks and spend your money testing three or more different heat ranges until you find the plug that best suits your riding demands.

Throttle Maintenance

It's the feeling all dirt riders dread! A total loss of control! Your throttle is stuck at the worst possible time. The engine is revving so high that the kill switch is ineffective and you have to pull the carb's choke just to stop the engine!

Many top riders are cautious about their throttles. The 1995 British champion, Paul Cooper, disassembles and cleans his throttle between practice sessions and motos. It gives him peace of mind and confidence. Use the following tips on how to clean a throttle and identify trouble signs and you'll have the same peace of mind and confidence.

Basic Cleaning and Inspection

After removing the throttle's rubber dust cover and plastic housing, examine the throttle pulley and cable for frays in the cable or dirt in the pulley. Examine the plastic guide for cracks, which can cause the cable to fray or catch on a tree branch, pulling the throttle wide open. If this happens to your cable, don't try to fix it with tape, just replace it with an OEM part.

The throttle pulley is made of nylon and doesn't require lube, but the cable does. Use a cable lubing tool to force chain lube down the throttle cable. Remove the carburetor slide and stuff a rag into the top of the carburetor to prevent any dirt from entering the carburetor. Make sure you disconnect the cable from the carburetor slide first, otherwise you will force dirt and lube from the cable down into the slide, and that can cause the throttle to stick open.

Clean the throttle grip and pulley with brake cleaner. Lube the grip and bar with penetrating oil, unless the throttle contains one of the new Teflon throttle tubes, which are self-lubing.

Inspecting the Slide and Carb

Check the corners of Keihin PWK carbs for dents or deep wear marks. Newer-model slides are chrome plated; older models are a dull gray color. The gray PWK slides tend to wear at the corners and can cock and jam in the carb's slide bore when the throttle is turned wide open. This is a common

Maintenance Interval Chart

The following are recommended intervals for maintaining different components of your bike. Keep in mind that these are averages; if you are riding in extremely dusty, muddy, or wet conditions, times will be shorter.

RIDING HOURS

COMPONENT	2	5	10	20	50
Chain	C&I	-	-	-	R
Air filter	C&I	-	-	R	-
Brake pads	C&I	-	-	R	-
Cables	C&I	-	L	-	-
Brake fluid	-	-	R	-	-
Radiator coolant	-	R	-	-	-
Transmission oil	R	-	-	-	-
Top end	-	C&I	RB	-	-
Reed valve	-	C&I	-	-	-
Air boot	-	C&I	-	-	-
Magneto	-	C&I	-	-	-
Crank seals	-	-	-	R	-
Clutch plates	-	-	R	-	-
Bottom end	-	-	-	C&I	-
Shock fluid	-	-	C&I	RF	-
Fork fluid	-	-	-	RF	-
Wheel bearings	-	C&I	R	-	-
Spokes	-	-	C&I	-	-
Steering head bearings	-	-	L	-	-
Swingarm and linkage bearings	L	RB	-	-	-

KEY: Clean and Inspect (C&I)   Replace Fluid (RF)   Lubricate (L)   Rebuild (RB)   Replace (R)

problem on older KX 250s and 500s. Replace the gray slides with chrome-plated ones when they get worn. The chrome slides are the standard OEM part for 1993-and-later KXs and are available from accessory carburetor parts companies such as DG, White Bros., and Sudco in America.

Replacing the Throttle Grip

The stock throttle grips on modern off-road bikes are molded to the throttle tube. If you damage the grip and need to replace it, it's a very tedious job to remove the old grip. Here are some tips on removing and replacing the grip:
1. Use a pocket knife to strip off the grip.
2. Use a file, a wire wheel, or a lathe to remove the plastic splines and the remains of the rubber grip.
3. Apply a thin coating of grip cement to the throttle tube and slide the new grip onto the tube and let it dry for 24 hours.
4. As an extra safety precaution, wrap the grip with 0.020-inch or 0.5mm stainless steel safety wire. Wrap the grip at two equidistant points and twist the wire end and clip it with 1/4 inch remaining. Position the wire end so it faces on the lower palm side of the grip. This way it won't stick to the rider's glove.

Fixing Sticking Throttles

You should have a factory-trained technician disassemble and clean the carb, throttle grip, slide, and cable. If the cable is dry or rusted, replace it with an OEM part. Sometimes, the slide will have dirt wedged between it and the carb. The dirt indicates that the air filter was leaking.

◗ O-Ring Chain Care

Question: What is the best way to clean and lube an O-ring chain? Should I use detergent when I power-wash the chain? Is there a special chain lube I should use?

Answer: Lightly power-wash the chain with water only, while periodically brushing it with a soft wire brush. Then, spray it with some type of water-displacing chemical such as WD40 or LPS to bring out the water so you can apply a chain lube designed to protect the rubber O-rings in the chain links. Go to your local dirt bike shop; they'll have chain-lube for O-ring chains.

◗ Master Link Problems

Question: Every few times I ride my 1989 KD80X, my master link will pop off. I don't mean pop; I mean break apart and *fly* off. I have tried tightening and loosening the chain tension, but nothing works. It is getting very costly having to buy new master links so often (three times a month). It's also hard work pushing my bike home when even my spare link breaks.

Answer: The most basic problem could be that the master-link clip isn't positioned correctly. Make sure that the open side of the clip faces opposite of the direction of rotation. The next thing to check is the wheel alignment in the swingarm. There are marks on the swingarm at the rear axle, but those marks could be inaccurate, so use a tape measure to check the distance between the rear axle and the swingarm pivot. Adjust the wheel to the same distance on both sides of the swingarm. The proper chain free-play is 3/4 inch when the swingarm is parallel to the ground. Also, if the swingarm and wheel bearings are worn, the wheel could twist out of alignment when you accelerate. Check the swingarm or wheel by trying to move the components back and forth with the bike on a stand. There shouldn't be any movement in the swingarm or wheel. If there is, then the bearings need to be replaced.

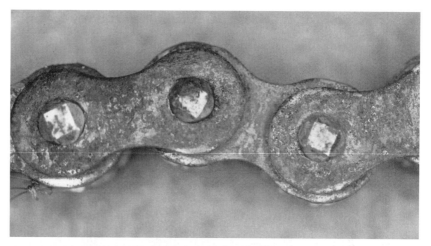

This is an example of a chain that has links that are corroded internally. The links are permanently kinked and frequently derailed from the rear sprocket.

Several aftermarket companies make sprockets that are designed for extended life. This Tallon Radialite sprocket has a groove that runs around the circumference of the sprocket to help channel dirt from the chain.

When the teeth of the rear sprocket are broken and pitched in the direction of the chain's rotation, the sprocket needs to be replaced. This is an extreme example; you should replace your sprockets before they get this bad.

degrees—oil, moly, lithe grease, and even chain wax. However, each is designed for a specific use. Chain lube made from moly is good for street bikes because it doesn't make a mess, but it offers little resistance to water. Spray-lithe grease lasts a long time and offers protection against water damage, so it is good for enduro and trail riding. Chain wax was designed for motocross race bikes that are serviced every moto or practice session. Chain wax is a light coating that seals the link and doesn't fly off or attract dirt. This type of lube is easily stripped off when the bike is power-washed.

Tips on Chain Adjusting

The two most important things to know about chain adjusting are to maintain alignment of the sprockets and to correctly set the chain free-play when the swingarm is parallel to the ground.

There are a few ways to set the sprockets in alignment—by adjusting the axle to stamped marks or using an alignment gauge. All dirt bikes have marks stamped in the swingarm at the axle mounts. The chain adjusters have corresponding marks denoting the center of the rear axle. Normally, you would use the marks to keep the rear wheel centered in the swingarm while adjusting the chain's free-play. However, production frames are robot-welded, and there are slight tolerance differences that can put the stamped marks out of alignment. That's why race mechanics prefer to use an alignment gauge, which fits into the centers of the rear axle and swingarm pivot bolt. Race Tools in New York makes a simple alignment bar that fits all dirt bikes. You just fit it in the centers of the axle and pivot while you adjust the wheel position for the proper chain free-play.

No matter how much travel a dirt bike has, the ideal chain free-play is 1/2 inch or 13mm, measured when the swingarm is parallel to the ground. At that point, the rear axle is at the farthest point from the swingarm pivot. The chain free-play will be at it's minimum, and it should never be less than 1/2 inch or 13mm.

Just because the wheel is aligned when the bike is still doesn't mean it will stay in alignment when the bike is accelerated up a bumpy hill. Whenever you

Sometimes the slide is worn and scratched so bad that it needs to be replaced in order to fix the problem. If there is any dirt in your carb, carefully inspect the air filter for tears at the seams. Also check the air boot that links the air box and carb. Sometimes the air boots will leak at the bolted flange that fastens the boot to the air box. Honda makes a special sealer for the boot flange. Automotive weather-strip adhesive works well, too. Never use silicone products to seal any parts in the intake system of a motorcycle because silicone deteriorates when exposed to fuel vapor.

Chain and Sprocket Basics

The condition of the drivetrain is the one thing that has a significant effect on both the handling and the engine performance of a dirt bike. The simple chain-and-sprocket drivetrain is still the most efficient way to transfer power from the engine to the rear wheel, especially on a motor vehicle with 12 inches of travel. The forces transferred through the chain and into the suspension can have a positive effect on handling. During acceleration, the chain forces push the rear wheel into the ground. That's why when you land from a jump with the throttle on, the rear suspension has more resistance to bottoming. Pro racers

depend on the chain forces when prejumping and landing. If the chain is too tight, too loose, or the wheel is not aligned in the swingarm, a good rider will notice the difference. When the chain and sprockets get packed with mud or corroded from lack of lubrication, they can generate a significant amount of friction to load the engine. A poor set of chain and sprockets could absorb as much as five horsepower from the average 250cc dirt bike. Learning the basics of drivetrain maintenance can improve your riding performance because you'll be able to use the chain forces to your advantage.

Clean and Lube

After each ride, spray the chain and sprockets with degreaser, rinse the chain with water while scrubbing it with a wire brush, and then spray the chain with a water-displacement chemical such as WD40 or LPS. When you scrub the chain and sprockets, make sure you remove the dirt and oil deposits that become embedded near the teeth of the sprockets. If you don't clean off this debris, the sprocket will wear faster.

The ideal chain lube is a spray lube with a chemical that penetrates the chain's links but doesn't fly off or attract dirt, and there are many different types of chain lube that fit this ideal, to varying

▶ Coolant Clinkers

Question: I removed the water pump cover on my bike and was shocked to find these white and green clinkers (deposits). I use a popular brand of antifreeze and tap water. What did I do wrong and how can I flush the system of these clinkers?

Answer: There are only three brands of coolant additives that prevent the magnesium water pump covers from corroding: Moose Juice, Spectro Coolant, and Peak. Use one of these. Also, you should only use steam-distilled water, which you can buy at the grocery store. Regarding flushing agents, auto parts stores sell several different brands, just make sure the flushing agent is formulated for use in aluminum radiators and engine blocks.

▶ Gray Bubbly Trans Oil

Question: My KX60 has a little window mounted in the right side cover. I poured brown oil in the transmission, and after a couple of rides, the oil changed to a gray, bubbly color. Now the engine is overheating easily. Could these problems be related?

Answer: This is a common problem on older water-cooled dirt bikes. There is a rubber seal between the water pump and the transmission. When the seal wears out, coolant leaks into the trans, causing the oil to turn that bubbly, gray color. When any volume of coolant is lost from the system, the engine overheats easily. Replace the bearing and seals for the water pump, and that will fix the problem.

set the chain free-play, try to wiggle the rear wheel and the swingarm. If any of the bearings are worn, the drivetrain can run out of alignment, causing a big power drain.

Types of Chains

There are two types of chain, conventional and O-ring. Conventional chains use steel pins with some type of press-fit soft-metal bushing to form each link. These chains use a mechanical seal to protect the link. Mechanical seal means that there is minimal clearance between the rollers and links. O-ring chains use the O-ring to seal lubrication in the link and keep dirt and water out. O-ring chains are more durable, more expensive, and heavier. These chains are great for long-distance off-road riding because the chain doesn't require as much maintenance as a conventional chain.

Some chains are advertised as having the ability to resist stretching, but this claim is misleading. No chain really stretches because metal doesn't stretch and stay at a larger size. When you turn the bike's rear wheel and the chain has points where the free-play varies, that is due to chain wear not stretch. It's normal for a chain to wear at different rates at different points. The variance of the wear is greatly dependent on sprocket alignment and the chain's free-play.

Checking a Chain for Wear

There are a few different ways to determine if a chain needs to be replaced. Examine the chain for kinks—points where the link and roller have seized, preventing them from freely rotating—and replace the chain if kinks are found. Then, with the chain installed, cleaned, lubed, and adjusted, rotate the wheel and check the chain's free-play at different points. If the chain needs to be adjusted frequently and has many points where the free-play varies, then the chain needs to be replaced. Normally, the sprockets wear twice as fast as the chain, but replace the chain, too, when the sprockets are worn enough to need replacement. If you install a new chain on worn sprockets, the chain will wear prematurely.

Master Links

There are two types of master links, slip-fit and press-fit, but both use a clip. Conventional chains use slip-fit links, and O-ring chains use press-fit links. The clips should be positioned so the opening faces opposite the direction of rotation. Press-fit links can be installed by pressing against the link with the end of a hammer handle and pressing the link plate on by placing an 8mm socket over the link pins and tapping on the socket with another hammer. Tap on the socket alternately until the link-plate is pressed-on so far that the entire clip notch is exposed.

Types of Sprockets

Sprockets or chain rings come in many different colors, patterns, tooth designs, materials, and sizes. Patterns and colors don't mean anything, but some sprocket designs can be problematic, especially those that have grooves that allow dirt to flow into the chain. Well-designed sprockets have relief grooves positioned around the circumference of the sprocket, allowing the dirt to be channeled away from the chain. Tallon Engineering's Radialite design is a good example of the proper type of channel groove. Sprockets are made of either steel or aluminum. Steel is a better material for longevity, but aluminum is lighter and more expensive. The individual teeth of the sprocket tend to wear in the pattern of a wave. When the profiles of the front and rear sides of the teeth look different, the sprocket is worn out. Once the teeth wear so far, they allow the chain links to skip over the top of them. Don't let your sprocket get worn so far that the chain skips. If the chain derails while you're riding it, you could get injured!

Tips for Changing the Sprockets

Countershaft Sprocket

There are two different types of front-sprocket retaining methods, bolt/nut and circlip. Circlip retainers can be easily removed with a circlip pliers, available at any hardware store. The bolt/nut retainers are often over-tightened so that special tools and knowledge are needed to remove and tighten them, but the job is much easier if the chain is left in place while the bolt/nut is loos-

These are some "soft tools" that can help you with cooling system repairs. From left to right, Duro Master Mend epoxy for sealing external leaks, Alumaseal to help seal internal leaks at seals and gaskets, Radiator Cleaner to flush the radiator of mineral deposits, and Enginkool to help the engine run cooler in hot weather.

Final-Drive Gear-Ratio Chart

Match the front and rear sprocket size to determine the final-drive ratio. The formula is to divide the number of teeth of the rear sprocket by the number of teeth of the front sprocket.

	12	13	14
49	4.08	3.76	3.50
50	4.16	3.84	3.57
51	4.25	3.92	3.64
52	4.33	4.00	3.71
53	4.41	4.07	3.78

Cooling Systems

A dirt bike's cooling system is such a compromise of design. Because of the emphasis on low weight and compactness, motorcycle designers are forced to fit aluminum radiators to one small area at the front of the motorcycle chassis, an area that is constantly hammered with sticks, stones, and crashing. At the 1990 500cc USGP, Rodney Smith collided with another rider. The other bike nailed Rodney's KX500 and crushed three channels of one radiator. I was working as Smith's mechanic, and we had to repair the bike before the next practice session. I applied epoxy to the damaged area of the radiator, and it held for the entire race!

Here are some tips on how to maintain a cooling system for maximum performance, and how to do emergency repairs to a punctured radiator.

Soft Tools

There are several excellent products that are invaluable to have on hand when you need to repair your coolant system. Duro Master Mend epoxy can be used to make temporary repairs to the outside of the radiator. Alumaseal can be used to make temporary repairs to the inside of the coolant system, and it works great for chronic head-gasket leaks. Radiator cleaner should be used to flush out the coolant system on a yearly basis because corrosion, debris, and waste products from combustion gases leaking into the coolant system can accumulate in the tiny channels of the radiator and reduce the cooling efficiency.

Enginekool, Moose Juice, or Spectro coolant products transfer more BTUs of heat to the radiator than an equal mix of water and antifreeze. These products are

ened. The average torque setting for the front sprocket is 24 foot-pounds. If you don't have an electric or pneumatic impact wrench to remove the sprocket's retaining bolt/nut, you'll need to prevent the sprocket from turning so you can loosen the retainer with a hand wrench. The best way to do this is to apply the rear brake so that the chain will prevent the sprocket from turning—assuming, of course, that you did not remove the chain first. Never wedge anything between the chain and sprocket while removing or tightening the front sprocket bolt/nut because the wedge can come out and injure you or damage the chain and sprocket.

Once you remove the sprocket, I recommend that you clean the inside and outside of the countershaft bushing, which is the spacer that fits between the bearing and the sprocket on the countershaft. The bushing is sealed on the outer edge by the countershaft seal that fits into the crankcase and by an O-ring on the inside. After cleaning, apply a dab of Bel Ray waterproof grease to the inner and outer faces of the bushing to help keep out water and dirt.

Rear Sprocket

Rear sprockets are bolted to the wheel hub. Normally, a tapered-head bolt with a flanged nut is used to fasten the sprocket to the hub. Sprocket bolts tend to loosen up. That makes mechanics overtighten them, causing the Allen hex head or the nut to strip. Avoid these problems by using blue Loctite on the threads of the bolts. Always use a six-point box wrench on the sprocket nuts, and tighten the bolts in an alternating diagonal pattern.

Gearing Tips

You'll have to change gearing to suit different tracks. Tracks with steep hills, many tight turns, and long whoop sections will require higher final-drive ratios. Fast tracks require a lower ratio. A simple rule of thumb: For more top speed, switch to a countershaft sprocket with one more tooth than stock; for quicker acceleration, switch to a rear sprocket with two more teeth than stock. Use this gearing chart to find the difference between different combinations of sprockets for your model bike.

This is an example of how epoxy can be used to seal leaks in radiator cores. Duro Master Mend epoxy or Alumaseal work well and can be found at auto parts stores. Bear in mind that this is probably only a short-term solution.

This is a Devol Racing radiator guard. It protects the radiator from branches poking through the cores, and prevents the radiator from being crushed when the bike is crashed on its side.

available from most auto parts stores. Moose Juice is available from Moose Racing or your local dirt bike shop.

Basic Cleaning and Inspection

A dirt bike's cooling system should be flushed and changed once a year. Before you drain the cooling system, add four ounces of an aluminum radiator flushing fluid. Several companies make these products, and they are available from any auto parts store. Run the engine for about 10 minutes and then drain the cooling system. Take care when disposing of the old coolant. Some states have severe EPA regulations regarding the disposal of used coolant. Call your local auto repair garage and ask if they have a recycling drum for used coolant.

Remove the water pump cover and check for corrosion and debris. Check the water pump's bearings by grasping the water impeller with your fingers and trying to move it up and down. If you feel any movement, then the water pump bearings and seals need to be replaced. If you see oil leaking into the water pump housing, that is a sign that the seals and

bearings are worn too. Sometimes, the bearings will be so worn that they cut a groove in the water pump shaft. In most cases, when the water pump seals and bearings are worn, so is the shaft. It's best to replace these parts as a set because they aren't that expensive. The water pump is gear-driven by the crankshaft. Some bikes use gears made of plastic, but other bikes use metal gears. Metal gears are more durable but are very noisy. Plastic gears are vulnerable to melting, especially when the gearbox oil is low and at very high temperatures.

Filling and Bleeding Tips

Some bikes have bolts located on top of the cylinder head or water spigot that are used for bleeding trapped air in the coolant system. If the air isn't bled from the system, the air pocket will prevent the coolant from circulating and the temperature will rise until the radiator cap releases. The proper way to bleed the trapped air is to fill the system to the top of the radiator, leave the cap off, then loosen the bolt until coolant streams out. Then top off the radiator, install the cap, and run the engine for 10 minutes before checking the coolant level. CAUTION: Let

the engine cool down before releasing the radiator cap; otherwise, the hot coolant could rush out and burn your hand.

Damage Control

The radiators of dirt bikes seem to mysteriously attract rocks and branches. Crashing a bike can damage the radiators, too. Radiators and exhaust pipes are like bumpers for dirt bikes, so chances are you will have to perform emergency repairs on your bike's cooling system. It may be at a race, on the trail, or in the wilderness several miles from any roads. Every trail rider should carry epoxy in his or her tool bag and every mechanic should carry it in the tool box.

Any type of quick-setting epoxy works great for radiator repairs. Epoxy isn't an adhesive in that it isn't sticky. Epoxy bonds when it can wrap around the edges of surfaces. It's easy to get epoxy to bond on a radiator because

With the right side cover removed, grasp the water pump shaft and try to move it back and forth. If you feel any movement then the water pump bearings and seals need to be replaced.

Some engines have air-bleed bolts located on top of the head so as to allow you to bleed the trapped air from the cooling system. If the air isn't released from the system the engine could seize from overheating.

there are so many edges on the cores and the surrounding fins, but the area affected must be cleaned before the epoxy is applied. Quick-setting epoxies need only about 30 minutes of drying time when air temperatures are over 75 degrees Fahrenheit, longer in colder weather.

Epoxy radiator repairs should be regarded only as temporary fixes. When you get your bike home, replace the damaged radiator or have it heli-arc welded by one of the many companies who specialize in radiator repair, such as Myler's in Utah and Fontana Radiator Works in California.

Protection for Radiators

Radiators can be protected on the front and on the sides. Aluminum bars are used to protect the sides of the radiator from damage if the bike is dropped on its side. Screens are used in place of the plastic louvers in front, to protect the radiator cores from being punctured by tree branches, but this protection comes at a cost, because the cooling system will not work as efficiently when the louvers are removed and replaced with screens. The louvers serve to collect and channel air at high velocity into the cores. DeVol Racing makes guards for radiators, and they may have models to fit your machine.

Troubleshooting Tips

Use this guide of common symptoms and problems to aid in the troubleshooting of coolant systems.

Symptom: Coolant flows out of overflow tube

Problem: Leaking head gasket, trapped air in system, or stripped water pump gear

Symptom: Engine overheats quickly

Problem: Coolant is low or radiator is clogged

Symptom: Grinding noise from right side of the engine increases with rpm

Problem: Water pump bearings and seals are worn

Symptom: Clutch slipping, water in transmission oil

Problem: Water pump bearings and seals worn

Symptom: Coolant leaks from rear of cylinder head.

Problem: Chronic head gasket leaks are usually due to frame problems.

▶ Clutch Slips and Drags

Question: My bike's clutch has the strangest problem. The clutch slips and drags. I've tried adjusting the cable several different ways and it has no dramatic effect. The bike is five years old. Could that have something to do with this problem?

Answer: The problem is either the outer pressure plate or the clutch basket. The pressure plate could be worn too thin. That will affect the clutch-lever free-play and the dragging problem. The clutch basket can cause the same problems because the drive plates (fiber) wear grooves in the clutch basket. The grooves prevent the plates from shifting position when the clutch is disengaged. Conversely, the grooves prevent the plates from moving closer together and providing the necessary friction.

▶ Clutch Nut Gets Loose

Question: My bike has a recurring problem. The center nut that holds the clutch to the transmission main shaft gets loose and nearly falls off! What do I have to do to keep this nut tight? Does anyone make Nylok nuts large enough to fix this problem?

Answer: Most modern dirt bikes use a nut and a tab washer to secure the clutch. The washer has two tabs, one to align with the inner clutch hub and one that bends over one flat side of the nut. If you torque the nut to the manufacturer's specification and use a new tab washer, the nut will stay tight. However, if the problem continues, then check the engine's main bearings and the bearings that support the transmission shafts. Worn bearings could be the source of excessive vibration, which would cause the clutch nut to unthread.

Remove the top cover of the throttle and inspect the cable for kinks and frays. If there is any dirt on the pulley or cable, disassemble the parts. Clean the inside of the throttle tube with brake or contact cleaner.

Clutch Repair

A motorcycle's clutch has a significant effect on power delivery and handling. If the clutch doesn't engage and disengage smoothly, the bike's rear wheel could break loose and compromise traction or, worse, cause the rider to crash.

Does your bike lurch when you fan the clutch? Do the clutch plates break or burn out fast? Does the clutch make a grinding noise when the engine is idling in neutral? This section will give you insight into the problems that affect clutches, and some tips on how to permanently fix clutch problems.

Common Clutch Problems

Too many riders replace their clutch plates before they are worn out. They don't measure the plate thickness, plate warpage, or the spring free length. One guy called me on the telephone complaining that he had spent over $600 in clutch plates in one riding season. He said his bike burned up clutch plates on every ride. I asked him to send me the entire clutch and all the old plates and springs. The problem was that the springs were sacked-out and didn't exert adequate spring tension on the plates. That allowed the plates to slip, causing them to burn. All of his clutch plates were the standard thickness and none of the plates were warped. The plates all

had a minor surface glazing problem. That was easily fixed using medium-grit sandpaper. The average cost of replacing a set of clutch plates is about $90, which brings up the moral of this story: Spend some time looking for the cause of a clutch problem rather than just throwing money at it.

Measuring Tools

There are three inexpensive tools that you need to perform basic measuring of clutch parts. A flat surface, such as a piece of glass or preferably a thick piece of steel, will give you a surface to check plate warpage and deglaze the plates. A feeler gauge will enable you to measure the plate warpage. A dial caliper will enable you to measure the free length of the clutch springs and the plate thickness. Dial calipers are available from Sears, auto parts stores, or Enco.

How to Measure the Parts

Before you attempt to measure the clutch parts, you will need the manufacturer's recommended dimensions for the parts. The factory service manual lists this information, or you can call your local motorcycle dealer. The dimensions for parts such as the clutch-plate thickness or the spring free length will be listed as standard and minimum. The standard dimension refers to the dimension of a new part, while the minimum dimension refers to the worn-out dimension of the part.

Measuring the Plates

Clutch plates wear thinner with use and can warp if they become overheated. Use the caliper to measure the thickness of the face of the plates. If the plate thickness is within spec, then place it on a flat surface such as glass or steel. Press the plate down evenly and try to insert a 0.020-inch feeler gauge between the plate and the flat surface. If the feeler gauge can be inserted under the plate, then the plate is warped and cannot be repaired.

Measuring the Springs

Clutch springs sack out with use, meaning that they become shorter in length. Measuring the free length of the spring is the best way to determine if the springs should be replaced. Use the caliper to measure the free length of the spring and compare the dimension to the minimum-length spec listed by the manufacturer. Sacked-out clutch springs will cause the plates to become glazed and the clutch to slip.

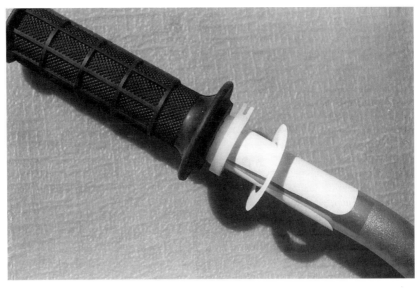

A new product for throttles is a Teflon sleeve that wraps around the handle bar end so you don't have to lubricate the throttle tube. The lubrication attracts dirt and requires you to clean the throttle often.

Troubleshooting Clutch Problems

The previous section covered basic clutch service, but what happens when you have a serious clutch problem such as a grinding noise or a combination of both dragging and slipping? This section provides some insight into troubleshooting common and serious clutch problems.

Grinding Noises

Warm up your engine, put the transmission in neutral, and turn the throttle so the engine runs steadily, just over idle. Pull the clutch lever in slightly. Check for a significant reduction in vibration and the grinding noise. If the noise is reduced, then the needle bearing and bushing that fit between the clutch basket and main transmission shaft are slightly worn. This is very common on KX250s, but it isn't a serious problem. There is no way to measure the needle bearing, but the service manual will list a dimension for the bushing diameter. Always replace the needle bearing and bushing as a set.

If the grinding noise isn't affected by engaging the clutch, then the problem may be more serious. Check the bolt that retains the primary gear to the crankshaft and the nut that retains the clutch hub. If the nut and bolt are tight, then the crankshaft main bearings may be worn out. In 1991 and 1992, Suzuki RM125s and 250s had a characteristic problem with bad primary-gear bolts. Suzuki has corrected the problem, and the new bolts are available from any

Throttle grips are molded on to the plastic throttle tube. If you want to change the grip, you have to remove the old grip. Sometimes, you can cut the grip with a utility knife and peel it away from the throttle tube. If it is particularly stubborn, you can mount a piece of handlebar and the tube in a lathe to strip off the old grip. The finished grip is shown on the left.

◆ Stator Plates

Question: My YZ125 has become increasingly harder to start over the last two months. The bike is three years old and I haven't had any problems with the bike's electrical system. Is there any component that steadily wears out?

Answer: All Kawasakis and Yamahas have Mitsubishi stator plates. The coils on Mitsubishi stators have poor insulating characteristics, causing the coil windings to break down over time. Your bike's stator coils are probably breaking down. If you do an ohms test you might find that the ohms values are lower than the manufacturer's specification range (10 percent variance). The Mitsubishi stator plate is rebuildable. Shoup Enterprises in Colorado offers a service of wet-wrapping for better insulation properties. This service sells for about half the cost of a new stator plate.

◆ Factory Ignitions

Question: I sneaked into the pits at the Red Bud motocross National last summer, to check out the factory bikes. I noticed a factory mechanic flipping some switches mounted near the igniter black box of the bike. When I asked the mechanic what he was doing, he noticed that I didn't have a pit pass and he chased me out. What do you think the mechanic was doing with those electrical switches?

Answer: Many of the factory bikes use the latest type of digital igniter boxes that can be switched to one of eight different ignition timing curves. There is a dip-switch module mounted away from the igniter box, in a safe place such as under the fuel tank. The factory tuners adjust the dip switches to change to an ignition timing curve that best suits the track conditions. In Japan, factory test riders have been using a two-position switch mounted to the handlebars. The rider can switch the timing curve on the fly. That gives riders the ability to change the timing for different sections of the track—slow whoops sections and fast straights. Now don't go bothering those hard-working factory mechanics anymore.

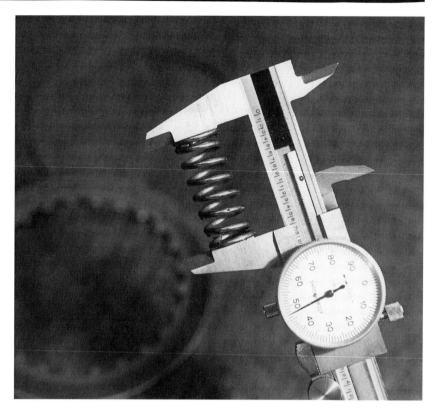

Measure the free length of the springs and the thickness of the clutch plates with a dial caliper. All the springs should be the same length. Springs sack-out with use and plates wear, so check your manual for the recommended free length of the springs and plate thickness.

Suzuki dealer. There is no implied warranty from Suzuki, but I suggest replacing the bolt just for safety's sake.

Dragging or Lurching Problems

These problems are primarily caused by deep notch marks that form in the clutch basket and inner hub. The notch marks are the result of wear caused by the splined teeth of the clutch plates. Eventually, the notch marks become so deep that the plates just stick in one place and resist engaging or disengaging. If the notch marks are less than 0.020 inch deep, then it's possible to draw-file down the high spots of the notches. Be careful, though, because if you file too much aluminum from the clutch basket or inner hub, then the clutch will be prone to dragging. A common symptom of dragging is the bike creeping forward when you put it in gear.

Before you attempt to draw-file the notches from your clutch basket, you must check the basket for hair-line fractures at the base of each of the fingers. If you find any cracks, replace the basket. If the fingers break off, the debris will cause catastrophic engine damage. If you draw-file a basket with fracture cracks, it will fail much faster! Late-model KX125s (pre-1993) and 1992 RM250s have characteristic problems with clutch baskets. The manufacturers have redesigned the clutch baskets, and they are available from your local dealer.

Draw-filing refers to a filing method whereby you stroke the file in one direction, evenly, along the length of a surface. This will enable you to file down only the high spots of the notches equally. You will need two types of files, a flat file for the clutch basket and a triangulated file for the inner hub. You'll also need a file-card to clean the aluminum debris from the file; otherwise, the file grooves will become clogged with aluminum and prevent the file from cutting.

Over time, the clutch plates will make chatter marks in the splines of the clutch basket and inner hub. These marks should be carefully filed off (see next photo).

The chatter marks can be draw-filed to take the high spots off the chatter marks. If you file down the clutch parts too far, the clutch will drag.

The clutch plates may become glazed with a coating of oil. This glazing can be removed by lightly sanding the plates with 320 grit sand paper placed on a flat surface.

Sometimes the clutch plates will get so hot that they warp. You can check the plate warpage by placing the plates on a piece of glass and trying to slip a feeler gauge (.020 inch) between the plate and the glass.

This is what a clutch basket looks like when it is disassembled. The primary driven gear fits on the clutch basket with rubber bushings. A plate is riveted over the top of these parts to allow a certain amount of side clearance.

Electrical and Ignition Systems

Electrical systems fail for the stupidest reasons. Water, heat, and vibration are the three main causes of electrical component failure. Simple preventative maintenance can save you hundreds of dollars in electrical parts. Simple tasks such as cleaning the dirt and condensation from the flywheel and stator to prevent corrosion, applying dielectric grease to the connectors, and periodically

checking the spark plug cap for tightness may save you from pushing your bike rather than riding it. This section will show you how to care for your motorcycle's electrical system and what can go wrong if you neglect a problem. It also provides a troubleshooting guide for detecting fluke electrical problems.

Ignition System

Modern ignition systems are designed with specific timing curves. The typical

Japanese ignition system fires at about 6 degrees before top dead center (BTDC) at idle, then advances to 20 degrees BTDC at the rpm of peak torque. At high rpm, the timing changes back to the retarded position of 6 BTDC. This reduces the heat in the cylinder and shifts it into the pipe to prevent the engine from overheating and seizing. The timing curve is controlled by the "black box" or "igniter." That is the small plastic box located under the fuel tank on most dirt bikes.

Dielectric grease should be applied to all the wire connectors to prevent them from corroding.

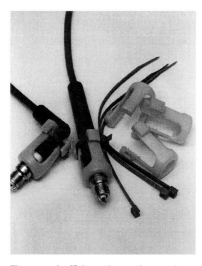

These are the Nology aftermarket spark plug wires, caps, and Silver Beru spark plugs. This system replaces the original parts and offers superior performance through higher discharge voltage and shorted spark duration.

An inexpensive multitester can be used to check the condition of electrical parts such as a kill button. Simple items such as kill buttons and spark plug caps are the first electrical parts to suspect when the engine is hard to start or misfires.

The black box has either analog or digital circuitry. Analog circuitry uses a series of zener diodes to trigger the spark based on the amount of voltage generated by the rotor magnets and stator coils. Analog black boxes produce and are vulnerable to heat. Digital ignition systems use chips that sense rpm and adjust the ignition timing to suit. It isn't possible for us to change the timing curves of digital or analog black boxes, but it is possible to change ignition timing by adjusting the position of the stator plate.

Basic Ignition System Maintenance

Apply Dielectric Grease to Connectors

Auto parts stores sell dielectric grease. If you apply it to the wire connectors, they will never corrode. Clean the connectors with brake or contact cleaner, let the connectors dry, then apply a light coating of the grease. Wipe the plastic covers of the connectors to seal out water. Take care to route the wires and connectors clear of the exhaust system and away from the rider's boots. Electrical tape can be used to route the wires, but zip ties should not be used because the wires can get pinched or severed and can then ground to the frame.

Cleaning and Checking the Magneto

The magneto of a dirt bike consists of the stator plate for mounting the generator and signal coils and the flywheel rotor that houses the magnets. Japanese dirt bikes have plastic magneto covers that are flexible and prone to leaking. That can allow water and dirt to enter the magneto and cause corrosion. If you want to protect the magneto on your Japanese dirt bike, I suggest installing a Boyesen Factory Racing side cover.

To clean the magneto properly, you'll need a flywheel puller (K&N sells flywheel pullers for under $10). First you remove the flywheel nut and thread the puller into the flywheel, in the counterclockwise direction. Most flywheel pullers use left-hand threads on the main bolt that threads on to the flywheel. The center bolt is right-hand thread. This bolt pushes up against the crankshaft end, forcing the flywheel off the crankshaft's tapered end. It's best to apply a dab of grease to the crankshaft end so the puller's bolt doesn't damage the end of the crankshaft.

With the stator plate removed from the engine, you can use fine-grit sandpaper to remove the corrosion from the coil pick-ups. Clean the stator plate coils with brake cleaner. Check the coils for dark spots that would indicate a shorted wire and a heat build-up.

How to Adjust the Ignition Timing

The timing is changed by rotating the stator plate relative to the crankcases. Most manufacturers stamp the stator plate with three marks, near the plate's mounting holes. The center mark is the standard timing. If you loosen the plate mounting bolts and rotate the stator plate clockwise to the flywheel's rotation, that will advance the ignition timing. If you rotate the stator plate counterclockwise to the flywheel's rotation, that will retard the ignition timing. Never rotate the stator plate more than 0.028 inch or 0.7mms past the original standard timing mark. Kawasaki and Yamaha stator plates are marked. Honda stators have a sheetmetal plate riveted to one of the mount holes. This plate ensures that the stator can only be installed in one position. If you want to adjust the ignition timing on a Honda CR, you'll have to file the sheet metal plate with a 1/4-inch rattail file.

Lighting Systems

It is becoming popular to set-up motocross bikes with lighting systems. These systems range in complexity from lights powered by a total-loss 12-volt NiCad battery to ones with a lighting coil and a resistor. Companies such as UFO and Acerbis sell fenders with taillights and front number plates with headlights. These items are needed to make a motocross bike legal for enduro racing and riding in state off-road-vehicle (ORV) parks.

If you want to build a cheap temporary system, use a 12-volt, low-wattage bulb linked to a 12-volt rechargeable battery from a cordless drill, via a simple toggle switch. If you want to build a lighting system that will help you see in the deep woods, then you need to install a lighting coil.

There are three companies marketing lighting-coil systems: CRE, Pro-Racing, and A-Loop. CRE sells a high output system designed for the Honda CRs only. This system is made in Italy and features a ring of lighting coils positioned around the outside of the stock flywheel rotor. The coils are fastened to

This stator plate coil shorted out and burned the outer casing. It has to be replaced.

These are aftermarket lighting coils for Japanese dirt bikes, distributed by Pro-Racing of England. The individual coil on the left fits RMs, KXs, and YZs. The unit on the right is for Honda CRs. Because of the CR's stator plate design, you cannot just add a lighting coil, you have to buy the entire stator plate and then attach the original signal coil to the new plate.

an aluminum side cover that replaces the stock plastic cover. A-Loop and Pro-Racing sell similar products. They have bolt-on lighting coils that fasten to the stock stator plate, available for KXs, RMs, and YZs. The CR kit includes the lighting coils, generating coil, and a stator plate, but the stock signal coil must be swapped over to the new stator plate. The kit for the CR is more expensive than the kits are for the other bikes because Honda uses an unusual generating-coil design.

Also available for use with these lighting-coil kits are optional components such as wiring looms, resistors, brake-light switches, and handlebar switches. The maximum output of a lighting coil is about 140 watts. You must use a resistor in these systems,

otherwise you run the danger of burning out the light bulbs.

The average price of adapting your motocross bike to enduro or ORV park riding, is about $225 (slightly higher for a CR Honda). The includes the lighting coil, resistor, wire loom, number-plate headlight, and fender taillight.

Diagnosing Electrical Problems

The Kill Switch

A faulty kill switch is the most common electrical problem. The kill button can be easily checked with either a simple continuity light or a multimeter. Link the two test leads between the two wires from the kill switch. When the switch is depressed, the circuit will be continuous. Neither wire should ever be grounded to the handlebar.

Spark Plug Caps

Spark plug caps can break loose from the coil wire after repeated removal of the cap. Most caps thread into the wire. Whenever you reinstall a cap, first cut 1/4 inch from the end of the wire. This will insure that the cap threads are biting into fresh wire. Spark plugs can also be faulty. Refer to the section on spark plugs for more information.

Wire Connections

Poor wire connections or faulty ground eyelets are also a common cause of electrical problems. Check the wires from the magneto for burn marks or cuts. Often, the wires will be routed too close to the pipe and melt. Flying rocks can also hit the wire, causing it to break or fray. If the wire connectors aren't insulated properly, they could short out from moisture or corrode. Clean the connectors with contact cleaner and apply a thin coating of dielectric grease to protect the connectors from corrosion. Check the ground wires too. They are colored solid black or have a white stripe. These wires have eyelets that fasten to bolts such as those on the coil or black-box mounts.

Magneto

The magneto consists of a flywheel with magnets (rotor), and a stator plate with a few types of coils mounted to it. The

two basic coils are the generating coil and the signal coil. The generating coil is also known as a primary coil, and the signal coil is also known as a pick-up coil. The generating coil produces the primary AC voltage, and the signal coil is the trigger that releases the voltage to the igniter/black box. The additional coils mounted to the stator plate are charging coils for some type of lighting system. Some manufacturers put all the coils under the flywheel rotor, and some mount the signal coil outside of the flywheel.

The individual coils of the magneto can be tested two ways, for resistance (ohms) and AC voltage output. The resistance is measured with an ohm meter. The manufacturers publish resistance-testing specs in their factory service manuals. They specify what two wires to connect to the ohm meter, and what the ohms spec should be. The output of the generating coil can be tested with a multimeter set to AC volts. At the average kick-starting speed (spark plug removed) the AC voltage output of the generating coil should be at least 45 volts.

Igniter Box

The igniter or black box contains sensitive electronic circuitry that controls the ignition timing in accordance with changes in engine rpm. All sorts of things can cause a black box to fail, and it is very difficult to test them for anything but complete failure. The main causes of black box failure are heat and vibration. The electronic circuitry is encased in an epoxy material to insulate the components from the heat and vibration of the motorcycle.

Black boxes are usually mounted in areas of free air flow, such as the frame neck, under the tank, or under the seat. Sometimes water gets into the black box or the epoxy cracks and causes damage to the circuitry. There are some simple ways to test a black box for complete failure, using an ohm meter. The manufacturers publish wire connection and Ohms specs for their black boxes.

The black box can also be tested dynamically with an inductive pick-up timing light (plastic body). Remove the magneto cover, start the engine, and point the timing light at the flywheel. Look for timing marks to appear at one side of the flywheel, and focus the strobe light at that area. You should see a "T" and "F" and "|" marks. The T means TDC (top dead center) the F means fire at low and high rpm, and the | line means full advance. The F mark should line up with a fixed point on the crankcase at idle. When the engine is revved to mid throttle, the timing mark will advance to the | line. When the engine is revved higher the timing mark will jump back to the F mark. If the sparks is occurring after TDC, the engine may idle rough. If the ignition timing doesn't go to the F mark at high rpm, then the piston may seize from too much cylinder pressure and heat.

Troubleshooting Chart

Problem: The engine is hard to start and dies periodically.

Solution: Unplug the kill switch. If it cures the problem, then replace the switch with an OEM part.

Problem: The engine coughs under hard midrange acceleration and misfires at high rpm.

Solution: The stator coils are probably deteriorating. Use a multimeter on the ohm setting to check the coils. Ohms specs for the coils are listed in the service manual. Sometimes the coils become corroded from condensation and just need to be cleaned. Stator coils are rebuildable for about $125.

Problem: The engine runs fine on flat ground but misfires when riding over a series of whoops or braking bumps.

Solution: Check the top coil mounted under the fuel tank. Make sure the ground wire, coil mounts, and plug cap are tight and clean. There is also a slim possibility that the black box is faulty. These units are potted with epoxy to hold the fragile circuits from breaking apart. Sometimes the epoxy material breaks down, allowing the circuits to vibrate and short-out when you ride over rough terrain. Unfortunately, there is no reliable way to test an intermittently faulty black box, but an ohm test can determine if the unit has completely failed. See your factory service manual for testing procedures.

Problem: The engine overheats, the pipe turns blue in color, and the piston is melting in the front center of the dome.

Solution: The ignition timing is too far advanced at the stator plate or the black box is faulty and doesn't retard the ignition timing curve at high rpm. This is simple to check with the aid of an inductive pick-up timing light. See your local franchised dealer and a service technician can run a test for you.

Fitting Aluminum Handlebars

There is nothing worse than the sinking feeling you get when you land from a big downhill jump and the bars fall to the tank, preventing you from steering. This section provides tips on how to custom-fit aluminum handlebars and keep them tight in the clamps. First, determine the optimum width of the handlebars, based on your body positioning and riding needs. For example, if you are a tall guy with wide shoulders, you will leave your bars at the maximum width, but if you ride enduros through tight woods sections, then you will need to cut the bars down so the bike fits between trees.

Cutting and Polishing

In general, cut the bars to a width that matches the width of your shoulders. You may want the bar a bit wider or narrower than this to suit your personal taste and riding conditions. Motocross riders tend to use wider bars for a bit more leverage, and enduro riders tend to cut them narrower (down to about 28 inches) for maneuvering through tight trees.

Measure and mark the area of the bar that you need to cut, and wrap a piece of black tape around the bar. This will help guide your hacksaw and enable a smooth, straight cut. After cutting the bar with a hacksaw, wrap a piece of medium-grit emery cloth around the rough-sawed edge and polish it smooth. This must be done because the rough edge of the saw cut will gouge the inside of the rubber grip or plastic throttle grip, and may cause the throttle to stick wide open! Remember to install the end-plug in the bar after you have finished sawing and polishing. Some aluminum handlebars do not have diamond-shaped knurling for the handlebar clamps. It may be

Team Honda mechanic Fred Bramblett recommends tapping threads in the bar ends to prevent handguards from tearing out when bumping trees.

difficult to keep these bars tight, especially if the clamp and bar surfaces have deformities. It may be necessary to lap these surfaces together to increase the clamping surface area.

Lapping and Fitting the Bars and Clamps

Factory mechanics in Europe recommend using medium-grit valve-lapping compound ($3 at auto parts stores) to lap the surfaces of the bars and clamps so the clamps can get a tighter grip on the bars. To begin the process, apply the compound between the handlebar and clamps, then snug the clamps down and rotate the handlebars back and forth. This procedure polishes the high spots off the surfaces of the bar and clamp and effectively increases the clamping surface area. After lapping, the handlebars will stay tight in the clamps, eliminating any chance of slipping. This method of clamp-to-bar lapping is also recommended for the cross-bar clamps. Normally they have a locking agent applied to the clamp from the manufacturer, but a couple of hard landings causes the locking agent to break bond with the bar. The lapping method is a reliable way to keep the cross-bar tight.

Race Tools in New York, has developed an excellent method for matching the triple clamps to the handlebars. They recommend using a 7/8-inch reamer to line-bore true the top clamp and handlebar clamps. The amount of material removed varies from bike to bike. The handlebar clamps should also be draw-filed flat. Race Tools recommends using one-piece bar clamps for extra rigidity. Race Tools offers a service at AMA National motocross races of fitting Renthal handlebars with one-piece clamps. They are stationed at the race headquarters on Saturdays and the track on Sundays.

Handlebar Tightening Warnings

Pay attention to the manufacturer's recommendation on how to tighten your handlebar clamps and to the torque specification. Some handlebar clamps are designed for equal-distance gaps on each side of the bar and some are designed for zero gap on one side. For example, Honda stamps one side of the clamp with a dot mark. That indicates that the dot

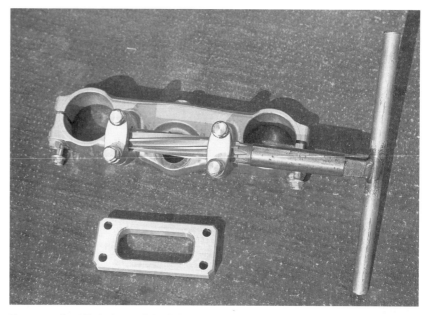

The guys at Race Tools designed this 7/8 inch reamer T-handle to line-bore the handlebar clamps with the triple clamp. This method is used by all the pros on the Supercross circuit. Those riders have chronic problems with their handlebars slipping down because of hard landings from jumps.

should face the front of the bike and that clamp bolt should be tightened until the clamp has zero gap. This is a common clamping system used on late-model Japanese motorcycles. Honda uses this system on all the front-end clamps from the handlebars to the controls and the front-axle clamp. Some other manufacturers use arrows to denote directions of forward or up. If you are ever unsure of which direction a clamp should face, refer to your factory service manual or call your local franchised motorcycle dealer.

Fitting Radiator Guard and Tank Stickers

Are you a little nervous about trying to apply those expensive radiator and tank stickers to your bike? Here are some tips on how to reduce the chances of misaligning the stickers, making bubbles, or having them peel off the first time you ride your bike.

Clean and Prep

If the plastic panels are scratched, you should consider replacing them. If your bike has an exposed fuel tank and it is deeply scratched, you can repair it by sanding down the scratches with 220-grit sandpaper. Clean all the plastic parts

with contact or brake cleaner and wipe dry with a clean cloth. When applying stickers to an exposed fuel tank, it's best to drain the fuel first because the fuel vapors seep through the plastic and deteriorate the adhesive.

Some sticker manufacturers include an acetone-soaked swatch so you can clean the outside of the plastic. The acetone actually dissolves the substrate of the plastic, sealing it from leaking fuel vapors while the stickers are applied.

Keep It Straight!

The best way to keep the stickers straight while applying them is to remove a small section of the backing paper and align the covered part of the sticker on the plastic. Then press down the exposed part of the sticker. Now carefully peel off the backing while pressing down the sticker. This will ensure that no air bubbles get trapped between the sticker and the plastic. If some air bubbles get trapped under the sticker, you can remove them by popping them with a pin and pressing out the air. Popping the bubbles results in a slight distortion in the sticker but nothing compared to what would happen if you tried to press the air bubble across the sticker to bleed it out at the edge.

These are the materials you'll need for installing the stickers. Fresh plastic parts, a razor knife, contact cleaner, and some clean towels. Clean the plastic with contact cleaner. Clean fuel tanks with acetone to seal the surface of the plastic.

Graphic FAQs

▶ Stained Fuel Tank

Question: My bike has a white fuel tank. It is stained with fuel residue that has turned the white plastic brown in color. I want to cover the stains with rad and tank stickers. How should I prep the tank before I install the stickers?

Answer: You will never get the brown stains off the tank. However, you can prep the tank surface for installation of the stickers. Wet-sand the tank with 320-grit wet/dry sandpaper and Soft Scrub brand kitchen tile cleaner. Rinse the tank, being careful not to allow any water to enter the tank. Then use a clean cloth and acetone to wipe the surface area where the sticker will bond to the tank. Acetone seals the pores in the surface of the tank and removes the soap film.

▶ Fix Peeled Stickers?

Question: The edges of the rad stickers on my bike are peeling off. What can I do to rebond the sticker?

Answer: I suggest using a razor knife to trim the part of the sticker that has peeled off. There is no aftermarket adhesive that will bond to the stickers.

Care for New Stickers

Stickers will eventually start to peel at the edges. Here are some tips on reducing the wear and tear on stickers. Don't pressure-wash the stickers directly at the edges. Also, be careful not to use harsh detergents meant for use on stripping grease from metal parts. These detergents will deteriorate the adhesives in the stickers. The best way to clean the stickers is with a sponge and water. If the edges of the sticker start peeling, use a razor knife to remove the peeled part of the sticker.

Use the razor knife to cut a small section of the backing paper off so you can start to apply the sticker. Once you have the small section applied, remove the paper and apply the rest of the sticker. Press the entire sticker down with your fingers especially at the edges.

Fitting Seat Covers and Foam

Have you ever spent $50 on a seat cover and botched the installation, leaving it looking like the ruffled trousers of a wobbly old man?

There are two different opinions on how seat covers should be installed. Some people believe you should install a new seat cover over the top of an old cover. That may work on a cheap seat cover, but not on one that is designed to fit properly. One important thing to consider when installing a new cover is the foam. Seat foam deteriorates when you power-wash the seat with detergent. When you strip off the old cover, you may find pieces of foam have crumbled off. This is an indication that the foam is gone bad and that the foam must be replaced, too.

Aftermarket Seat Foam

There are many different types of seat foams available from aftermarket companies. You have the option of stiffer foam in two degrees, or foam of different heights both shorter and taller than stock. Before you buy a new seat cover and foam, consider your height, weight, and riding style. A very tall, heavy rider will need the tallest stiffest foam possible. Stiffer foam will make the seat seem taller.

MXA specializes in making tall stiff foam for riders over 74 inches in height. MXA foam is stiffer than stock foam and is more resilient over time. They have two different foam heights to choose from. The taller foam will help, but extremely tall riders might also find that higher handlebars (ATV bars have a lot more rise), extended foot pegs (TUF racing can modify pegs to fit), and the taller foam and cover will better match your bike to your size and be more comfortable to ride.

Tecnosel foam is very stiff and is designed for riders who stand often and use their inner thigh muscles to grip the seat and turn the bike. That is why Tecnosel seat covers have the grip material up on the top front edges. Riders who sit down all the time (enduro or hare scrambles riders in particular) may experience lower back pain because Tecnosel foam is not designed to absorb impacts. Conversely, soft,

It is possible to use a hand-operated staple gun to install a seat cover, but you need a strong grip and a lot of pressure to punch through the plastic seat base.

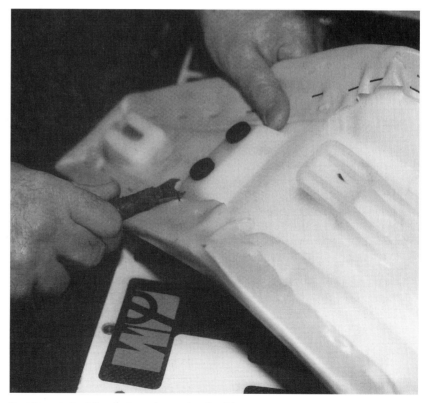

Start by prying out the staples and removing the old seat cover.

worn-out foam can have the same effect on your back.

If you are not a tall rider and want to lower the stock seat foam, you may want to trim the foam. This will enable the rider to rest his foot flat on the ground when coming to a stop or waiting at the starting line. Trimming the foam lower is accomplished with a "hot-wire." Most upholstery shops can handle this task. Then, you will need to stretch the seat cover tighter and reposition it on the seat base.

Fitting the Seat Cover

You will need some tools to fit a seat cover right. You need a staple remover, a razor knife, and a staple gun. A pneumatic staple gun is best because it requires significant force to inject the staple into the plastic seat base. If you try to do it with a hand-squeeze stapler it will be difficult to get the staple to bite into the base while keeping the cover taut. If the staple doesn't seat into the base, the cover will just tear apart and the staples will fall out. If you doubt your abilities, take the seat and cover to an upholstery shop and make a copy of this section on seat-cover installation tips to guide the person doing the work.

1. Remove the old seat cover by extracting the old staples with a hooked staple remover. You can also use a flat-blade screwdriver and a side-cutter pliers.
2. Hook the seat cover to the front of the seat and pull it tight at the back. Remove all the wrinkles along the length of the seat before you staple it.
3. Start stapling the seat at the back. Just put four staples in to begin.
4. The next point to staple the seat is at the front corners. Pull the cover tight and put two staples on each side.
5. Now take a razor knife and cut the cover to accommodate the seat mounting tabs. Just cut two vertical lines on each side of the tabs. Pull the cover tight on each side equally and put a staple on each side of the tabs. Take care in aligning the seat equally on each side. Now that the cover is set into position you can staple it every 1/2 inch around the perimeter.

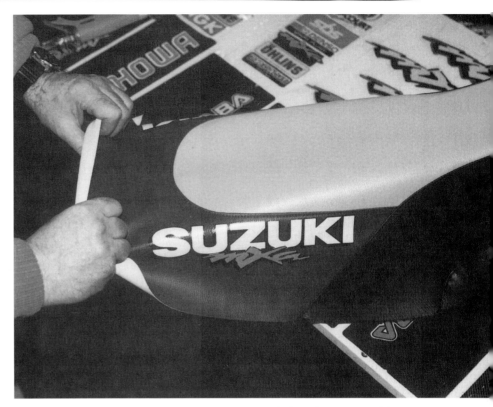

The seat cover should be looped over the front edge and stretched tightly to the rear of the seat.

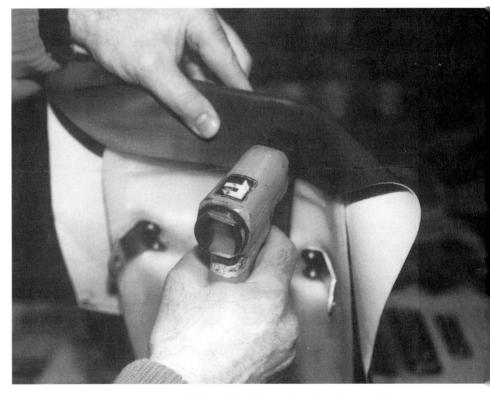

Holding the seat cover tight, staple it to the back edge of the seat base first. The rest of the cover should be stapled on to the bottom of the seat base, working around the seat taking care that no wrinkles develop.

Race Day Preparations

Every time I go to the races, I see racers fumbling around with their bikes for hours between motos; later, they push their bikes back from the second moto because their bike broke down for some silly reason. It only takes about 20 minutes to thoroughly inspect and service a bike between motos. Servicing a bike can give a rider confidence and peace of mind. It's also a great way to channel "nervous energy." Many talented professional riders share some of the maintenance duties with their mechanics as a way of preparing for the next moto. Paul Cooper cleans his throttle, Jeff Stanton adjusts his bars and levers, and Danny "Magoo" Chandler used to change his own tires just to psyche-out other racers. Too many riders and mechanics are unorganized when performing between-moto maintenance. This section is a guide to help you become more organized and build your mechanical confidence.

Start During the Race

A good mechanic prepares during the race for the tasks he will need to do between motos. For example, if the rider gets involved in a crash but continues the race, the mechanic will think of what parts were damaged in the crash. If the mechanic hears that the engine is detonating at the end of a long straight, he'll know that he must increase the carb's main jet size between motos. If the first race starts muddy but the sun begins to shine and the wind starts blowing, he'll know that in the next moto the track will dry out. This will require him to change the suspension settings and perhaps even the tires in order for his rider to have a competitive advantage in the next race. Here is a checklist for moto maintenance, listed by priority.

Washing the Bike

This seems like a very simple thing, but washing a bike incorrectly can cause more damage than racing. Start by scraping the majority of the mud from the bike. This will reduce the amount of water needed to wash the bike and keep your pit area clean. Remove the seat and air filter then cap the silencer end and

Use a razor knife to slit the seat cover to accommodate the seat mounts.

After you power wash the bike, you should lube the clutch cable. A dry clutch cable is the most common reason that a lever is hard to operate.

This mechanic is using an alignment bar to check the distance between the axle and swingarm pivot bolt center. The mechanic will check both sides of the swingarm when he is adjusting the chain tension.

the air boot. Seat foam manufacturers warn not to power-wash seats because the foam acts like a sponge to absorb water (added weight) and the water and detergent can break down the seat foam to make it "mushy." Never point the power-washing wand directly at rubber seals (forks, shock, sprocket, wheel bearings). Never spray detergent on the brake pads or discs in order to clean them. The detergent bonds to the disc and glazes the first time you use the brakes, rendering the pads useless. The best way to wash the bike between races is with a stiff brush, sponge, and a bucket of water.

At the 1993 USGP, a Castrol Honda mechanic criticized my bike for not being perfectly clean. He spent a lot of time making his bikes perfectly clean, but that reduced the amount of time he could spend doing maintenance. This mechanic was later made famous for forgetting to put gas in his bike, costing his rider the British championship. However, the bike was clean when the rider pushed it back to the pits!

After you wash the bike you need to do some things immediately. Drain the carb's float bowl just in case water seeped past the air-filter cover. Dry the air box and boot with a towel. Grease the air-filter flange and install a clean filter to prevent anything from accidentally falling into the exposed air boot. Finally, use a wire brush on the chain and spray it with chain lube to prevent it from corroding.

For race days when the dust and water are minimal, you can use a thin disposable sock over the filter. Rather than changing your filter between motos, you can simply pull off the sock and have a clean filter. Some systems allow you to pull off the sock without even removing your seat. Several companies sell them in America and Europe.

Fuel Precautions

If you use petroleum or synthetic pre-mix oil, you should immediately top up the tank with fuel-oil mix after washing the bike so you don't forget. If

Race Day Log

Before you can figure how to improve your bike, you need to know what it is doing. Although the seat of your pants will give you some general impressions, a race log is the hot ticket to pinpointing areas that are lacking performance. Ideally, fill out a race log for each race of the season. This will give you baseline settings for the track and an excellent picture of how your bike is working in different conditions.

General Data
Date:
Location:
Air temperature:
Humidity:
Elevation:
Terrain and conditions:

Suspension Fork
Spring rate:
Oil level:
Compression (clicks out):
Rebound damping (clicks out):
Fork tube height in triple clamp:

Shock
Spring rate:
Low-speed compression (clicks out):
High-speed compression (clicks out):
Rebound damping (clicks out):
Shock sag:
Shock preload:

Chassis
Front tire:
Front tire pressure:
Inner tube or bib mousse:
Rear tire:
Rear tire pressure:
Inner tube or bib mousse:
Front brake pad brand and type:
Rear brake pad brand and type:
Accessories (handguards, skid plate, etc.):

Engine
Fuel type:
Premix oil brand and ratio:
Main jet:
Needle jet:
Pilot jet:
Clip position (from top):
Air screw (turns out):

Comments
What obstacles or parts of the track did the suspension work well on:

Where did the suspension perform poorly and what was happening:

Where did the engine work perfectly:

Where did the engine work poorly and what were the problems:

you use a castor-based pre-mix oil, then you should dump the fuel from the previous moto and mix your fresh batch of fuel just prior to staging. Castor-based oils separate quickly from fuel and that can cause either spark plug fouling or piston seizures. On very hot days, place a wet white towel over the fuel tank so the sun doesn't heat the fuel. Cool fuel gives a definite advantage on the start of a race.

Quick Check

Grab a set of T-handles and check all the bolts on the bike. This will force you to look over the entire bike, enabling you to find problems such as worn, bent, or broken parts. Check the brake pads at the wear-indicator lines scribed on the sides of the pads after every moto because mud races can wear out a set of pads in one moto. Check the chain adjustment. Look for oil leaks at the suspension components. Adjust the clutch cable if the lever has too much free-play.

Wheels and Tires

Check the tire pressure and make corrections based on track conditions. Here are some basic guidelines. Muddy conditions: front 8 psi, rear 6 psi. Dry conditions: front 14 psi, rear 12 psi. Always use heavy-duty inner tubes because they allow you to run lower tire pressure without the threat of a puncture.

If you can't afford a new rear tire for every moto, use a hacksaw to cut the rounded edge from the knobs. Don't ignore the braking edge of the knobs (backside) because it's just as important to stop as to go. There are some goods tools available for the purpose of restoring the edges on the knobs between motos.

The best way to tighten the spokes is to start at the valve stem and tighten every third spoke 1/8 turn. When you get to the stem again, start with the next spoke and repeat the procedure. Once you have tightened three spokes from the stem you will have tightened every spoke equally. Check the spokes for loose ones, then tighten them to the same tension as all the others. Don't use the "tap the spoke and listen to the pitch of the sound method." It doesn't work! You

After the normal maintenance is finished, the mechanic uses T-handles to check all the exposed nuts, bolts, and screws on the bike.

have to develop a sense of feel for spoke tension. If the spoke is too tight, you'll hear stress-relief sounds.

Involve the Rider

I make it a practice to always involve the rider in the final sequence of between-moto maintenance. Have the rider sit on the bike and check the rear spring sag, handlebar, and lever positions, and brake- and clutch-lever adjustments.

Ask him how the bike worked in the race and if there is anything he wants you to check or change. This is mainly

done for psychological reasons. You are showing the rider that you care about what he thinks and proving to him that the bike is in great working order. This will give him confidence and also prevent him from making up some bogus mechanical problem as a reason for quitting during the next moto.

The Rider-Mechanic Relationship

I place a lot of emphasis on being willing to do whatever it takes to give the rider an advantage. I've been able to get

better-than-normal results out of riders just by being an emphatic listener between motos. I like to finish the bike maintenance as quickly as possible so I can talk to the rider and help him prepare for the next moto by doing things together, such as walking the track, watching the start, or even going up to the competitors and trying to psyche them out. Your mutual respect and confidence can help your rider boost his results in a race. The simple truth is, a good mechanic has to be able to respond to the rider's needs in an organized manner.

SUSPENSION AND CHASSIS

CHAPTER THREE

Your bike's handling is critical to your riding experience. If your bike handles badly, it destroys your confidence and can make your body ache for days after riding. The information presented in the latter part of this chapter is targeted to the needs of veteran riders and race mechanics who want to gain control over their suspension servicing and revalving needs. Novice riders and mechanics can benefit from this information, too, because it will make them a more informed consumer when shopping for suspension tuning services.

Baseline Settings

Every day I see people sending out their suspension for expensive revalving before they ever attempt to adjust and record the baseline settings—settings such as the front and rear spring sag, the compression and rebound clickers, the fork-tube overlap, or even the tire pressure. In many cases, the suspension components only need to be rebuilt and sprung correctly for the rider's weight and riding demands.

Measuring Sag

The rear sag should be measured and set before measuring the front sag. If the rear sag is too little and is corrected, more weight will then be placed on the front end and it will sag more than normal. Here are some guidelines for measuring the sag:

1. First measure the distance of the front and rear ends while fully extended on a bike stand. Measure the rear from the axle to the base of the back of the seat. Measure the front from the axle to the triple clamp. Be sure to measure from the same point each time.

Use a metric tape measure and record the extended lengths of the front and rear ends. A metric tape measure is ideal because millimeters are small increments and you won't have to deal with subtracting fractions of an inch, as you would with an American tape measure.

This is an example of the proper method of checking the rear sag. The bike has enough fuel to complete a moto, the rider sits in his normal racing posture with all his weight on the foot pegs. The mechanic measures the distance between the rear axle and a point on the fender directly above the axle while another person assists by holding the bike straight up. You can use a measuring tape to check the sag, but the Race Tools Sag Gauge has a pointer that fits into the axle to keep the measurements consistent and accurate.

Determining Spring Rates

Measuring the unladen sag of the rear shock, after you have set the race sag, is a good guide for the rear spring rate. The front is more difficult. You need to measure the fork sag and then compare the internal fork-spring preload. Expert riders may choose stiffer forks springs than the sag and preload indicates because they use the front brake hard and transfer more weight to the front end. One of the main causes of headshake is too soft of a fork spring rate or too low of an oil level in the forks.

Damping Circuits and Adjusters

The suspension circuits of the forks and shock are the HSC (high-speed compression), HSR (high-speed rebound), LSC (low-speed compression), and LSR (low-speed rebound). The compression adjuster for the shock is located on the reservoir, and the rebound adjuster is on the clevis (bottom shock mount). The compression adjuster for the forks is located on the bottom of the forks, and the rebound adjuster is located on the fork cap. Not all forks have rebound adjusters. Rebound adjusters were first used on production cartridge forks in 1989 by Kayaba.

LSR and LSC Circuits

The low-speed circuits work in two common track sections: braking for tight turns and accelerating on a straight with far-spaced, shallow whoops. All Japanese dirt bikes have suspension adjusting screws that affect the low-speed circuits only. Turning the adjusting screws clockwise will increase the damping and slow/stiffen the low-speed circuit. Turning the screws counterclockwise will decrease and speed-up/soften the low-speed circuit.

HSC and HSR Circuits

The high-speed circuits work in two common track sections: landing from big jumps and accelerating on a straight with tightly spaced, sharp-edged whoops. In 1996, Honda was the first to introduce HSC adjusters on the rear shock of the CR models. The adjuster has an inner screw for the LSC circuit and an outer ring for the HSC circuit. This

2. Set the sag after practice and refuel the bike with the normal amount of fuel that you race with. If it's a mud race, don't scrape the mud off the bike.

3. The rider should be fully dressed in his racing clothing.

4. The rider should get on the bike and bounce up and down while the mechanic pushes the bike. This will help work out the stiction from the suspension so you can get an accurate measurement. Coast the bike to a stop, tapping the brake will shift the bike's weight and give you a false measurement.

5. The rider should sit in his normal racing position and someone should hold the bike vertical. The bike should be on flat ground for best accuracy. The mechanic should measure the compressed distance on the rear suspension at the same two points where he measured the extended distance.

6. Increase or decrease shock-spring preload to set the rear sag at 90–105mm.

7. Measure the front-fork sag the same way, and if necessary, adjust the sag to 35–50mm with 5–15mm of fork spring preload (measured internally).

8. Finally, measure the unladen sag of the rear shock. Be sure to measure this AFTER you have the sag adjusted with the rider aboard. Let the bike sink under its own weight and measure the sag. It should sag 15–25mm if the spring rate is correct. If the sag is less than 15mm, then the spring is too soft for your weight. If the sag is greater than 25mm, then the spring is too stiff for your weight. It sounds backwards but think of it like this: If the sag is too little, then you had to preload the spring too much in order to get it to have the correct race sag for your weight.

Spring Rate/Rider Weight Chart

This chart will give you a starting point when trying to determine the proper spring rate for your weight.

	Shock-Spring Rate (kg)		Fork-Spring Rate (kg)	
	125cc	250cc	125cc	250cc
Rider Weight (pounds)				
130–140	4.6	4.8	0.36	0.38
140–150	4.6	4.8	0.36	0.38
150–160	4.8	5.0	0.38	0.39
160–170	5.0	5.2	0.39	0.40
170–180	5.2	5.4	0.40	0.41
180–190	5.4	5.6	0.41	0.42
190–200	5.6	5.8	0.42	0.43
200–210	5.8	6.0	0.43	0.43
210–220	6.0	6.3	0.43	0.44
220–230	6.3	6.7	0.44	0.45

adjuster can only make a slight difference in the high-speed damping.

White Power shock and fork adjusters are high-speed-only adjusters.

Tuning with Oil

There are three different weights of cartridge oil. Most bikes are valved by the manufacturer to use the middle weight. You can change the fork's damping slightly with different weight oils. The lighter weight oil will soften/speed up the compression and rebound damping. The heavier weight oil will stiffen/slow down the compression and rebound damping. On noncartridge forks, the oil level affects the compression damping and the oil viscosity affects the rebound damping.

The fork oil level determines the volume of the trapped air space in the top of the forks when fully compressed. The trapped air space acts as an extra spring to reduce bottoming when you land hard from big jumps. The manufacturer always lists a range of fork oil level settings in the service manual. The higher the fork oil level, the lower the trapped air volume and the higher the air pressure at full compression. Remember, the lower the fork oil-level setting number, the higher the oil level and smaller the air space. As a result, oil level will affect the last one-third of the suspension travel. Be careful when filling because it is possible to overfill the forks with oil and cause hydraulic lock before the forks bottom out. This could cause the seals to blow out. Always use an oil level setting tool, which makes it easy to set the level accurately in each fork leg.

This is an example of the proper method of checking the front sag. The Race Tools Sag Gauge is positioned parallel to the fork tube. The front sag should be checked after the rear sag is set to spec. If the front sag is incorrect, the spring preload may need to be set internally. True-Tech makes aftermarket fork caps with external adjusters similar to the factory Supercross bikes.

Suspension Data Log

Make some spare copies of this data log and record all of the pertinent data about your suspension, ideally at every track. This information is also vital for having work done on your suspension.

Personal Data
Rider's weight (with gear): _____ (lbs.)
Height _____
Skill Level _____

Type of riding
(circle those you do regularly)
motocross   enduro   DTX   Supercross   desert   hill-climb   dual sport

Terrain Data
(circle conditions you encounter frequently)
Soil content: sand mud rocks tree roots loam hard clay
Elevation: big hills   off-camber   many jumps   square-edged bumps
sand whoops

Motorcycle Data
Brand _____   Model _____   Year _____

Fork Data
Spring rate _____ kg
Spring Sag _____ mm
Unladen Sag _____ mm
Spring Preload _____ mm
Fork tube overlap _____ mm
Steering head tension set? _____
Compression adjuster: _____ clicks out
Rebound adjuster _____ clicks out/number

Maintenance history of the forks, including any crash damage
_____
_____
_____
_____
_____
_____
_____

Handling problems with the front end, including terrain condition and riding circumstances
_____
_____
_____
_____
_____
_____
_____
_____
_____

Shock Data
Spring rate _____ kg
Spring sag _____ mm
Unladen sag _____ mm
Oil brand
and weight _____
Compression adjuster _____ clicks out
Rebound adjuster _____ clicks out

Maintenance history of the shock, including frequency of link lubrication and bearing replacement
_____
_____
_____
_____
_____
_____
_____
_____
_____
_____

Handling problems with the rear end, including terrain condition and riding circumstances
_____
_____
_____
_____
_____
_____
_____
_____
_____
_____

Tire Data
FRONT Brand _____
Model _____
Pressure _____ psi
REAR Brand _____
Model _____
Pressure _____ psi

For a free consultation on your bike's handling, copy and send this form to: Jeremy Wilke, MX Tech, 4136 W. 6940 N. Rd., Bourbonais, IL 60914. Tel/FAX: 815/939-2196. E-mail: jwilkey@puma.olivet.edu

◗ Forks Rebound Fast

Question: The forks on my 1990 KX250 rebound very fast. When I hit bumps, they rebound so fast that my arms are getting pumped up. Also there is a clanking noise when the forks top out. I tried turning the rebound screws for more damping, but that made no difference. Could these problems be related? What do I have to do to fix these problems.

Answer: This is a common problem on Kayaba forks. The bushings that support and seal the piston rod and damper rod are worn. The worn bushings allow oil to bypass the rebound piston, causing a loss of damping. There is one bushing in each fork leg. It is located under the head cap of the damper rod. The head cap is threaded to the damper rod with normal right-hand threads. This is a difficult service job because the cartridge has to be removed from the forks and disassembled, and this disassembly requires special tools. Replacement bushings can be purchased from aftermarket companies such as Pro-Action, White Brothers, and Race Tech.

◗ Chronic Fork-Seal Leaks

Question: I'm having problems with leaky fork seals on my bike. I even bought the seals that claim to be leak-resistant. That didn't make any difference. What could I be doing wrong?

Answer: Check the fork tube for scratches or rust marks. There must be some imperfections in the tubes for it to leak after changing the seals and bushings. Also make sure you don't overfill the fork tubes with oil. Check the factory service manual for recommendations on oil volume. If the tubes are scratched, try polishing out the scratches with 400-grit wet/dry sanding paper.

Here is a tip to use when installing new seals: Place a plastic bag over the end of the fork tube so the seal doesn't get scratched during installation.

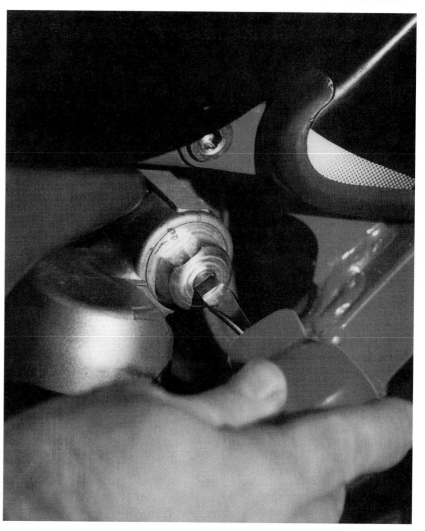

The rear shock's compression adjuster is located on top of the reservoir on most bikes. Turning the clicker clockwise will make the low-speed compression damping more slow/stiff. Turning the clicker counter-clockwise will make the damping more fast/soft.

Suspension Data Log

You should keep a log of suspension adjustments and settings to help you in tuning. The log should track the following data for the fork: oil level, spring rate, spring preload, oil weight, fork-tube overlap, compression-adjuster setting, rebound-adjuster setting, tire type, and tire pressure. Keep a similar log for the shock, with the following data: spring rate, spring sag, oil weight, compression-adjuster setting, rebound-adjuster setting, tire type, and tire pressure. You'll find a handy blank data log in this chapter in the section on video suspension tuning.

Final Tips on Basic Tuning

Remember to do the tasks that are listed earlier in this section for the best results. Record the race sag and adjuster positions in a race logbook. Check the sag every four races because shock springs loosen up and break in. Fork springs tend to sack out within about one season. Try setting your race sag first and install the correct springs for your weight and riding demands before you spend $500 on revalving.

The front fork's low-speed compression adjuster is located on the bottom of each fork leg. Sometimes this adjuster is covered with a rubber plug that prevents dirt from blocking the adjuster screw. All the clickers on Japanese dirt bikes use a slotted head so you can adjust the damping with a straight blade screw driver. The damping adjustments to the forks are performed the same as with a shock; as you look at the clicker, turning it clockwise will increase the damping (which will stiffen up the suspension, slowing down response).

Cartridge Fork Service and Tuning

More likely than not, your bike uses cartridge forks. They were introduced in 1986 on Kawasakis and were used by most bikes in 1987.

In this section I'll show you some tips for getting better performance out of any cartridge-type fork. Some tips involve just replacing worn bushings, while other tips are difficult to perform and require specialized knowledge and tools. Some parts of the cartridge are easily damaged and expensive to replace. Before you attempt any servicing of your bike's cartridge forks, purchase the factory service manual for details on assembly and tightening torque specs.

How a Cartridge Fork Works

The cartridge is basically two tubes with damping valves. The tubes slide together. The large tube is the damper rod, and it houses the compression valves. The small tube is the piston rod, and it houses the rebound valves. Cartridge forks rely on several plastic and metallic bushings to keep the telescopic rods from binding as they slide back and forth.

Cartridge fork valving consists of thin washers and cylindrical pistons with tiny bleed passages and slightly larger ports for the fluid to flow through. Damping is accomplished by restricting the fluid flow. An inherent problem with cartridge forks is that the debris from the bushings gets trapped between the valve washers and in the piston, thereby ruining the damping affect. This is the main reason why cartridge forks need to be cleaned and have the oil changed so often (every 10 to 15 hours of riding). The Twin Chamber design features improvements to extend the service time between cartridge servicing and improve the high-speed tuning (resistance to hard bottoming).

Evolution of the Cartridge Fork

Twin Chamber forks were a big deal when they appeared on the RMs in 1994, but the technology had been around since 1975. It developed when front fork travel went from 6 to 12 inches in 1975. Factory teams were scrambling to find forks that were soft enough for slow-speed bumpy off-camber turns yet stiff enough for hard landings from big jumps. Yamaha turned to a partnership with Steve Simons to try and make the long-travel suspension work. This alliance signaled the start of the best innovations in front forks.

In 1977, Yamaha adapted the accumulator from their monoshock to each fork cap on the front forks of the YZ250. Basically it consisted of a cylindrical chamber with a free-floating piston that separated two nitrogen gas-charged, spring-backed chambers. These accumulators worked as a pneumatic high-speed compression damping control. Modern cartridge forks use hydraulic damping controls (pistons and washers). Yamaha was bold to include this innovation on production bikes, but it was doomed to suffer the same fate as the Yamaha B.A.S.S system for rear shocks from the mid-1980s. The average mechanic had no tuning or service information so they weren't maintained properly.

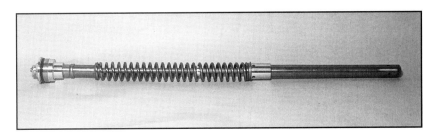

This is a fork cartridge. It consists of these main parts from left to right: fork cap, preload cone, spring, piston rod, damping rod, and base valve/compression adjuster bolt.

The damping rod is on the right. It has a castle fitting on the top of the rod so you can insert a holding tool (left) to prevent the damper rod from spinning when loosening the compression bolt assembly.

The top of the damping rod unthreads to uncover the piston rod bushing.

In 1978, Steve Simons invented and patented a hydraulic bottoming cone and cup design that is used in all Kayaba cartridge forks. In the mid-1990s, companies started selling aftermarket bottoming cones for cartridge forks. These products were based on the original Simons design but were slightly different than OEM parts. The forks still have a hydraulic lock, but it occurs more progressively than the stock part.

In 1981, Terry Davis' Two-Stage Reservoir product was popular with desert riders in the early 1980s. It was designed for noncartridge forks. It was a hydraulic/pneumatic version of Yamaha's accumulator fork cap. The main difference was that Terry Davis' design linked the fork tubes together with balance tubes and connected them to one giant aluminum-finned reservoir. It looked like you were riding with a beer-keg clamped to your crossbar. Despite the horrendous looks, it worked great if you had the patience to tune it.

This technology was used on Honda factory bikes in 1989 and nearly appeared on the 1990 CR250. These 1989 Showa factory forks were actually more advanced than the 1994 RM fork! Instead of using a floating piston and a spring, this design used a nitrogen-charged gas bladder (same as a rear shock). The gas pressure

This is the method used to remove the cartridge from the Suzuki Twin Chamber forks (1995 and later model RMs). The fork leg is clamped in a vise on the axle clamp while a deep well socket is used to loosen the bottom bolt. There is a jam nut located next to the bottom bolt and that is being held by a 14mm wrench. The only special tool needed to disassemble these forks is a 4mm thick flat plate with a 14mm slot cut into it. That tool holds the cartridge so it doesn't turn when the bottom bolt is loosened. These forks are actually easier to service than normal cartridge forks.

The trick to installing fork seals without ruining them is to place a plastic bag over the end of the fork tube, then slide the seal over it. Remember to remove the plastic bag after the seal is installed.

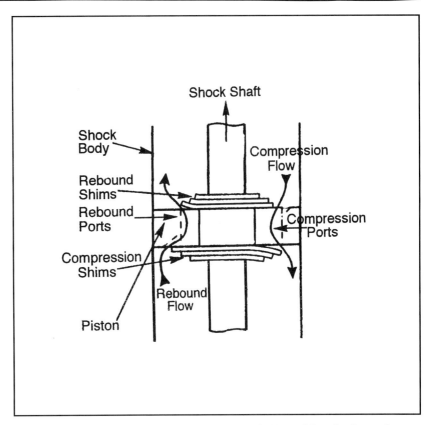

This illustration shows how the shim stack (or leaf stack) affects oil flow. By altering the size and number of shims, a suspension tuner can tailor dampening to specific needs.

was increased if more resistance to bottoming was needed. These forks were the factory riders' favorite for Supercross because they were specially developed for front wheel landings. This fork design was scheduled for the 1990 CR250, but Honda switched at the last moment because they didn't feel the average guy could service these forks, and was more likely to ruin something. They were right. Better to have bad damping than no damping.

In 1996, Kayaba revived the gas bladder concept and is rumored to be developing a fork for the 1998 Kaws that incorporates the bladder and the double-pumper damper rods.

1994 Twin Chamber Showa RM Forks

In 1994, one of the Japanese Manufacturers finally had the bullocks to select the Showa forks. The fork cap houses the compression valve at the top of a semisealed cartridge, so debris can't clog the valve. The fork cap also houses a free-floating piston-backed spring. The spring is used only during very high compression and full bottoming of the forks. This system offers track-side quick change capability of the compression-damping circuit. That is, once somebody figures out how to revalve and spring these forks for different types of riders.

1995

This was the year for aftermarket fork innovations. Bottoming cones became the rage. Products such as these replace the stock OEM hydraulic bottoming cones that fit on the piston rod of cartridge forks. The aftermarket cones are longer than the OEM cones and have more progressive angles that enable the forks to hydraulic lock at an earlier point in the travel. Another innovative product was designed by Terry Davis of Terry Products. Terry's Double-Pumper kit fits the Kayaba cartridge forks and enables compression damping from the rebound rod as well as the base valve.

The Double-Pumper kit also enables the cartridge to be replenished with oil during a series of high-speed compression impacts.

1996

This was the year that signaled the return of conventional cartridge forks that featured innovations similar to the Double Pumper. Two of these fork designs were the RM Suzuki Showa and the WP fork made in Holland.

The latest buzz in suspension is FMF's contractive suspension device. FMF licensed a patent from a European inventor that returns the forks and shock to the sag point of the suspension. The sag point for the shock is about 95mm and 55mm for the forks. The device is basically a spring-backed cartridge that enables a tuner to adjust the point to where the suspension components top out in travel. This eliminates some inherent problems associated with rear end kicking during braking or headshaking of the forks. Apparently a rider must adjust his pre-jumping skills because the suspension won't topout completely. Ohlins experimented with a similar device in the early 1990s, but abandoned it. During the 1996 GP season, Bob Moore of the Italian Magic Bike team is testing the FMF contractive suspension device that will be marketed in the States in September 1996.

To initially bleed the air from the forks, cap your hand over the top of the tube and compress the fork. Take care to release the air pressure from the tube slowly or it could spray in your face!

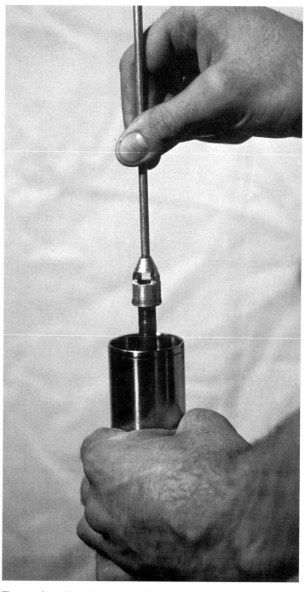

This is a Race Tools bleeder rod. It is used to stroke the piston rod up and down to bleed the air from the cartridge.

Special Tools for Servicing the Cartridge

It takes more special tools to service cartridge forks than to rebuild the motorcycle's engine. The basic tools include a damper rod holder, a bleeder rod, and a seal driver. Race Tools is the only company that sells suspension rebuilding tools, besides the Japanese motorcycle manufacturers. In addition, a tape measure can be used to set and measure the oil level, but a suction-type level-setting tool is more convenient.

Damper rod holding tools are used to prevent the rod from spinning when the base-valve bolt is unthreaded. These holding tools are not universal in size and flange shape because the flange shape on top of the damper rod is different from brand and model.

Bleeder-rod tools thread on to the top of the piston rod. During the final air-bleeding procedure, it's necessary to stroke the piston rod through its travel in order to facilitate bleeding of the cartridge. Four different sizes of bleeder

rods are made to service cartridge forks made from 1986–96.

Seal drivers are metal slugs machined to fit the outer diameter of the fork tube. There are two types of seal drivers—solid and split. Split drivers are needed for upside down forks because those types of fork tubes have axle clamps. Conventional cartridge forks can use solid seal drivers because the driver is installed from the top of the tube.

Servicing the Suzuki/Showa Twin Chamber forks does not require a hold-

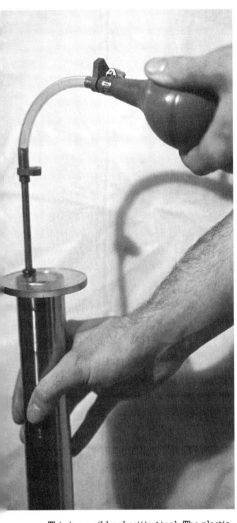

This is an oil level setting tool. The plastic disc is used to set the distance between the end of the tube so you can accurately set the oil level. The tool is placed on top of the compressed fork leg and the bulb is squeezed to remove the excess oil and set the oil level.

ing tool or a bleeder rod, you will need two tools that you can make from materials available from a hardware store—a shaft holder and an oil-level tool. The shaft holder is fitted to the bottom of the fork, to hold the damper rod from spinning while the bottom bolt is unthreaded, and it can be made from a 14mm wrench or a piece of flat stock with a maximum thickness of 5mms. The oil-level tool can be built from a 4-inch- or 100mm-long piece of 2-inch-inside-diameter PVC tubing. Suzuki

quotes oil level specs with the forks 4 inches or 100mm from bottom. The PVC can be inserted between the axle clamp and the fork tube wiper, to set the tube height. However you still need a seal driver to install the fork seals.

There are also some general tools that you'll need, including a vise with soft jaws, an assortment of large-diameter six-point sockets, a plastic mallet, a flat-blade screwdriver, an oil pan, and cleaning solvents.

If you are interested in revalving the fork valves, then you'll need some very special tools—such as digital calipers for measuring the shims and drivers to remove the peened tab on the bottoming cone. The bottoming cone is located in the middle of the piston rod. By removing the bottoming cone, you can separate the piston rod from the damper rod.

Changing Fork Oil

I strongly recommend that you completely disassemble and clean your cartridge forks every 20 riding hours. However, if you are sure that the forks are in good condition and you just want to change the oil, here is a simple method.

1. Remove the forks from the bike.
2. Unscrew the jam nut on the fork cap.
3. Unscrew the fork cap.
4. Remove the plastic spacer.
5. Slide out the spring.
6. Turn the fork upside down and drain the oil from the forks.
7. Stroke the piston rod to pump the oil out of the cartridge while draining the forks.
8. Add about four ounces of fork oil to each tube and use it to flush out the tubes.
9. After you have drained out the flushing oil, follow the procedure listed later in this section for filling the oil and bleeding air from the cartridge.
10. Reassemble the forks and put them back on your bike, being careful to torque the pinch bolts to recommended settings.

Disassembling Forks

Simply changing the oil is fine for periodic maintenance, but if your forks haven't been serviced in a season or more, you'll have to disassemble and clean the cartridge. Cartridge forks are especially susceptible to dirty oil, as gook tends to accumulate around the cartridge and the fork loses damping.

1. Remove your forks and drain the oil (see above).
2. Take the nut off the very bottom of the fork, either with an air impact wrench or by holding the damper rod in place with a damper rod holding tool (available at your dealer or from Race Tech).
3. Pull the cartridge out of the bottom of the fork.
4. Lay out all the parts and clean thoroughly with contact cleaner (note that at this point, the fork tube can be pulled from the fork slider to replace fork seals, etc.).
5. Replace any worn seals or bushings (see below).
6. Install the cartridge.
7. Tighten the nut on the bottom of the fork, using the special tool or an air impact wrench (be VERY careful with the impact wrench; you can blow the O-ring off of the cartridge and lose all damping).
8. Install the spring and spacer.
9. Follow the procedure listed later in this section for filling the forks with oil and bleeding air from the cartridge.
10. Reassemble the forks and put them back on your bike, being careful to torque the pinch bolts to recommended settings.

Replacing Bushings

The seals, wipers, and bushings should be replaced at least once a year. If you are looking for the highest level of performance, replace the bushing that fits in the head of the damper rod and supports the piston rod. The standard bushing has excess clearance that can cause the piston rod to go off-center and produce more stiction in the forks. After you have spent the time to polish the bearing surfaces of the damper and piston rods, then replace the standard bushing with an accessory bushing that has tighter clearances and a low coefficient of friction. Enzo Racing in America offers a racing bushing for Kayaba forks.

When your forks lose rebound damping, the main cause is worn piston rod bushings. When these bushings are worn out, they allow the cartridge fluid to bypass the bushing and piston rod, thereby losing the damping affect. If your bike's cartridge forks make a clunking sound when they extend, the piston-rod bushing is worn out.

The piston rod bushing can be replaced by unthreading the head from the damper rod, where the bushing is housed. This procedure is done by heating the steel head to break the bond of the locking agent on the threads. Then, use a chain-clamp wrench to grasp the steel head and unthread it from the aluminum damper rod. After the bushing is replaced, the threads of the damper rod and head must be carefully cleaned and a permanent locking agent applied. Then, tighten them with the chain-clamp-wrench. Warning: This procedure is very difficult and should only be entrusted to a professional suspension technician. The Teflon bushings support the fork tube to the slider. You can tell when they are worn because there will be discoloration on the load-bearing surface. These bushings are easy to replace and should be changed once a year. The slider bushing (large-diameter bushing) falls out when you separate the two tubes. The fork-tube bushing (small diameter) is under spring tension, so it must be removed by using a straight-blade screwdriver to spread the bushing at the side slit and slide it off the end of the fork tube. When you install the large-diameter bushings, take care to seat them properly in the slider before trying to install the fork seals. You do not need to use any special oil or grease on these bushings because they are Teflon coated.

Replacing Fork Seals

Once you have the forks disassembled and the fork slider and tube separated (see previous section), the fork seals can be removed. When installing the new seals, you must be very careful not to tear them when sliding them over the fork tube. Some grease and a plastic bag are key to getting your new seals installed without tearing.

1. Apply Teflon grease (Denicol or Noleen) to the wiper and seal.
2. Place a plastic bag over the end of the fork tube.

This is a seal-installing tool. It takes a bit of force to press the seal into the slider.

3. Slide the seal over the plastic bag and on to the fork tube. The plastic bag covers the bushing grooves and prevents the seal from tearing as it slides over the sharp edges of the bushing grooves.

Now, you can reassemble your forks and be confident that your new seals will hold.

Filling with Oil and Bleeding Air from the Cartridge

Here are some tips for filling Showa or Kayaba cartridge forks with oil and bleeding out the air.

1. During the initial filling and bleeding sequence, compress the fork tube and fill the fork to within 2 inches of the top.
2. Extend the fork, cap your hand over the end of the tube, and compress the fork. You'll feel air pressure building up under your hand. That is good because the oil is under pressure and that will help force tiny air bubbles through the shims of the compression valve and also displace the air that gets trapped between the fork tube and slider. Repeat this procedure at least four times, adding oil each time.

3. Use a stroker rod to grasp the piston rod and stroke the rod up and down until the tension through the stroke is equal. Equal tension is an indication that the air is bled from the cartridge.

4. To set the oil level, remove the spring and compress the fork. Use a thin ruler (preferably metric) to measure the distance between the top of the tube and the top of the oil. An oil level setting tool (or a large syringe with a bit of hose attached) is the quickest way to set your oil level. Also, make sure there is an excess amount of oil in the fork so the oil level setting tool can suck out oil to set the proper level.

5. The oil level should be set with the spring removed and the fork tube bottomed. Kawasaki recommends setting the oil level 10mm higher than the spec because that will compensate for the small amount of air trapped between the slider and tube. That bit of air works its way out when the bike is ridden.

Tips for Twin Chamber Forks

The Twin Chamber forks used on the RM models come in conventional and upside-down designs, but both use the same cartridge.

These forks are easy to service. A six-point socket and ratchet are all that are needed to unthread the bottom bolt. A thin, flat 14mm wrench is needed to hold the piston rod. Normally, you don't remove the fork cap from the cartridge because the cartridge can be removed as an assembly from the top of the fork tube. There is significant suction pressure on the fork cap because it is attached to the compression valve, which is submerged in oil.

Revalving of the compression valve is easy on the Twin Chamber forks because the compression valve can be removed without totally disassembling the forks. Another advantage to the Twin Chamber forks is that the compression valve can't get clogged by metal debris because it's mounted on top of the cartridge instead of the bottom. On normal cartridge forks the compression (base) valve is mounted in the bottom of the forks where the metal debris settles.

This is a WER steering damper. It attaches between the triple clamp and the frame to make the bike more stable and reduce headshake.

Twin-tube fork internals also generate less metal debris because the internal bushing and seal used to seal the bottom of the piston and cartridge rods is a very durable part. The way that you can tell that the bushing and seal are worn is the fork damping will be soft/fast and the outer tube's oil level will become higher. If you have to replace the bushing and seal, you'll need to wrap Teflon tape around the piston rod's threads. This will insure that the seal doesn't tear upon installation. This technique is similar to wrapping a plastic bag around the end of the fork tube to facilitate installation of the main fork tube seals. Teflon tape must be used on the Twin Chamber piston rod because the seal clearance to the shaft is very tight.

Problems that Mimic Poor Tuning

Mechanical problems, such as worn parts, can cause your forks to act as if they are poorly tuned when they are not. Before you spend a lot of money on revalving or other fork tuning, make sure there is not a mechanical cause for your fork's problems. The following is a list of potential trouble spots to check on your forks:

1. Oil breakdown can make the damping seem too fast or soft, especially when the fork oil gets hot. Debris can also accumulate in the valving to hinder the damping. Fix by cleaning the forks and changing the fork oil.

2. Blown oil seals cause a lack of damping and a number of other catastrophic problems such as worn bushings. Replace the seals.

3. Worn rebound piston rings. Most bikes use a plastic seamless band for a rebound piston ring. If your forks seem to rebound too quickly, the oil may be bypassing the rebound piston and shim valving. Unfortunately this seal band cannot be replaced; you must buy the entire piston-rod assembly.

4. Sacked fork springs. Fork springs become shorter in length with use, which can cause headshake or wobbling at high speed. Plan on replacing fork springs every season. Check to make sure they are even in length as a set.

5. Dented aluminum sliders. The sliders are made from thin-walled aluminum tubing, so the rocky roost from other bikes can easily cause dents in the sliders. These dents can cause the forks to bind, making the fork damping harsh. Replace the sliders when they get dented, and install plastic rock guards to prevent rock dents.

6. Worn bushing for the piston rod to damper rod. This bushing is located in the head of the damper rod and it supports the piston rod. If your forks appear to have lost rebound damping, this bushing is probably worn and must be replaced.

Revalving Cartridge Forks

The best performing forks are ones that have smooth, fitted bushings, clean cartridge fluid, the correct springs, and valving matched to the rider's ability and the spring rate. After you have used the previously described methods to make sure everything is working properly in your forks and are still dissatisfied with their performance, only then is it time to think about revalving your forks. The following guidelines will help you do it right.

Cartridge forks can be revalved by changing the washer dimensions. Base-valve kits are a replacement accessory that changes the compression damping. Race Tech's Gold Valve is also a (compression) base valve. The Gold Valve features different cross-over and bottom-plate washers, plus a revalving chart that provides washer-placement specs. These different specs are based on rider profiles, everyone from paddock-posers to GP riders. This system offers another level of "tuneability" for those tuners patient enough to experiment with it. There are other base-valve kits made by Pro-Action, Noleen Racing, and Pro-Racing that are simply bolted onto the compression bolt and take the place of the stock base valve. These aftermarket base valves have special pistons that are machined for better oil flow, and they have modified valve stacks to reduce problems such as mid-stroke spiking.

Polishing for Reduced Stiction

The largest bearing surface areas in the cartridge are the inside of the damper rod and the outside of the piston rod. Just by polishing these surfaces, you can reduce the stiction of the forks. The piston rod can be polished by hand or in a lathe. The best way to polish the inside of the damper rod is with an electric drill and a drill-rod with a slot in the end to accept a Scotch-Brite polishing pad (commonly used to scrub dishes).

Tuning with Oil Viscosity

There are two ways to rate suspension fluids, the Society of Automotive Engineers (SAE) weight and the viscosity index number. The SAE determines the weight number with a standard test that measures oil flow through a fixed orifice

at a certain temperature in a 30-minute period. The viscosity index number is a measurement of the oil's flow rate through a fixed orifice, over a specific temperature range in a set time period. The fluid velocities through the tiny steel shim valving and pistons of the cartridge forks are much greater than in the old-style forks, which used drilled jet passages.

Be sure to use a cartridge fork oil when you replace the oil; the weight is not that important. Cartridge fork oil is available from about 2 1/2 to 7 weight, and any of those work well. In general, the higher the weight, you'll get an incremental increase in compression and rebound damping. In reality, most riders wouldn't be able to notice these differences.

In general, raise the oil level when you're bottoming hard. Increased oil will help the last third of the stroke only.

Fork Oil Breakdown

The fork oil breaks down when its additives are depleted and it is contaminated with aluminum and bronze debris. The additives that enable the oil to have a low flow resistance are polymer particles, and they eventually accumulate as a varnish-like coating on the inside of the fork tubes. Consequently, the oil in new-style cartridge forks should be changed every 15 or 20 rides to maintain the best performance.

The main source of debris in the oil is spring flaking. Only Eibach aftermarket springs are coated with a flexible polymer that resists flaking. The aluminum damper rods and sliders, along with the plastic and bronze high-wear bearing parts, also slowly break down during use and contaminate the oil. Further debris is produced when steel preload rubs against the springs. Pro-Action sells aluminum preload cones of an updated design for the early 1990s Japanese dirt bikes. These cones greatly reduce the amount of debris produced by the cones rubbing on the springs.

Fork Spring Preload Tuning

Before you try to measure and set the preload, measure the length of both springs and compare the measurements to the manufacturer's spec for minimum length. If the springs are too short, it means they are sacked out and need to

be replaced. When you purchase new springs, make sure you get the proper spring rate for your bike and rider weight. The Japanese manufacturers have recommendations listed in the service manual for the best spring rate based on rider weight. If you are an expert rider and use the front brake hard or ride on tracks with big jumps, you should select the next stiffer spring rate from the one recommended in the service manual.

Here is how to measure and set the spring preload. Disassemble the fork. Let the fork tube bottom and extend the piston rod. Slide the spring over the piston rod. With the rod extended, measure the distance between the end of the spring and the point where the spring retaining collet clips into the rod. That gives you the preload measurement. Normally the preload should be 5–15mm. The only way for you to vary the preload is to adjust the jam nut height on the piston rod to set the correct preload.

White Power and Ohlins fork springs are available in a wide variety of spring rates, and are the proper length to replace extra-long Japanese springs that have too much preload. True-Tech sells aftermarket fork caps for 1990s models of Japanese dirt bikes.

These fork caps feature an adjusting screw to vary the spring preload. This is an excellent product but they require frequent maintenance. If you purchase a set of these fork caps, be sure to pick up a spare set of seals for the caps.

Front Suspension Troubleshooting

Diving

Problem: The bike suffers from too much front-end diving when braking for turns.

Possible causes: The fork's spring rate is too soft, spring preload is too low, compression damping is too soft/fast, or the compression clicker is turned out too far.

Headshake During Deceleration

Problem: The front end oscillates when you change the weight bias to the front end.

Possible causes: The tire's sidewalls are dry-rotted, the tire pressure is too low, the steering-head nut or bearings are too loose, the fork springs are too soft or sacked-out, the fork-spring preload is too low, the fork-tube overlap is too great, or the rebound damping is too slow/stiff.

Headshake During Acceleration

Problem: The front end oscillates when you accelerate out of a turn.

Possible causes: The low-speed damping is too stiff/slow or the spring preload is too great.

Spiking

Problem: You feel sharp jolts through the handlebars when the front tire rolls over square-edged bumps.

Possible causes: The fork oil level is too high, the compression damping is too stiff/slow, the fork spring rate is too stiff, or the compression-valve stack is too soft in the mid-speed range in relation to the oil height and the spring rate.

Bottoming

Problem: The front end bottoms out on small jumps.

Possible causes: The fork spring rate is too soft, the oil level is too low, the cartridge bushing is worn, or the compression adjuster is turned too far out, causing the low-speed damping to be too soft/fast.

Rear Shock Servicing

This section is a general overview for single-shock servicing. I'll show you what things you can clean and inspect yourself and how a professional service technician would service a shock. This section is also intended to give a thorough understanding of how suspension works and tell you all the things they leave out of the service manual. I want you to become a more informed consumer by learning when to have your shock serviced and how to shop for suspension services.

Total shock service with cleaning and oil changing should be performed every 15 to 20 riding hours. Servicing suspension components is a specialized task that requires knowledge, experience, and access to special tools and replacement parts. If you lack any of these important things, don't attempt to service your suspension components yourself. Trust revalving to a suspension technician.

Also, you should regularly clean,

This is a typical rear shock for a dirt bike. Starting from left to right, clevis (bottom shock mount), rebound adjuster, foam bumper, shock shaft, cover, seal pack, piston assembly, shock body, reservoir cap, reservoir piston or bladder, reservoir body, and compression adjuster.

inspect, and grease your rear linkage. See "Servicing Rear Suspension Linkage" section later in this chapter for more details.

Your bike's shock is constantly subjected to internal and external torture. Inside the shock, the bronze piston ring scrapes up against the hard-anodized aluminum shock body walls in oil that reaches temperatures of 450 degrees Fahrenheit. The bronze and aluminum particles quickly contaminate the small volume of shock oil, causing the oil to breakdown.

To make matters worse, the shock is also constantly subjected to external torture. The outside of the shock is constantly subjected to dirt particles being rammed into the shock seal by the foam bumper and the high strength detergents from the spray of a pressure washer.

Common Problems

The external elements cause the wiper and seal to fail. Small quantities of oil flow past the seal and you hardly notice until most of the oil is lost and the shock shaft turns blue from overheating. It's easy to forget about the shock because it's bolted into the center of the bike, but it's hard to forget about the replacement cost of a shock if it fails!

Basic Cleaning

This procedure should be performed every five riding hours:

1. Power-wash the shock clean. You want the dirt off the outside of the shock before you do the detail cleaning. Take care not to spray directly at the shock seal. Also, be sure to spray clean the fine threads on the shock body.
2. Spray penetrating oil on the threads and wait 15 minutes before you try to

unthread the spring retaining nut. Unthread the nut so you can remove the spring collet and the spring so you can remove the seal cap. There are two types of spring collets. One has an open slot and the other is a solid disc with a circlip. The circlip must be removed before you can remove the spring.

3. Use a plastic mallet and punch to rock the seal cap back and forth until the cap pops loose from the shock body. Notice how much dirt and debris is under the seal cap, jammed up against the seal wiper. It's very important to carefully clean under the foam bumper and the seal cap with detergent and water.
4. Check the seal wiper for oil seepage. Seepage indicates that the seal is worn and needs to be replaced.
5. Check the shock shaft for deep scratches and a blue color. The blue indicates that the shock was severely overheated probably from the loss of oil at the seal. The shaft can be re-plated or replaced if it is discolored or deeply scored.
6. Your factory service manual lists a minimum free-length for the shock spring. Measure it to make sure it hasn't sacked-out.
7. Remove the seals from the top shock mount and clean the dirt and old grease from the seals and spherical bearing. The bearing doesn't require lube, but you should pack the seals with grease to prevent dirt and water from reaching the bearing.
8. Check the lower shock-mount clevis for cracks at the bolt hole. Cracks are common on YZ shocks because the bottom shock mount protrudes below the frame tubes.

▶ Shock Rebound Adjuster Seized

Question: I have a 1989 CR250, and the rear shock's rebound adjuster is seized. I can't turn it with a screwdriver. What's wrong?

Answer: The problem you describe is common for Showa shocks on 1986–89 CR250s and CR500s. The rebound adjuster consists of a fine-threaded screw and a ramp-shaped nut. Condensation causes the fine threads to become corroded, and the corrosion keeps the adjuster screw from turning. It is possible to remove the rebound adjuster cartridge and clean the threads of the screw so the adjuster works, this task requires that you discharge the nitrogen gas pressure from the shock's bladder. If you do not have the special tools or knowledge required to service suspension components, then don't try to repair the adjuster. Instead, trust the job to a professional suspension technician.

▶ Rear Suspension Kicks

Question: I have a 1993 YZ250 with stock suspension. My problem is that the rear is kicking back at me. It seems to be kicking out to my left. All my suspension parts are in great shape, with no slack. This seems to happen only off of big jumps. The suspension feels pretty good on the rest of the track. Also, when I land from the big jumps my suspension springs up too quick, lifting me off of my foot pegs. If I change my shock rebound to 4, it seems to hang up too much on jumps.

Answer: Your shock is rebounding too fast, causing the sprung mass of the bike to accelerate rapidly and the rear tire to lose traction and slide the rear end sideways. When a bike kicks, that is an indication that the rebound damping is off.

The oil could be broken down, causing the too-fast rebound problem. Change the rear shock oil. If you don't have the knowledge or tools to rebuild the shock, trust your shock to a suspension technician.

Shock Disassembly

The following is a typical disassembly procedure that a professional service technician would follow when servicing a shock:

1. Depressurize the gas bladder, noting any oil mist escaping with the gas, which would indicate a perforated bladder that needs to be replaced.
2. Remove the compression adjuster bolt and let the oil drain. Take care when unthreading the compression bolt. Examine the first threads for three deep peen marks. You may need to drill the centers of the peen marks or the threads could be damaged.
3. Use a bladder-cap-removing T-handle to depress the bladder cap enough to remove the circlip. Now, the bladder cap can be removed. Enzo makes extended bladder caps that increase the oil volume of the shock.
4. Remove the shock shaft by popping up the seal cap, depressing the seal-pack assembly with two drift rods, and removing the circlip that holds the seal pack in place. Use a scraper to remove the burr left by the circlip because this burr could prevent the seal pack from lifting out of the shock body. Remove the shaft assembly from the shock body.
5. Clean all the shock parts thoroughly in mineral spirits solvent, but never in fuel. Fuels are explosive and will damage the rubber seal and foam bumper.
6. Smart technicians measure the inside bore of the shock body for excessive out-of-round wear. Although the shock bodies are hard-anodized, they can still wear out and let oil bypass the piston and shim valves, thereby reducing the damping affect.
7. Other high-wear parts of the shock include the seal pack and piston ring. The seal pack has a bushing built into the inside of it, along with the seal and wiper. When the wiper fails, the seal and bushing wear out fast. They should be replaced as a set. Average replacement cost of a seal pack is $50. The best way to install the seal pack on the shock shaft without damaging the seal is to wrap a piece of Teflon tape over the end of the shaft threads. Piston rings are made of either bronze or plastic. The bronze ones wear fast and should be replaced every time you have the oil changed.

A circlip holds the damper rod assembly into the shock body. The circlip can be removed by pushing down the seal pack with a drift rod and then wedging a scribe between the circlip and shock body and lightly prying it out of its groove.

8. Check the shock shaft for deep scratches, straightness, and bluing. If the shaft is bent, blued, or deeply scratched, repair or replace it. European manufacturers offer replacement shafts, but some Japanese manufacturers don't offer any replacement parts for their shocks. Luckily, some companies offer re-chroming and polishing services for shock shafts. The best method of shaft plating is titanium-nitrate. The material is gold in color and is very hard and resistant to chipping from rock roost.

Assembling the Shock and Bleeding Air

While reassembling the shock, it is critical for good damping performance that you make sure that no air is trapped in the shock. If air is trapped in the shock, the oil will become aerated and break down faster. Also, the air travels through the piston and shim valves, reducing the damping effect. That can be dangerous because the shock will rebound faster and cause the rear end of the bike to kick. The following is a gen-

Clean the shock parts in mineral spirits solvent with a soft nylon brush.

When installing the damper assembly on Ohlins or older YZ shocks, the position of the floating piston in the reservoir must be maintained at a constant position with a special tool. On Japanese shocks with rubber bladders, you need to pressurize the bladder with 10 psi of nitrogen or air in order to prevent the bladder from collapsing when the damper assembly is installed.

eral procedure that technicians use when reassembling shocks:

1. Pour shock oil into a cup and set the compression adjuster bolt and the piston side of the shock shaft assembly in the oil for at least 30 minutes before assembling the shock. This will reduce the chances of air becoming trapped between the tiny shim-valve washers.

2. Now pour some oil into both the shock body and reservoir, and install the compression bolt. Clamp the top shock mount in a vise, and pour shock oil in both the reservoir and shaft sides of the shock body.

3. Pour oil to within a 1/2 inch of the top of the reservoir. Apply Denicol or Noleen seal grease to the top edge of the bladder. Install the bladder and its retaining circlip.

4. Pressurize the bladder with 10 psi of nitrogen gas. This will make the bladder inflate to full size and force oil through the reservoir, past the compression bolt, and into the shaft side of the shock body. This also helps to force tiny air bubbles out of the

shock. Let the air flow up out of the shock for at least 30 minutes.

5. Pour oil to within 1 inch of the top of the shock body and install the shaft assembly. It will be difficult to depress the seal pack in order to install the circlip because you are compressing the inflated bladder. The shock is now overfilled with oil. This is done to facilitate the final air-bleeding procedure.

6. Some shocks, such as those built by Kayaba, have a 5mm Allen bolt on the top shock mount of the body that is used for bleeding air from the shock. Others, such as older Showa shocks, do not. These shocks must be bled though the compression adjuster bolt. Take care when removing the compression adjuster bolt. You must use a tiny drill bit to drill down the center of the three center-punch points, where the threads of the shock body and the compression adjuster are threaded together. Drill into center-punch points about 0.030 inch—just enough to drill through the points. The compression adjuster can then be unthreaded with-

out the threat of damaging the fine threads. In either case, position the top shock mount in the vise so the bleeder bolt or the compression adjuster is at the highest point. This will insure that no air enters into the shock during the final bleeding procedure.

7. Compress and extend the shock shaft several times so the trapped air congregates at the highest point on the shock, near the bleeder bolt. Lightly tap on the shock body and reservoir with a hammer. This will help tiny air bubbles to break loose from the sides of the body. If you feel any tight and loose spots during the shaft's travel, then there must be a lot of air trapped in the shock and you must start completely over.

8. If the shaft travels smoothly, then you can extend the shaft and slowly remove the bleeder bolt. The excess oil and air will flow out of the shock.

9. Set the bladder pressure to the factory-recommended spec. Normally that is 150 psi of nitrogen. Never use air to pressurize the bladder.

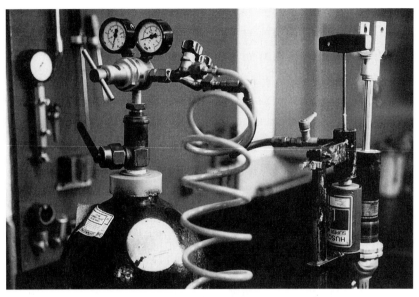

This is the nitrogen gas charging rig for a White Power shock. For most shocks, all you need is an air chuck for a Schraeder valve to pressurize the shock with nitrogen.

Installation Tips

Check the shock linkage and steering-head bearings for wear and grease. Also, be sure to reset the race sag on the back end. On full-size bikes, the rear race sag should be 90 to 105mms with unladen sag of 17 to 25 mm. Always check race sag with your full riding gear on, the fuel tank at race volume, and your feet on the pegs! If you go to a mud race, set the rear race sag after the bike gets muddy in practice. You'll be surprised how much it varies from when the bike is clean.

Servicing Rear Suspension Linkage

Remove the link bolt that fastens the linkage to the swingarm and elevate the rear wheel with the 10-inch block. This allows greater access to the shock bolt and other link pivot bolts. Take care when removing the links because some bikes use thin shim washers between the link-ages. The linkage consists of two main parts, the frame-mounted link arms and the swingarm-mounted link bar.

Remove the rubbers seals from the ends of the pivot bushings. Push the bushings halfway out and use degreaser and a shop towel to remove the old grease and dirt build-up. If the needle bearings are dry or corroded, then the seals are leaking, so the bearings and seals should be replaced. If

the bearings still have grease on them, then use a small brush to apply new grease to the bearings. Take care not to displace any of the needle bearings because they don't have a race-cage to hold them in place. Repeat this procedure to the bearings on the other side of the linkage.

To grease the swingarm pivots, you'll have to remove the swingarm pivot bolt. You may have to remove the brake pedal to remove the pivot bolt, and you should grease the brake pivot, too. Remove the chain or you won't be able to extend the swingarm back far enough to reach the pivot bearings. The pivot bolt may be difficult to remove, so use a brass drift rod and a hammer to drive the bolt out. The brass rod is softer than the pivot bolt and won't damage the threads. If the bolt is still very difficult to remove, then loosen the engine mounting bolts. Clean and grease the bearings and bushings the same way as you did the linkage parts.

Quick Link Lubing

Follow these steps to quickly lubricate the rear suspension link:

1. Place the bike on a stand and remove the linkage pivot bolt that goes through the swingarm.
2. Elevate the rear wheel with a 6-inch-tall block.

Shock springs are calibrated in many different spring rates. The only way to measure a spring's rate is with a digital spring tester.

3. Unbolt the link stay bars from the frame.
4. Clean the old grease and dirt from the seals and bearings with a rag and re-grease the bearings with wheel-bearing grease.
5. Reinstall the parts and torque the linkage pivots to factory specs.

This is a close-up view of the typical rebound adjuster of a Japanese shock. The adjusting screw slides through a spring and ball collar that acts as a detent so the screw stays in whatever position you set it to. The screw then threads into a ramp nut that changes the position of a long tapered rod that regulates the oil flow of a passageway in the shock shaft, located near the shock piston.

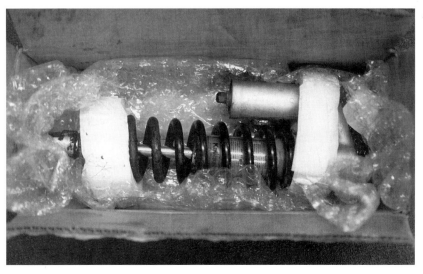

If you want to send your shock in for service, pack it in a sturdy cardboard box with lots of bubble wrap.

Rear Suspension Troubleshooting

Bottoming

Problem: The rear shock bottoms hard when landing from big jumps.

Possible causes: The spring rate is too soft, the spring sag is too great, the shock oil or nitrogen pressure has leaked out, the piston ring is worn (allowing the oil to bypass the piston), or the compression valve stack is too soft/fast for the rider's needs.

Kicking

Problem: The rear shock rebounds too fast. Every time you hit a bump the rear end bounces up and down several times before stabilizing.

Possible causes: The rebound damping is too fast/soft, the spring sag is too low, the rebound adjuster is turned out too far, or the piston ring or shock body are worn, allowing oil to bypass the piston.

Rear Wheel Hopping

Problem: The rear wheel hops and spins when accelerating out of a turn. The tire is repeatedly gaining and losing traction. The rear end makes a high-frequency wallowing motion.

Possible causes: The shock spring sag is too great, the rebound damping is too stiff/slow, the compression damping is too stiff/slow, or the linkage-ratio curve is too progressive.

Video Suspension Tuning

Suspension tuning can be a mystery for both the rider and his mechanic. As a rider on race day, you go out for your practice session and your suspension nearly kills you! You come back to the pits and your mechanic asks you if the high-speed rebound feels too fast. You haven't got a clue because for the last 20 minutes you tried to keep your motorcycle on two wheels! After riding and tuning motorcycles for years, I still cannot diagnose suspension problems by riding or watching the bike on a race track.

The best suspension tuners in the world have a well-developed sense of high-speed vision. They can watch a bike and rider on various sections of the track to determine how well the four different suspension circuits are working. You can acquire that same sense of high-speed vision with the help of a video camera. After video-taping the rider attacking various sections of the track, you can replay the tape one frame at a time and see exactly how the four different suspension circuits damp the impacts of jumps, whoops, and other track irregularities.

This section tells you how to use a videotape to tune your suspension. First, I'll explain the four suspension circuits and the track sections that help isolate each circuit. At the end of this section is a troubleshooting chart that will help you to identify problems with each circuit. A suspension-data log sheet is also provided so you can record all the pertinent information on your bike and have the data reviewed by a suspension tuning expert. The data log will help you to develop a mental framework for setting up your suspension properly. Finally, I will explain what changes suspension tuners make during revalving. A warning though: Do not try to revalve your own suspension! One small mistake can put you over the bars! First, set up your suspension with the proper springs, settings, oil heights, and so on. If you still need revalving performed, at least then you will know exactly what your suspension needs. Too many people have their suspension parts revalved without first trying to set up the bike properly.

Put the bike on a stand, remove the swingarm linkage bolt, and elevate the rear wheel with a
10 inch block so you can access the linkage.

Bel-Ray Waterproof Grease is great for the linkage bearings,
bushings, and seals. Wipe the old grease away before applying the
new grease.

Some links use circlips to retain the needle bearings. The clips are
easily covered in dirt and grudge. Use a scribe to scratch the area
around the bearing to check for a circlip, or check the parts
microfiche for placement of the circlip.

In this photo, the link is positioned over an open vise and a bearing driver is used to push the new bearings in place. Companies like Harbor Freight sells universal bearing/bushing/seal driver kits for as little as $15.

Video suspension tuning begins with someone shooting a video of you riding. Ideally, the video operator will catch you launching and landing off some bike jumps, going over deep whoops, hitting braking bumps, and accelerating over stutter bumps. The more different conditions you record, the more you will be able to figure out about your shocks. This mechanic films his rider taking a big jump to check the high-speed damping circuits.

Tuning with the Damping Circuits

As previously mentioned, the four suspension circuits of the forks and shock are the high-speed compression (HSC), high-speed rebound (HSR), low-speed compression (LSC), and low-speed rebound (LSR). Your main objective in video suspension tuning is to make video samples of the rider on sections of the track that best isolate two of these circuits at a time. Before you start riding and taping, change the suspension fluids, grease the linkage, and have the proper spring rates and sag settings on the shock and forks.

Low-Speed Compression (LSC) and Low-Speed Rebound (LSR) Tuning

The low-speed circuits work in two common track sections, braking for tight turns and accelerating on a straight with far-spaced, shallow whoops. When taping a rider, be sure to have the whole bike and part of the ground in the film frame. Stand far enough back from the track section and pan with the rider for at least 25 yards. Replay the tape one frame at a time and pay attention to how the wheel follows the ground as the bike hits the bumps. The wheel shouldn't compress quickly or rebound abruptly. All Japanese dirt bikes have suspension adjusting screws that affect the low-speed circuits only. Turning the adjusting screws clockwise will increase the damping and slow/stiffen the low-speed circuit. Turning the screws counterclockwise will decrease damping and speed-up/soften the low-speed circuit.

High-Speed Compression (HSC) and High-Speed Rebound (HSR) Tuning

The high-speed circuits work in two common track sections, landing from big jumps and accelerating on a straight with tightly spaced, sharp-edged whoops. Videotape a rider as he lands from a big jump and for about 15 yards after he lands. That is important because there are usually many small bumps in the landing path after a big jump. Replay the tape one frame at a time and watch to see how equally both the front and rear suspension compress and rebound. If the rear shock rebounds too fast, the rear end may spring up so fast that it loads the forks. If both ends rebound too fast, the whole bike may spring up off the ground. That can be hazardous if there is a turn after the jump.

Kicks like a mule! The low-speed rebound and compression are so stiff/slow on this bike that the rear wheel springs up off the ground. If your wheels are kicking high off the ground, your suspension needs tuning. If your rear wheel is off the ground a lot, you are losing drive.

When taping in whoop sections, try to pan the rider in as much of the section as possible. Watch how the suspension reacts to the sharp-edged whoops at speed. The rear wheel shouldn't pack-up. Packing is caused when the HSC and HSR are too slow to react to the terrain. The wheel will stay compressed as it hits the next whoop. Eventually the rider loses control and must slow down. Taping in whoops also helps the rider; if the bike is reacting properly, he may gain enough confidence to go faster through the section

If the videotape indicates that you need to change the high-speed circuits, you must take the suspension to an expert in revalving because there are no external adjustments that you can make to the high-speed circuits. Some suspension tuners are starting to encourage riders to make video samples for review.

World Champion Stefan Everts' bike is tuned so well that the wheels follow the terrain very well.

Notice that Everts' bike is well-balanced as it hits the bumps. This is the sign of well-tuned suspension.

This single-photo sequence shows the take-off and landing on a big jump. When tuning your suspension with a video recorder, watch for what happens during and after these two critical times.

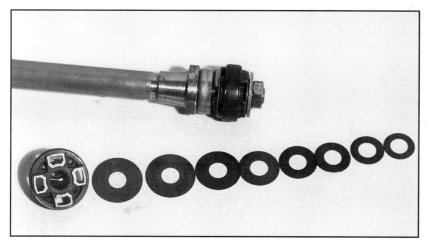

This is a fork's valve stack. Shown disassembled is the compression valve stack that comprises the base-valve assembly. Oil flows through the piston's ports and against the shims. The shims provide progressive resistance as the load increases. The rebound piston and valve stack is fastened to the end of the piston rod. That is a very simple valve stack because the load posed by the spring is linear and based on the spring rate.

Suspension Revalving

The forks and shock are supposed to keep the motorcycle's wheels in contact with the terrain and isolate the rider from the terrain's impact on the suspension—these are the ultimate goals of a suspension tuner. Easier said than done! When the rear wheel follows the terrain, the knobbies get a better bite on the dirt, so more of the engine's power drives the bike and less is lost to wheel spin. Similarly, when the front wheel follows the terrain, the knobbies bite deeply, so the front wheel steers rather than washing out.

This is a rear shock disassembled to show the different shims used for damping. On the left is the rebound valve stack. The larger diameter shims are mounted closest to the piston and they control the low speed damping. The small diameter shims are usually thicker in diameter than the low speed shims. They control the high speed damping. On the right is the compression stack. Notice how the shims taper in diameter to a very small diameter shim? That is the transition or cross-over shim. The transition shim separates the low and high speed valve stacks.

How Damping Works

Suspension fluid (oil) flows through the ports of the piston and up against the shims. The shims pose a resistance to the oil flow, which provides a damping effect. The damping effect is directly related to the diameter and the thickness of the shim. The shims act as a series of tiny springs, flexing to increase the flow area for the oil. The greater the flow area, the greater the oil flow and less the damping effect. The first shims that the oil encounters are the ones that affect the low-speed damping. These shims are large in diameter and thin in thickness. The oil deflects these shims easily because of their large surface area and the relatively thin steel poses low spring tension. The shim stack or valving is arranged in a taper shape. The large-diameter low-speed shims are positioned closest to the piston and the small-diameter high-speed shims are positioned farthest away from the piston.

Revalving 101

Revalving is a fine-tuning service performed to the compression and rebound valve stacks to effect a certain damping characteristic. The valve stack comprises many individual shims of various thicknesses and diameters. Revalving, then, is the manipulation or replacement of shims in the valve stack of cartridge forks or shocks.

All dirt bikes are originally built with springs and valving to suit one particular "average" rider profile. Therefore, it is almost certain that your bike will need adjustments, revalving, or different spring rates to suit your particular weight and riding style. In most cases, riders who are extremely light or heavy will need to change to different spring rates and valving to match. For example, a 175-pound expert motocross rider racing a 125cc bike will need to use stiffer-than-stock springs because those bikes are sprung for 150-pound intermediate riders. Using stiffer springs means that the dampers (forks and shock) will rebound faster because the spring has more stored energy when the travel is bottomed. Because of this, the rebound valving will need to be stiffer to prevent the dampers from rebounding too fast.

Revalving is performed by changing the combinations of shims on the compression and rebound valve stacks. It's a simple concept, but there are 20 different diameters of shims and 6 different thicknesses of shims, which allows for thousands of different combinations of shim stacks. You might wonder how suspension technicians know exactly what shims to change to fix handling problems. The answer is they don't know; they have to work it out by one or more of these three methods: trial and error, video camera, or data acquisition

The trial-and-error method requires a tuner to pair up with a rider who can give them accurate feedback on tuning changes.

The videocamera method requires the tuner to film a rider and review the tape footage in slow motion. Then the tuner can use the trial-and-error method to fine-tune the suspension. The video method can be very helpful for separating rider skill deficiencies from motorcycle handling problems. Sometimes, rider and handling problems can occur at the same time. A rider might try to compensate for the motorcycle's handling problem, and it is easily noticed when the video is played in slow motion. For more information on this method, see the section on video suspension tuning.

The data-acquisition method usually involves the use of a video camera and some trial-and-error testing. Matching the data with videotape footage is the quickest way to troubleshoot handling problems. Sensors are attached to the forks and shock to measure damper travel over time to calculate shaft-speed. Data-acquisition systems were first used in auto racing, then in motorcycle road racing, and then on dirt bikes.

Suspension Design Software

In 1993, Showa, a suspension component manufacturer in Japan, published a technical paper in the *JSAE Quarterly*. The paper was a case study on their development of a computer design program for shock tuning. Showa's program is designed to run on a mainframe computer, but there are programs designed for PCs. A line of three programs is available from Kevin Stillwell of Dirt Bike Specialties in Texas. Stillwell offers programs on springs, linkage ratios, and shim load. These programs are an excellent tool for simulating proposed changes to the suspension components, but they won't give you exact specs on how to revalve suspension for every combination of conditions and rider profiles. That can only be done the hard way, by trial and error. Even so, the spring program helps you to determine what the spring rate of any given spring is. Another part of the program calculates the estimated spring rate for a particular rider. The link-ratio program enables you to visualize the differences in linkage ratios and speculate as to the effect on the valving. It also helps you simulate simple things such as the effect of the wheelbase on the link ratio.

Frame Care

Most people think of frames as the thing that all the rest of the motorcycle parts bolt to. That is true in a sense, but a frame can be a tunable component of the suspension system. The stiffness of the frame is one thing that distinguishes a new bike from an old bike. A stiff frame gives you confidence when you ride, the confidence of knowing that you can bottom the bike from jumps or stuff it into a berm without losing control.

Let's think about what makes a frame feel worn out and twitchy. The front forks, shock linkage, and swingarm are fastened to the frame with large bolts that pivot on bearings. When the bolts loosen up, the bearings lose the side tension needed to keep the components in alignment. If the bearings are worn on the linkage, dangerous side forces will be applied to the shock as it compresses, increasing rear stiction, causing a handling problem or, worse, a bent shock shaft. Also, the tapered roller bearings that support the triple-clamp assembly loosen up over time, and too little tension will allow the fork assembly to rock back and forth when the bike hits bumps and when braking for turns. Slop in the steering-head bearings is the major reason for side-to-side shaking of the front end.

This section is a guide to inspecting and protecting a frame and its attached components. I'll give you tips on how to care for the bearings and tension pivot bolts, and I'll show you how the factory race teams gusset frames for greater strength.

Inspecting the Frame

Most dirt bike frames are made of mild steel with only 2 percent chrome-moly. Metal fatigue can occur when the engine-mount bolts or pivot bolts get loose. Excessive vibration from the engine and flex forces from the swingarm and steering head can cause frame cracks. Check for frame cracks where the neck is welded to the top and down tubes. Also check the engine-mount sleeve flanges that are welded on each side of the tube because cracks can form around the circumference of the tube. This is a common failure on early model KX perimeter frames. Some bikes have thin plates for engine mounts. The manufacturer doesn't weld along the entire seam of the plate and frame tube; they only spot-weld the plate at key places. Look for cracks on the spot welds. The frame can crack at both the motor mounts and the top shock mounting plate. Also, if the bottom frame tubes aren't covered with a skid plate, they may be susceptible to water corrosion, so inspect the bottom of the frame, too.

Frames become sprung with use, the most common evidence of which is a "spreading" apart at the engine cradle. That's why you often hear a cracking noise and see gaps open up between the mounts and the engine when you loosen the engine mounts.

Tightening Pivot Bolts

The torque on the pivot bolts is critical because if it is too high, the swingarm and linkage will bind. If the torque is too low, the swingarm and linkage will twist when the suspension is bottomed, making the bike handle twitchy. See your service manual for correct torque figures.

Shimming the mounts is as important as tightening the bolts to the proper torque. As mentioned earlier, frames tend to spread out near the engine cradle, which results in gaps between the mounts and the engine, swingarm, or top shock mounting plate that bolts to the mounts. If you tighten the bolts on perimeter frames without shimming these gaps, you put the frame under considerable stress, and the stress may cause the frame to crack faster than normal. Kawasaki makes thin engine-mount shims (8mm and 10mm inside diameter) that can be inserted between the engine and frame to take up the excess clearance and reduce the stress on the frame. These shims fit the motor mounts of any Japanese dirt bike.

Basic Maintenance and Greasing

Like the rest of the bike, the frame needs periodic maintenance. An ideal time is when the engine is out being serviced, or during the off-season.

Hard and Soft Tools

If you want to maintain and lube your frame right, you need the right tools. For hard tools, you'll need a ratchet, torque wrench, and 6-point sockets in sizes to fit the swingarm nut and linkage bolts. These bolts are tightened to torque in the range of 25 to 77 foot pounds. If you use 12-point sockets, they might strip the hex head of the bolt. Also, the swingarm bolt will need to be driven out of the frame. Because the bolt is so long, you'll need a one-foot-long brass drift rod with a slightly smaller diameter than the pivot bolt. You can buy one at Sears or from auto parts stores. For soft tools, you will need clean rags, spray degreaser, a thread-locking agent, and bearing grease.

Prepping the Bike

Spray degreaser on the outside of the linkage and power-wash the bike. Before washing, it's best to position the bike on a mat-like indoor-outdoor carpet available at hardware stores. That way, if parts such as shim washers or needle bearings fall off the link parts, they can be found easily. Set the bike up on a stand and get a 10-inch-tall block to elevate the rear wheel when the bolts are removed from the linkage.

Checking the Swingarm and Bearings

First, check the bearing flanges for cracks. If the swingarm became loose or the bearings seized, the flanges could have become overstressed and cracked. Second, check the bearings to see that they are still in good condition. The main cause of bearing failure is lack of lubrication from too much power-washing. The left side bearing wears out first because chain lube accumulates on that side, and clean-freaks go crazy blasting away the dirt and oil, taking the grease out of the bearing at the same time.

Remove the swingarm and check the bearings by trying to rotate them with your finger. If they move, clean the bearings with mineral spirits solvent and regrease. If the bearings are rusty and seized, you must install new ones.

For easy bearing removal, use a propane torch to heat the aluminum bearing holders. Heat the holders for three minutes, and then insert an ice cube into the bearing to contract it. Support the swingarm in a vise and use a deep-well socket and a plastic mallet to drive out the bearing. If it's really stuck, you will need to carefully slit the outer race of the bearing with a sharp-edged triangle file. Never use too much force when driving out the bearings; you could bend the bearing holders. To install the new bearings, you should slowly press them in so the outer race doesn't bend. Better yet, use the Suzuki bearing alignment tool. It comes as a universal kit to install swingarm, linkage, wheel, and tapered roller bearings. Check the swingarm pivot for shear marks where the bearings ride. Shear marks are sharp divot lines that are only about 0.010 inch deep. Also, place the pivot on a thick piece of glass or a flat surface, roll the pivot, and check for run-out. If the pivot is bent or has shear marks, replace it. Never try to polish out the marks or straighten the pivot. The axles and the linkage pivots should be checked this same way.

Chain Tension and Acceleration *By Rick Johnson*

Rick is an engineer who has worked with dirt bike suspensions since 1982. He raced the local Pro class in the 1980s and still rides and competes regularly. Rick continues to perform shock tuning track side at a variety of southern California tracks. Contact Rick at Too Tech Suspension, Tel: 310-371-3887, Fax: 310-371-7839.

Chain tension has a significant effect on a bike's rear suspension, but there is a lot of confusion about exactly what it does. Contrary to popular belief, chain tension during acceleration does not cause the rear end to sag; it simply reduces the frame's tendency to squat. To prove this, perform this simple experiment. Put your bike in first gear directly in front of some immovable object such as a tree. Rev up the motor and slowly let out the clutch. Notice how the rear fender rises under this load. Squat during acceleration is caused by the vehicle's weight being transferred to the rear wheel, not by chain tension. In fact, chain tension reduces the amount of squat during acceleration.

Chain Tension Calculation

In order to analyze why the suspension reacts during maximum acceleration, we are going to examine the physical relationship between tension and rear suspension. First, assume the bike and rider weigh 400 pounds and the swingarm is in a horizontal position.

A 250cc motocross engine produces about 25 foot-pounds of torque. Assuming the rider is in second gear with the throttle wide open and factoring in final drive ratio, swingarm length, and a bit of rear wheelspin, we come up with approximately 700 pounds of tension exerted on the chain by a 250cc bike.

This photo shows the forces acting on the bike when the rider accelerates. The bottom line is that chain tension during acceleration takes weight off the rear shock and applies it to the rear wheel. The suspension is stiffer, and a bit of lift is applied to the rear wheel. Try riding through a set of stutter bumps off the gas in a high gear and then accelerate hard through the bumps in first or second gear. You'll notice the stiffening effect right away! The lift provided by the chain is apparent on jumps.

Chain Tension and Acceleration

Effect on Rear Suspension

In Sketch A, we see a diagram of the two sprockets with a chain drawn between them. Note the actual rise (vertical component) between the sprockets is 1.75 inches. Sketch B converts the chain angle into X and Y components (distances) so we can calculate the angle of the chain. The angle calculates to eight degrees, thus the 700 pounds of chain tension is at an eight-degree angle with respect to the swingarm.

In order to determine the effects of 700 pounds of chain tension at the rear wheel and at the frame, we must convert the chain tension into its perpendicular components with respect to the swingarm. Note from our example that the horizontal force "Fx" calculates to 693 pounds. The vertical force "Fy" calculates to 100 pounds.

Sketch D shows the forces acting on the rear wheel and the frame that hold the system in equilibrium. First note the horizontal force labeled Fx at the rear wheel. It is held in equilibrium by an equal and opposite Fx1 force exerted by the eight-degree angle of the chain tension at the front sprocket. These two forces cancel each other and combine to compress the swingarm some negligible amount. The vertical forces are much more interesting. The Fy force acts at the rear wheel and its associated equilibrium combine for a "couple" or torque, which would exert a torque or twisting force on the entire bike. However, in our case, the swingarm is attached with bearings at both ends, so our two vertical forces are separated by a pivoting link system. This link allows the two opposite vertical forces to cause vertical displacement instead of a torque. The rear wheel Fy tries to make the swingarm swing down in the rear. The ground prevents this motion. The opposite vertical force at the front sprocket Fy1 tends to lift the frame which unloads the rear shock spring. By applying 100 pounds of lifting force directly to the frame, the rear spring is relieved of 100 of the total 400 pounds of rider and bike weight. This causes the bike to rise.

Out on the track, when the throttle is applied quickly, chain tension effectively lifts the bike as if the rider had suddenly lost 100 pounds. This sudden loss of a 100-pound load from the rear spring causes the bike to accelerate upward to its new equilibrium point.

Discussion and Application

Remember, we chose 400 pounds for the total bike weight and we said all the weight would be transferred to the rear wheel during acceleration. Without chain tension forces, all 400 pounds is transferred to the rear wheel through the rear shock spring. When we consider the chain tension and analyze the resulting vertical forces at the rear wheel and frame, we realize that 100 of the 400 pounds of bike weight is applied

This is an early prototype of Eyvind Boyesen's Z-Link suspension. Notice the absence of a conventional swingarm pivot. Eyvind's invention neutralizes the chain forces that act on a bike.

directly to the rear wheel via the tension in the chain. The remaining 300 pounds are supported by the rear shock spring. The advantage of the conventional chain layout is the rider's ability to use this upward force to his advantage for prejumping obstacles and clearing double jumps. As discussed earlier, this 100 pounds of upward force reduces the weight carried by the spring. When you relieve the spring of part of its load, it accelerates to a new equilibrium position. When the rider coordinates this upward frame acceleration with a jump takeoff, the result is more upward motion and more distance. Chain tension also tends to reduce bottoming when landing from large jumps. Landing with the throttle on reduces suspension bottoming because the shock spring only has to support the impact forces from 300 pounds rather than 400 pounds combined weight of the bike and rider. The remaining 100 pounds is supported by the tension of the chain. Note that the "Torque Eliminator" system eliminates these forces so the rider can not "dial in" frame lift or antibottoming with the throttle.

The disadvantage of the traditional chain alignment is that 100 pounds of the bike weight are carried by the "rigid" chain connection between the frame and rear wheel, thus the rear wheel behaves as if is had 100 extra pounds of "unsprung" weight during acceleration. Any "unsprung" weight has trouble following the changes in terrain. Adding another 100 pounds to this "unsprung" weight during acceleration adversely affects the rear tire's ability to follow the terrain. (This adds another reason to exit a turn one gear higher. The higher the gear, the less engine torque is multiplied; thus, the rigid connection between the frame and rear wheel is minimized!)

The "Torque Eliminator" product effectively eliminates the rigid connection between the frame and rear wheel. By aligning the chain parallel to the swing arm, the chain tension becomes parallel to the swing arm.

Chain Tension and Acceleration

continued from page 67
Without an angle between the chain and swingarm, the forces are purely horizontal with no vertical components. No vertical forces mean no frame lift and no rigid connection between the frame and rear wheel—all 400 pounds of bike spring. This also explains why the "Torque Eliminator" product requires a stiffer shock spring. Without the 100 pounds of vertical force at the frame to counter rear-end squat during acceleration, the bike requires a stiffer spring rate to eliminate excessive rear squat. Most riders experimenting with this "Torque Eliminator" system found that they preferred the potential for frame life over a smoother ride.

It should be noted that a 500cc bike has 1.5 times more torque than a 250cc bike and proportionately greater chain tension. Conversely, a 125cc bike would have about half the potential chain tension of a 250cc bike. Additionally, there is more engine torque multiplication and chain tension in the lower gears and less in the higher gears. This explains why reactions at the rear wheel and frame will be more noticeable in the lower gears with large displacement bikes.

Happy trails, and don't forget to gas it to clear that next obstacle or double jump!

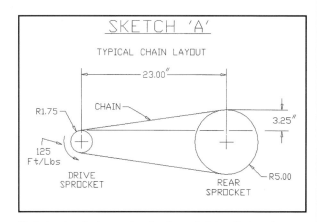

Chain tension during acceleration has a definite effect on the rear suspension. By calculating the amount of force applied to the chain, the effect can be calculated. Straight lines with arrows indicate forces and their direction of application. The numbers indicate magnitude.

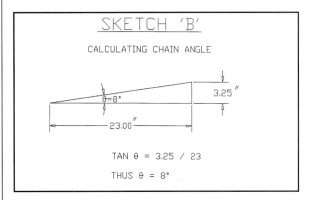

Sketch B shows how to calculate chain angle, which affects both the force going to the rear wheel and through the swingarm to the rear shock.

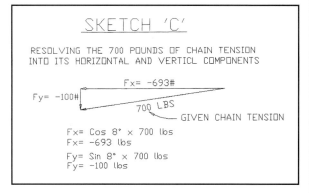

To understand the effects of a force (straight arrows) drawn at some angle other than vertical or horizontal, we "resolve" the angled force into its horizontal and vertical components. In our example, "X" will indicate horizontal and "Y" will indicate vertical forces.

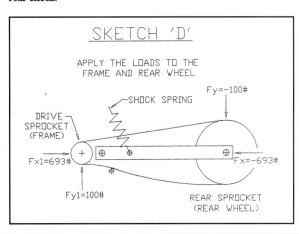

All forces must balance at some equilibrium condition. When we twist the throttle, the tension in the chain is added to the force equilibrium analysis. This added force causes a new equilibrium condition and a short-term vertical acceleration to get to this point.

Don't forget to grease the steering head bearings. You can loosen the stem nut and drop the steering stem down about an inch so you can brush grease on the lower bearing. Apply grease to the upper bearing by removing it and pressing the bearing into a dab of grease.

Steering Head

Modern dirt bikes have tapered roller bearings in the steering head. These bearings should be greased when the bike is new and twice a year using high-temperature bearing grease. The top bearing can be greased by wiping some grease into the palm of your hand, then wiping the large-diameter side of the bearing into your hand. Rotate and wipe the bearing until grease forces through the rollers all around the bearing. To grease the lower bearing, you must try to force some grease into the bearing from the outside because this bearing is pressed onto the steering stem and cannot be removed easily.

You must also periodically check the bearing preload because if the steering head bearing preload becomes too loose, the steering head will rock back

and forth while you are riding through whoops and during braking. The bike will have a headshake problem and eventually the bearing races will develop divot marks. You can tell if the races are damaged by slowly turning the front end while the bike is on a stand. If the steering stops in one spot easily, the races are worn. The bearings and races should be replaced as a complete set, top and bottom. A tapered race alignment tool should be used to install the races because it is easy to install the races crooked and not deep enough, with the result that the first time you land from a big jump, the bearings will seat and the front end will become loose.

Use the following procedure to check and adjust bearing preload. With the bike on a stand, remove the handlebars, and loosen the top-clamp pinch bolts and the

large stem hex nut. Grasp the upper fork tubes and try to rock the tubes back and forth. If you feel any movement, you should tighten the spanner nut that tensions the steering-head bearings. Be careful, though: If you overtighten the spanner nut, the tension will be too great and the bearings will fail. Some riders prefer to test the tension by turning the forks and feeling the resistance to rotation; others prefer to grasp the upper fork tubes and check for movement. After adjusting the bearing preload, tighten the hex stem nut, but again, be careful because when you tighten the nut, the steering-head tension will increase slightly. Tighten the top-clamp pinch bolts after you tighten the hex nut, or the top clamp will be stressed. Always use blue Loctite locking agent on the hex nut because they tend to vibrate loose easily.

Suspension Terminology

Have you ever read a magazine test on a new bike and been confused by the words used to describe the bike's handling? The reason is that suspension terminology is a mixture of engineering and slang words. Read this section before you read any of the sections on suspension servicing.

Angular Motions

Pitch—A motion fore or aft, when the front end dives or when the rear end squats.

Roll—A motion where the motorcycle leans left or right from straight-up riding.

Yaw—A motion that veers left or right from the motorcycle's heading angle.

General Terms

Anti-squat Ratio—A formula that calculates the relation between the drive sprocket, rear-tire contact patch, swingarm pivot height, and the chain force lines to determine the rear suspension's resistance to squatting under acceleration.

Arm pump—When the muscles in a rider's forearms tense up to the point that hand-grip is weakened or uncontrollable. This can be caused by forks that are transferring the impacts to the wheel to the rider's arms rather than absorbing the bumps.

Axle—The axis about which a wheel spins.

Base valve—The compression piston and valving that fits onto the compression-bolt assembly.

Bladder—A closed-end, thick rubber, cylindrical-shaped piece that contains the nitrogen gas in a rear shock. The bladder works like an extra cushion on HSC.

Bottoming—A riding situation in which all the suspension travel is used.

Bumper—A tapered, dense foam piece that fits on the shock shaft and provides last-ditch resistance to bottoming.

Bushing—A bronze or plastic ring used as a load-bearing surface in forks or shocks.

Center of gravity/mass center—The center point of the motorcycle's mass, normally located somewhere behind the cylinder and below the carburetor of a dirt bike.

Chassis—The frame, swingarm, suspension, and wheels of a motorcycle.

Clevis—A fork-shaped piece of aluminum used as the bottom mount for most shocks.

Clickers—The knobs or screws that control the LSC and LSR circuits of the forks or shock. Also aerial maneuvers.

Compression damping—The damping circuit that absorbs the energy of compression forces on the damper.

Compression-bolt assembly—A large-diameter bolt that houses a LSC adjusting screw and the compression-valve assembly.

Counter steering—When the rider applies steering pressure in the opposite direction of the turn.

Damper assembly—The parts of a shock comprised of the clevis, shaft, bumper, piston, and shims.

Damper rod—The large-diameter aluminum tube in the lower leg of telescopic forks.

Damper speed—The relative speed at which the moving end of a damper compresses or rebounds. The two different speeds are high and low.

Damper—A fluid chamber with a means of regulating the fluid flow to restrain the speed of the moving end of the damper during the compression or rebound strokes. A set of forks and a rear shock are considered dampers.

Damping circuits—There are normally four damping circuits that affect the damper's speed: both a low-speed compression (LSC), high-speed compression (HSC), low-speed rebound (LSR), and high-speed rebound (HSR).

Damping—The process of absorbing the energy of impacts transmitted through the forks or rear shock on the compression stroke, and the process of absorbing the energy of the spring on the rebound stroke.

Flicking—The action of putting the bike into a full-lean position quickly.

Front-end diving—This is what happens when the front forks compress quickly. It usually occurs when braking for turns.

Handling—The quality of response from the chassis of a motorcycle while riding through a variety of obstacles such as turns, jumps, hills, whoops, and bumps.

Harshness—An undesirable quality of the damping that results in sharp shocks being transferred through the suspension to the chassis.

Headshake—The high-speed oscillation of the forks when braking for a bend at the end of a fast straightaway. Every motorcycle has a certain frequency band in which its front end oscillates. This frequency can be tuned to a higher vehicle speed with a sacrifice in the bike's ability to turn.

High side—What happens when a bike falls to the outside of a turn.

Hopping—When the tire bounces up off the ground due to a reaction from a bump.

HSC—The high-speed compression circuit is affected most when riding fast over square-edged bumps.

HSR—The high-speed rebound circuit is affected in the same riding circumstances as HSC.

Kicking—Describes both "pogoing" and "packing."

Low siding—What happens when a motorcycle falls to the inside of a turn.

LSC—The low-speed compression circuit is affected most when riding through turns.

LSR—The low-speed rebound circuit is affected in the same riding circumstances as LSC.

◗ 1990 CR250 Fork Base Valves Clogged

Question: Every time I disassemble and clean the forks on my CR250, the base valve is clogged with gray metal debris. If I spend the money to hard anodize the forks, will that reduce the debris that clogs the base valve?

Answer: The source of the metal debris that clogs the base valve will surprise you. The debris isn't from the inside of the aluminum slider, it originates from the springs and the preload cones. The coating on Japanese fork springs flake off through use and vibration. The preload cones fit between the fork cap and the springs. The stock Showa cone is made of steel, and that wears on the spring.

The best fix is to install Eibach springs and Pro-Action preload cones.

Eibach springs don't flake and the preload cones are made of aluminum. You can buy these parts mail-order from Pro-Action. Call 412-846-9055

◗ Antibottoming Devices

Question: I've seen products advertised as antibottoming devices for forks. How do these devices work? I'm a big guy (275 pounds) and I ride a big bike (CR500). I've installed the stiffest fork springs available for my CR and I can still bottom the forks on front-wheel landings. Would an antibottoming cone solve my problem?

Answer: The anti-bottoming devices for cartridge forks consist of an angled cone and a cup. This product replaces the stock hydraulic bottoming cone and cup. The aftermarket products have more progressive angles machined into the cone and cup. These products require that you disassemble the cartridge. The rider types that this product benefits most are heavy riders who are experiencing fork bottoming with stiffer fork springs.

◗ Retro Honda Cartridge Forks

Question: I have a question about an older bike. I have a 1985 CR250 and I'm looking for better performance from the forks. Is there a cartridge fork kit for these older bikes?

Answer: The Race-Tech Emulator Valve is well known as a fork kit for modern mini cycles and it fits into the older noncartridge forks. The kit is easy to install because it just slides in from the top of the fork and is held in place by the fork spring. When you install the Emulator Valve, clean the fork's internal parts. Check and replace the fork bushings, seals, and add new fork oil. New fork springs will reduce front-end diving and head-shaking at the end of fast straight away. All fork spring manufacturers have recommendations for the correct spring rate for your model bike and your riding weight. Guides such as these are published and printed in catalogs.

◗ Depressurized Shock

Question: I accidentally let the nitrogen out of the rear shock. What do you suggest I do about that?

Answer: If the pressure is released from the bladder and you ride the bike, the bladder will be permanently damaged and so may the shock. Your bike is too dangerous to ride. Ask a suspension technician to examine your shock and give you an estimate on the repairs. Pro-Action 412-846-9055 has several franchised suspension repair shops all over North America. Call for the location of the Pro-Action suspension technician in your area.

Suspension FAQs

Midturn wobble—When the bike wobbles or weaves near the apex of a turn.

Nitrogen—An inert gas used to pressurize the bladder or reservoir of shocks.

Packing—When the rear shock is compressed by the wheel hitting one bump and cannot rebound quickly enough to absorb the impact of the second or third bump.

Piston ring—A ring that fits around the piston and prevents oil from bypassing the piston and shims.

Piston rod—A small-diameter steel rod that fits into the upper legs of cartridge forks. It fastens to the fork cap on one end and holds the rebound piston and shims on the other end.

Piston—A cylindrical piece of steel with several ports arranged around the periphery so as to direct oil towards the face of shocks.

Pivot—A fixed point about which a lever rotates. Examples: swingarm or suspension linkage.

Pogoing—When the rear shock rebounds so quickly that the rear wheel leaves the ground.

Preload—Preload is applied to the fork and shock springs to bring the bike to the proper ride height or race-sag dimension. The preload can be biased to change the bike's steering geometry. For example, high preload/less sag in the front forks will make the steering heavy/slow and more stable at high speed.

Race sag—The number of millimeters that the forks or shock sag with the rider on the bike in full riding gear. This is essential to proper suspension tuning but is often overlooked or adjusted incorrectly.

Rake—The angle between the steering axis and a vertical line.

Rear-end squatting—When you accelerate the motorcycle, the chain forces push down on the rear wheel, and the resultant forces are transferred up the swingarm into the main frame, causing a lifting force that extends the front end, causing a weight shift backwards.

Rebound damping—The damping circuit that restrains the release of the stored energy in the compressed spring to reduce the rebounding speed of the damper.

Reservoir—A cylindrical device that contains oil and nitrogen gas.

Revalving—Altering the compression and rebound shims in order to fine-tune damping characteristics.

Seal—A rubber or plastic cylindrical piece that prevents oil from being lost from the damper.

Shaft—The chrome-plated rod on the rear shock that has a clevis on one end and the piston and shims fastened to the other end.

Shim—A circular flat washer of thin steel, used to exert resistance on the oil flow through a piston. A series of shims (valve stack or valving) with varying outer diameters and thicknesses are arranged in sequence to provide a damping affect.

Shock body—The aluminum cylinder that contains the damper assembly.

Shock dyno—A machine that cycles a shock absorber at different damper speeds and measures the resistance posed by the four damping circuits.

Shock fade—When the shock oil becomes so hot that the damping effect is reduced, so the shock compresses easily and rebounds quickly.

Speed wobble—When a motorcycle wavers back and forth rapidly at high speeds.

Spiking—How the forks work when the damping is too stiff/slow. This is also associated with arm pump.

Spring—A steel wire that is wound into a coil shape and tempered to provide resistance to compression forces and store energy for expansion to the extended position.

Steering angle—The angle of the handlebars as you rotate them left or right about the steering axis.

Steering axis—The axis about which the forks rotate.

Stiction—A combination of the words "static" and "friction." This word is used to describe the drag exerted on the moving damper parts by the stationary parts such as the bushings, seals, and wipers. Low stiction is desirable because it results in more responsive suspension.

Stiff/slow or soft/fast—Describes the damping characteristics of the forks or shock. With regard to the clickers, these words refer to the direction of rotation that you will turn the clickers in order to improve the damping. Turning the clickers clockwise will make the damping stiff/slow. Turning the clickers counterclockwise will make the damping soft/fast.

Swapping—When the rear end of the bike skips from side to side very quickly.

Swingarm angle—The angle of rotational motion about the swingarm pivot axis.

Swingarm pivot axis—The point where the swingarm mounts to the frame and about which the swingarm rotates.

Swingarm—The rear fork that connects the rear wheel to the frame.

Tank slapper—When the forks rotate from stop to stop rapidly and your arms and body slap back and forth against the motorcycle's gas tank.

Trail—On the front end, the horizontal distance between the point where the steering axis reaches the road surface and the center of the front tire's contact patch. Generally, forks with offset axles have more trail than forks with straight-through axles.

Transition shims—These are shims with very small outer diameters that are used to separate the normal shims of the low- and high-speed valve stacks.

Transmittability—This term refers to the suspension oil's ability to transmit shock loads. As the oil's temperature rises, the transmitability falls. For example, with every increase in temperature of 18 degrees Fahrenheit, the transmitability of the oil falls 50 percent.

Trapped air space—The height of the air space that forms in the top of the fork tube between the fork cap and the oil.

Triple-clamp assembly—Includes the steering stem, bottom clamp, and top clamp. The triple-clamp assembly connects the forks to the frame.

Unladen sag—The number of millimeters that the bike sags under its own weight without a rider.

Unsprung/sprung weight—The unsprung weight of the motorcycle comprises many parts such as the wheels, brakes, swingarm and suspension linkage, and the lower front fork legs, the weight of which does not bear down on the fork and shock springs. The sprung weight is all the parts of the motorcycle that are supported by the suspension.

Valves—Refers to a series of shims either for the compression or the rebound damping.

Viscosity index—The flow rate characteristic of the oil over a range of temperatures. The VI rating of an oil is directly linked to the oil's transmittability. Cartridge-fork oil has a VI number of 115. Shock oil normally has a much higher average operating temperature so its VI number is 300.

Viscosity—A rating system for oils that measures the oil's flow rate through a fixed orifice at a certain temperature. Also known as the oil's weight, as in 30-weight oil.

Washout—A term used to describe what happens when the bike's tires lose traction and slide to the outside of a turn, causing the bike and rider to fall to the inside of a turn.

Weight bias—Also called weight distribution. The amount of weight on each wheel of the motorcycle.

Wheelbase—The distance between the front and rear axle centers.

Wheelie—A motorcycle in motion with the front wheel off the ground.

CARBURETOR TUNING

CHAPTER FOUR

Carburetor tuning has the greatest effect on engine performance. When a motorcycle manufacturer builds a bike, it usually install jets in the carb that are too rich. The manufacturers sell the same model worldwide, so they couldn't afford to install different jets in the carb to suit all the different climates and types of fuel. In addition to the climate and fuel, the manufacturer would also have to consider many other factors, such as the terrain and type of riding. And then there is the most important jetting consideration, the rider.

When I worked as a mechanic, I was in charge of jetting the bike over the course of the day. During morning practice sessions, the track was usually muddy and the air temperature was at its lowest point. I had to jet the bike rich for practice because the air density was greater and the mud put more of a load on the engine. Then I had to watch the rider and the bike perform on different sections of the track. I would go to the obstacle on the track that presented the greatest load on the bike, typically an uphill straight section. I'd listen to my engine and watch the rider. I'd listen for pinging or knocking noises or excessive smoke from the pipe. I would watch to see if the rider had to fan the clutch a lot and how my bike pulled in comparison to others. Getting feedback from the rider is difficult because they are concentrating on riding, not the bike's performance. At

a pro national there is one practice session, followed by a series of qualifiers and eventually two race motos. The time spacing of the riding sessions over the course of the day was such that the I had to compensate the jetting two or three times. Otherwise, the bike would either seize from being too lean in the morning or run too rich for the second moto.

Race mechanics have different techniques for carb jetting. The techniques range from asking other mechanics what jets they are running to using precise measuring gauges to monitor the engine performance. In motocross races, where most of the riders are of equal skill levels, a holeshot in the start can mean the difference between a place on the podium and 30 minutes of roost in your face! The difference in horsepower between the bike that gets the holeshot and the bike that brings up the back of the pack may only be a few ponies! The race mechanic can give his rider an awesome advantage if he carefully monitors the carb jetting.

This section will give you insight into the carb tuning process, from diagnosing mechanical problems that mimic poor jetting to tuning tools such as gauges. It will also give you tips on a jetting method that I've developed called the "ride-and-feel" method, which I consider to be the best method. It's a technique that I teach to all the riders I've worked with. You don't need any fancy tools, just the ability to make observations while you ride.

Carburetor Parts and Function

A carburetor is a device that enables fuel to mix with air in a precise ratio while being throttled over a wide range. Jets are calibrated orifices that take the form of parts such as pilot/slow jets, pilot air screw, throttle valve/slide, jet needle, needle jet/spray-bar, air jet, and main jet. Fuel jets have matching air jets, and these jets are available in many sizes to fine-tune the air-fuel mixture to the optimum ratio for a two-stroke engine, which is 12.5: 1.

Fuel Jets, Air Jets, and Throttle Positions

Three circuits control the air: the air screw, the throttle slide, and the air jet. Four circuits control the fuel: the pilot/slow jet, the spray-bar/needle jet, the jet needle, and the main jet. The different air and fuel circuits affect the carb jetting for the different throttle-opening positions, as follows:

Closed to one-eighth throttle—air screw and pilot/slow jet

One-eighth to one-fourth throttle—air screw, pilot/slow jet, and throttle slide

One-fourth to one-half throttle—throttle slide and jet needle

One-half to full open—jet needle, spray-bar/needle jet, main jet, and air jet

(Note: On many modern carbs the spray-bar/needle jet and air jet are fixed-diameter passages in the carburetor body and cannot be altered.)

Mechanical Problems

The process of jetting—changing air or fuel jets in order to fine-tune engine performance—is very simple. Jetting becomes complicated because mechanical problems sometimes mimic improper jetting. This causes you to waste time and money trying to correct the problem with expensive carburetor jets.

Before you ever attempt to jet a carb, make sure the engine doesn't have any of the problems in the following list. If you are in the process of jetting a carb

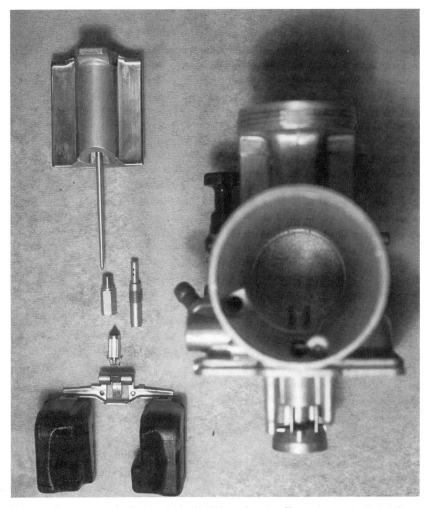

These are the components of a two-stroke dirt bike carburetor. The parts are, starting at the right and working clockwise, carb body, float assembly, fuel inlet needle, hex main jet, pilot/slow jet, jet needle, and the throttle slide.

and you are stumped with a chronic problem, use this section as a guide to enlightenment!

Crankcase air leaks—Air leaks can occur at the cylinder base, reed valve, or the magneto seal. Air leaks make the throttle response sluggish and may produce a pinging sound. That sound occurs when the air-fuel mixture is too lean.

Crankcase oil leaks—The right-side crankcase seal is submerged in the transmission oil. When this seal becomes worn out, oil can leak into the crankcase. The oil is transferred up to the combustion chamber and burned with the air-fuel mixture. The oil causes the spark plug to carbon-foul. This mechanical problem makes the jetting seem to be too rich.

Coolant-system leaks—Coolant systems leaks commonly occur at the cylinder-head gasket. When the coolant leaks into the combustion chamber, it pollutes the air-fuel mixture and causes a misfire or popping sound at the exhaust pipe. Check the engine's coolant level frequently. Hondas and Kawasakis have characteristic coolant leaks because they use steel head gaskets. Yamahas and Suzukis use O-rings to seal the head and cylinder. Coolant-system leaks lower the engine's peak horsepower. It makes the engine run as if the air-fuel mixture is too rich.

Carbon-seized exhaust valves—The exhaust valves sometimes become carbon-seized in the full-open posi-

tion. This mechanical problem can make the engine run flat at low rpm and make the slow-speed jetting seem lean. The carbon can be removed from the exhaust valves with oven cleaner. Clean the exhaust valves whenever you replace the piston and rings.

Blown silencer—When the fiberglass packing material blows out of the silencer, excess turbulence forms in the silencer and the turbulence causes a restriction in the exhaust system. This restriction makes the engine run flat at high rpm.

Broken reed-valve petals—The petals of the reed-valve can crack or shatter when the engine is revved too high. This mechanical problem makes the engine difficult to start and can also have a loss of torque. Expert riders should switch to carbon fiber reed petals because they resist breaking at high rpm. Novice riders should use dual-stage fiberglass reeds (Aktive or Boyesen). These types of reed petals provide an increase in torque.

Weak spark—When the ignition coils deteriorate, the engine performance will become erratic. Normally, the engine will develop a high-rpm misfire problem. Check the condition of the coils with a multimeter.

Clogged carburetor vent hoses—When the carburetor vent hoses get clogged with dirt or pinched closed, the jetting will seem to be too lean, so the engine will run sluggishly. Always check the condition of your carburetor vent hoses. Make sure there is no mud in the hoses and that the hoses are not pinched between the suspension linkage.

Carburetor float level—When the float level is too low, the jetting will seem to be too lean, so the engine performance will be sluggish. When the float level is too high, the jetting will seem to be too rich.

Worn carburetor fuel-inlet needle— When the fuel-inlet needle wears out, excess fuel enters the float bowl and travels up the slow jet and into the engine. This makes the carb jetting seem to be too rich. Replace the fuel-inlet needle and seat every two years.

◗ Fuel Additives

Question: I've seen some press releases lately on products that are race gas concentrates. Are these products worth the money? What type of fuel do I mix them with?

Answer: Reputable companies such as Powermist and Klotz sell a 5-gallon concentrate that mixes with super unleaded premium pump gas to make a total of 20 gallons of safe race gas, Safe meaning that the octane rating is at least 102 and the volatility rating is low. That means you don't have to worry about your engine detonating, causing catastrophic engine damage.

◗ Hot and Hard to Start

Question: My 1988 RM250 is so hard to start when it is hot that I have to push-start it. The bike also fouls plugs. I don't understand it, I use the choke each time to start it. Should I crack the throttle a few times before I try to start it just to get some gas in the engine?

Answer: Most 250s have a strong fuel signal. In other words, they spew raw gas just when you open the throttle during kick-starting. When the engine is cold and you open the throttle with the choke on, it will cancel the effect of the choke and make the engine harder to start. The best procedure for warm-starting a dirt bike is to leave the choke off, hold the throttle wide open, and kick-start it. Also try installing a spark plug with a hotter heat range. That will prevent the plug from cold fouling.

◗ Too Noisy for Neighbors

Question: My brother and I are taking a lot of flak from our neighbors. We ride on our own property with our 1988 CR and KX 80s. The neighbors complain that our bikes are too loud. Our friend has an XR100. Can we make our bikes as quiet as his just by using aluminum silencers? Aren't aluminum silencers quieter than the stock steel silencers?

Answer: You're right that the steel silencers are louder, but the main reason is that you cannot repack them with good silencer packing material such as Silent Sport. Those stock silencers are nonrebuildable. My suggestion is to get an FMF silencer and a Sparky. The Sparky is a clamp-on attachment to the end of the silencer that will really quiet down the bike (90 decibels). It may be louder than your friend's XR100, but two-stroke engines produce different pressure waves than four-stroke engines and they are inherently louder. The Sparky can be quickly clamped on for trail riding in your neighborhood and removed for racing use. The best part is that your bikes will make more power because there will be less turbulence in the new packed silencers than in those worn-out steel silencers.

◗ YZ490 Runs Erratic

Question: I trail ride an old Yamaha YZ490. The bike has been very reliable for me, but lately it has started to run erratically. This is the jetting I'm using: 35 pilot, needle in the middle, and a 420 main jet. The bike has also become difficult to start. It backfires constantly, causing my knee to slam into the handlebars. I'm starting to think that my bike is possessed!

Answer: Chill out biking brother; your 490 is just a piece of metal not a character from an *Excorcist* movie! I noticed that you haven't changed the slide. Yamaha's *Wrench Report* bulletins suggest that changing to a leaner slide and a richer needle jet can make your bike accelerate smoother off the bottom, with less chance of pinging in the midrange. I've found this jetting to work best for eliminating the pinging and the erratic running: 45 pilot, 3.5 slide, Q-8 needle jet, stock needle in the second position, 440 main, NGK BP6ES spark plug, and a premix ratio of 60:1 with Yamalube R.

Be advised that the Woodruff key that aligns the flywheel to the crankshaft tends to shear when the bike backfires or kicks back during starting, which allows the flywheel to shift position and effectively change the ignition timing. Your timing could be way off right now and that could be causing the majority of your problems. Remove the flywheel and examine the Woodruff key, it should have sharp edges. If the edge on one side of the key is rounded, then the flywheel has probably shifted. Replace the key and tighten the flywheel nut to factory torque specs.

The Effect of the Weather

The weather can have a profound effect on the carb jetting because variable weather brings variable air density. When the air density increases, you will need to richen the air-fuel mixture to compensate. When the air density decreases, you will need lean-out the air-fuel mixture to compensate. Use the following as a guide to correcting your jetting when the weather changes:

Air temperature—When the air temperature increases, the air density becomes lower. This will make the air-fuel mixture richer. You must select jet sizes with a lower number to compensate for the lower air density. When the barometric pressure decreases, the opposite effect occurs.

Humidity—When the percentage of humidity in the air increases, the engine draws in a lower percentage of oxygen during each revolution because the water molecules (humidity) take the place of oxygen molecules in a given volume of air. High humidity will make the air-fuel mixture richer, so you should change to smaller jets.

Altitude—In general, the higher the altitude, the lower the air density. When riding at race-tracks that are at high altitude, you should change to smaller jets and increase the engine's compression ratio to compensate for the lower air density.

Jetting

The most basic method of determining correct carburetor jetting is "ride and feel." This method requires you to determine if the carburetor tuning is too rich or too lean by the sound and feel of the engine. The first step is to mark the throttle body in one-fourth-throttle increments, from closed to full open. Then, this method requires that you ride the motorcycle on a flat, circular course. To check the carb jetting for throttle positions up to one-half throttle, ride the motorcycle in second or third gear. Roll on the throttle slowly from one-fourth to one-half open. If the engine is slow to respond and bogs (engine makes a *booooowah* sound) then the carb jetting is too lean. You can verify lean jetting by engaging the carb's choke to the halfway position. This will make the air-fuel mixture more rich and the engine should respond better. If the carb jetting is too rich, then the engine will

The Keihin PWK carbs have a removable component that houses the needle jet, main jet, and pilot/slow jet. This component is bolted to the carb body and sealed with O-rings. Over time the O-rings will wear out, causing some strange jetting problems similar to a rich condition.

This is the inlet needle (also called the float valve). It has a Viton rubber tip. Replace this part every two years.

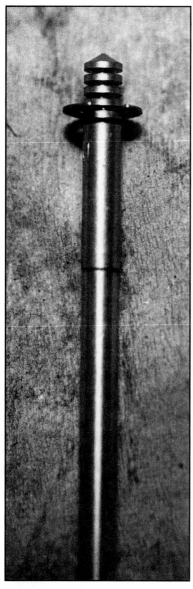

The proper float level setting on any carburetor is with the center line of the floats parallel or slightly angled away from the carb's float bowl gasket surface. In this photo, a caliper is used to measure the float height from the bottom of the float to the float bowl gasket surface. All float level specs quoted in Japanese service manuals use this measuring technique.

This is the jet needle. There are five clip positions. The top position (#1) is the leanest and the bottom position (#5) is the richest.

make a crackling sound; the exhaust smoke will be excessive and the engine will run as if the choke is engaged.

To check the jetting for throttle positions from one-half to full open, ride the motorcycle in third and fourth gear. (You may need to increase the diameter of the circular riding course for riding in the higher gears.) Check the jetting in the same manner as listed above. The carb jets that affect the jetting from one-half to full throttle are the jet-needle, main jet, and the air jet.

Note: Most models of dirt bikes have a fixed orifice for the air jet, and it cannot be removed like a main jet.

Tuning Gauges

There are three types of gauges that professional tuners use to aid carb jetting:

1. Relative-air-density (RAD) gauge
2. Air-fuel (AF) ratio meter
3. Exhaust-gas-temperature (EGT) gauge

The following is a description of how each gauge functions and their advantages.

RAD gauge—This gauge provides the tuner with an indication of how much the air density changes, helping the tuner compensate for the effects of changes in the air temperature, altitude, and barometric pressure. The gauge is calibrated in percentage points. Its main advantage is that once the tuner sets the carburetor tuning perfectly, he can then set the RAD calibration screw so the RAD needle is 100 percent. When the air density changes, the RAD gauge will show the relative percent of change. The tuner can multiply the percentage change shown on the RAD-gauge by the main jet size and determine the corrected main jet size for the air density.

AF ratio meter—The AF meter is an electronic gauge that measures the percentage of oxygen in the exhaust gasses, and displays the approximate air-fuel ratio of the carb. The gauge displays AF ratios from 10-16:1 The optimum AF ratio for a two-stroke

This is the magneto-side crank seal. The oil and dirt accumulating outside the seal indicates it is leaking. On some bikes, it can be replaced without splitting the cases.

engine is 12:1 The AF gauge utilizes a sensor that is inserted into the center of the exhaust stream, approximately 6 inches from the piston. A permanent female pipe fitting (1/4 inch) must be welded to the side of the header on the exhaust pipe in order to fasten the sensor. The weld-on fitting set-up is also used on the temperature gauges, and the fitting can be plugged with a 1/4 inch male pipe fitting when the gauge is not in use.

EGT gauge—The EGT gauge measures the temperature of the gasses in the exhaust pipe by means of a temperature probe fastened into the exhaust pipe, six inches from the piston. This type of gauge is my favorite because it enables me to tune the carb jetting and the pipe together, taking advantage of the fact that exhaust pipes are designed with a precise temperature in mind.

An exhaust pipe is designed to return a compression wave to the combustion chamber just before the exhaust port closes. Most pipes are designed for a peak temperature of 1,200 degrees Fahrenheit. Most dirt bikes are jetted too rich, which prevents the exhaust gasses from reaching their design temperature, so power output suffers. Sometimes just leaning the main jet and the needle-clip position makes a dramatic difference.

I use the Optak brand of EGT gauge. It measures both EGT and rpm. This gauge is really tough and is sealed so water and mud can't damage it. It is designed to mount on the handlebars, but I prefer to mount it to the front fender. That way the rider can focus in on it. Once I have performed my baseline jetting, I'll send the rider out on the bike with the Optak. The rider

observes the EGT to give me feedback on the necessary jetting changes. Once the jetting is dialed, we use the Optak to check the peak rpm of the engine on the longest straight of the race track. For example, if the peak rpm exceeds the point of the engine's power-peak rpm, then I'll change the rear sprocket to a higher final-drive ratio (rear sprocket with less teeth) until the rpm drops into the target range. The first time I used an Optak was at the 1992 500cc USGP. I was a race mechanic for Jorgen Nilsson. My European mechanic friends joked about the Optak. They weren't laughing much when Jorgen pulled the holeshot in all three motos!

Carburetor Tuning for Riding in Sand and Mud

Sand and mud tracks exert a greater load exerted on the engine, so the engine requires more fuel. Normally, you need to increase the jet sizes for these conditions. Other changes might include changing to a lower final-drive ratio (rear sprocket with more teeth) to reduce the load on the engine and help prevent it from overheating. Advancing the ignition timing will make the engine more responsive at low to middle rpm.

Fuel and Oil Mixture Ratios

When we talk about the "fuel" in the air-fuel mixture for a two-stroke engine, we are really talking about a mixture of fuel and oil. If you richen the pre-mix ratio (20:1 as opposed to 30:1) there is more oil and less fuel in the same volume of liquid, which effectively leans the air-fuel ratio. And this fact gives the clever tuner one more tool to use when the correct jet is not available or when none of the standard jets are exactly right: You can richen the jetting by slightly leaning the pre-mix ratio (less oil) and lean out the jetting by slightly richening the pre-mix ratio (more oil). The best part is that changes in the pre-mix ratio affect the jetting over the entire throttle-opening range, but the changes in ratio must be small to prevent excess wear from lack of lubricating oil or fouled plugs from too much oil.

Pre-mix oils are formulated for a fairly narrow range of pre-mix ratios. You should examine the oil bottle for the oil manufacturer's suggestion on the pre-mix ratio. All production two-stroke dirt bikes have a sticker on the rear fender suggesting that you set the pre-mix ratio to 20:1 That sticker is put there for legal purposes. Always refer to the oil manufacturer's suggestion on pre-mix ratios. In general, small-displacement engines require a richer pre-mix ratio than do large-displacement engines because smaller engines have a higher peak rpm than larger engines.

The higher the engine revs, the more lubrication it requires.

Fuel Recommendations

The fuel for a dirt bike should be selected based on the bike's compression ratio, the bike's peak rpm, the rider profile, and the riding conditions. For example, engines with high compression ratios that are run at high rpm and in heavy-load situations (such as sand or mud tracks) by aggressive riders require expensive, high-octane race fuel to prevent the engine from pinging, but less-demanding riders on low-compression bikes in less-demanding terrain can probably get by with pump gas. Use the following guidelines to select the fuel you need. A warning, though: When selecting fuel, keep in mind that there is no advantage to being extravagant by buying overpriced race fuel when you don't really need it, but being cheap by trying to make do with pump gas when you really need race fuel can lead to the ruin of your engine.

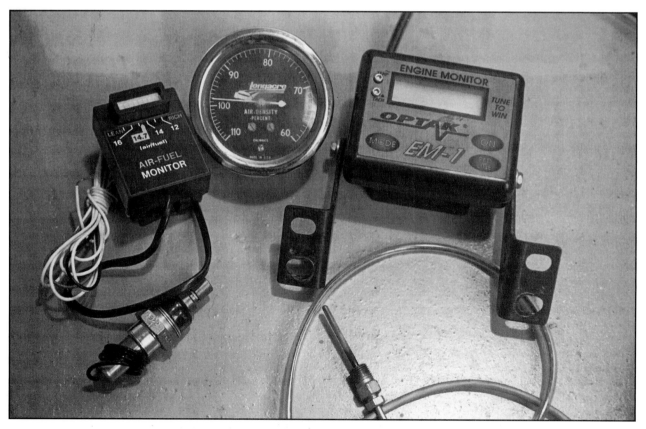

These are the high-tech carburetor jetting tools. From left to right, oxygen sensor, RAD gauge, and OPTAK exhaust gas temperature and tachometer gauge.

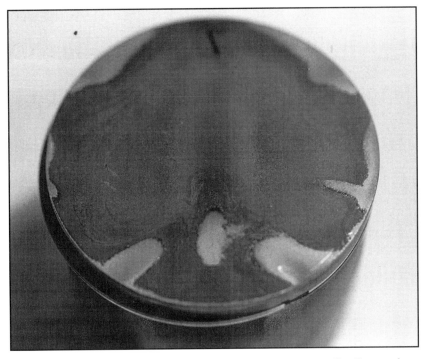

Roadrace tuners prefer to observe the carbon patterns on piston crowns rather than spark plugs. The color and shape of the carbon pattern can give an indication of carb jetting and cylinder scavenging. The color of the piston crown should be mocha brown and the pattern should be consistent from side to side. If the pattern is concentrated on one side, then the cylinder transfer ports probably aren't balanced with regards to width or opening timing.

If you ride a 250cc bike in slow-speed enduros, you will want quick throttle response at low to middle throttle openings. The best fuel for that is super unleaded premium (about 92 octane, depending on where you buy the fuel). Most of these fuels contain oxygents (such as alcohol), so you will have to jet the carb richer to compensate. Running pump gas on a dirt-tracker or desert racer will probably cause the engine to detonate and eventually melt the piston crown. For these riding situations you will need race gas, which has a relatively slow burn speed that makes them resistant to detonation. If you need a high-octane fuel but do not have access to race fuel, then consider using a concentrate mixed with pump fuel. Power-Mist and Klotz sell concentrates via mail-order. These products are very cost effective and safe to mix with popular brands of super unleaded pump fuel.

But high-octane fuels are not appropriate for every engine. Using fuel with too high an octane rating in a low-compression engine, or one that is ridden at low rpm will cause the engine to run sluggishly. It's best to experiment with different types of fuel and carb jetting in deciding what fuel is best suited to riding needs and style.

This is the OPTAK's temperature probe. It fits into the exhaust pipe, 6 inches from the piston face. Jetting with the aid of an EGT gauge is the most accurate method of jetting a racing two-stroke engine.

TWO-STROKE TOP END

CHAPTER FIVE

Top-end rebuilding is the most frequent and costly service routine on two-stroke dirt bikes. Every year, dirt bike riders waste loads of money on top-end parts that didn't need to be replaced, or make costly mistakes while performing repairs. This section will give you the dos and don'ts to easy top-end rebuilding, plus some tips that aren't printed in your factory service manual.

Before You Start

Thoroughly wash your bike because dirt stuck to the underside of the top frame tube could break loose when servicing and fall into the engine! Use a stiff plastic brush and hot, soapy water to clean off the grit and grime around the base of the cylinder, on the carburetor and intake boot, and especially underneath the top frame rail. Degreaser can be used on metal surfaces, but be careful not to let it sit on rubber or gasket surfaces.

Tools

You'll need at least some 3/8-inch-drive metric sockets and box wrenches (open-end wrenches will round-off the edges on the cylinder or head nuts and shouldn't be used for top-end rebuilding), a needle-nose pliers for removing circlips, and a gasket tool to scrape the old gaskets away. For soft tools you'll need shop towels, aerosol oven cleaner, a Scotch-Brite pad, a locking agent such as Loctite, a gasket scraper, a brush, and a bucket of soapy water.

Maintenance and Inspection

A thorough top-end rebuild requires removing the reed valve, cylinder head, and cylinder. You should tear down your top end periodically and inspect the reed valve, cylinder head, cylinder, piston, and so on. Use the following chart to determine when you should tear down your bike:

Displacement:	Tear down after:
80cc	5 hours
125cc	10 hours
250cc	20 hours
500cc	40 hours

Note that air-cooled bikes should be inspected more frequently. Also, you may want to inspect more often if you are riding in fine sand or lots of mud. When you tear down the engine, inspect each system and look for the following trouble signs.

Reed Valve

Check the reed petals for open gaps between the sealing surfaces. In time, the reed petals lose their spring tension, and the backflow can cause a flat-spot in the throttle response. Stock nylon reeds tend to split at the edges on bikes that are constantly overrevved. Expert riders find that carbon fiber reeds last much longer.

Cylinder Head

Check the head at the edge of the chamber for erosion marks—a sign that the head gasket was leaking. If the head or top edge of the cylinder is eroded, it must be turned on a lathe to be resurfaced.

Never use a hammer and chisel to separate the head or cylinder from the engine. Use a plastic mallet to rock the cylinder up off the alignment pins that center it on the crankcases.

Cylinder

All cylinder bases use aligning dowel pins around two of the cylinder base studs. These pins are made of steel, and after heavy power-washing, they get corroded. That makes it difficult to remove the cylinder from the crankcases. Never use a pry bar! That will damage the cylinder. Instead use a plastic mallet to hit upward on the sides of the cylinder at a 45-degree angle. Alternate from left to right sides so the cylinder lifts up evenly. After you remove the cylinder, stuff a shop towel into the open crankcases to prevent debris from entering the engine.

The Piston

Some unfortunate guys cause more damage replacing the piston than the actual wear on the piston! Remove the circlips with a small needle-nose pliers and throw them away. It is a common mistake to reuse circlips, but the cheap spring-steel wire clips will fatigue and break if you install them for a second time.

After removing the circlips, you have to remove the piston pin. Never use a hammer and punch to remove the pin. That will damage the connecting rod and

needle bearings. Instead, use one of the pin-extractor tools available from your local franchised motorcycle shop. You can also grasp the piston with one hand and use a 3/8-inch socket extension to push the pin out with your other hand.

Too many people replace their pistons too often. The exact service interval for your bike depends on how hard the bike was run, for how many hours, the quality of the lubrication, and the amount of dirt or other debris in the intake air. Bikes that are run hard with dirty air filters may wear out pistons in only 6 hours, while bikes that are ridden easy with clean filters and adequate fuel octane may last 60 hours.

Measuring the Piston

The best thing to do is measure the piston with a caliper. Digital calipers cost about $100 at industrial tool companies such as Enco or Harbor Freight. A digital caliper is easy to use and gives accurate measurements on the piston diameter and cylinder bore. Measure the width of the piston (front to back) just above the intake cutaway because this is the widest point of the piston. Check the maximum wear specs in your service

Top End FAQs

▶ **Thin Sleeve Causing Seizures**

Question: My 1987 CR125 has chronic piston seizure problems. The cylinder is bored 1mm oversize. The lower end was rebuilt so I know it doesn't have a crankcase air leak. What could the problem be?

Answer: The original cylinder for your model bike had a very thin steel sleeve. Honda only offers one oversized piston. When the sleeve is overbored too far, the sleeve cannot transfer out heat into the water jacket efficiently. The heat builds up over the exhaust port, and the piston melts. You have two repair options: buy a new cylinder or install a new thicker sleeve in the old cylinder. Wiseco offers thick sleeves and forged piston kits.

▶ **Top-End Big Bore**

Question: I have an old cylinder for my 250. The bore was ruined when the head gasket leaked, and there is severe erosion on the top edge of the cylinder. I read your article on top-end rebuilding and had an idea and a related question. I compete in amateur enduro events and the rules state that the displacement of bikes competing in the open class must be a minimum of 251cc. My question is, can I salvage this old junk cylinder by overboring the cylinder to fit a Wiseco piston kit and have the bore replated? If yes, will my bike be legal for the open class?

Answer: There are a number of companies offering cylinder repair services and replating. The way to fix the erosion problem is to heli-arc weld aluminum over the erosion and then re-face and bore the cylinder. WISECO and L.A. Sleeve make oversized piston kits and gaskets for most Japanese dirt bikes. The common overbore displacement sizes for 250s are 265, 285, and 310cc. After the cylinder is replated, the exhaust valves and the cylinder head must be matched to the larger bore size. This involves special metal machining and should be trusted to a qualified tuner or machinist. This type of mod will enable you to race your 250 in the open class.

manual. Check the piston for detonation marks in the crown, cracks in the skirt, or seizure marks. Look at the underside of the piston crown for a large black spot. The spot is burnt oil deposits that adhered to the piston because the piston crown temperature was too hot. This is an indication that the carb's main jet needs to be richer.

Measuring the Ring Gap

The best way to know if the rings are worn is to measure the ring end gap. Put the ring in the cylinder and use the piston to push it down about 1/2 inch from the top, evenly spaced. Now use a feeler gauge to measure the width of the ring gap. Normally, the maximum gap is 0.018 to 0.025 inch. Very narrow! Too narrow for you to measure with the naked eye.

Cylinder and Exhaust Valve Cleaning

Does your cylinder have burnt-on mud on the outside, heavy brown oil glazing on the cylinder bore, or gooey oil on the exhaust valves? If so, here is a tip for cleaning those parts without flammable cleaners. Go to the grocery store and get a can of aerosol oven cleaner. This stuff is great for cleaning the carbon from the exhaust valves without completely disassembling them. Caution: Oven cleaner attacks aluminum, so don't leave it on the cylinder for more than 20 minutes. Oven cleaner can be used on both steel and plated bores.

The oven cleaner will help loosen the oil glazing on the cylinder walls. Then, you can use a Scotch-Brite pad to hone the cylinder walls in a crisscross pattern. Wear rubber gloves when you use oven cleaner and flush the cylinder afterwards with soapy water. This will neutralize the acid in the oven cleaner and break the molecular bond of the oil, so the debris can be rinsed away. Sleeved (especially Kawasaki cylinder bores) are vulnerable to corrosion after cleaning. Spray some penetrating oil on the cylinder bore to prevent it from rusting.

Caution: Certain types of cylinders corrode quickly after the cleaning process, so spray the bore area with penetrating oil to displace the water.

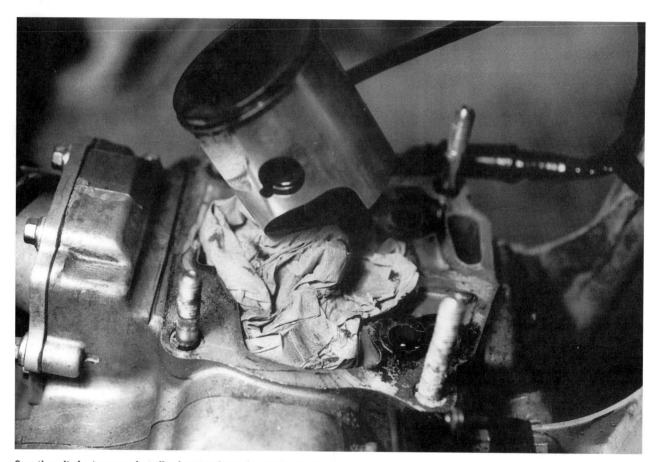

Once the cylinder is removed, stuff a clean towel into the crankcases to prevent dirt from contaminating the engine.

Top-End Assembly Tips

1. Install the circlips with the openings straight up or down.
2. Grease the cylinder-base alignment pins.
3. Set the exhaust valves in the closed position.
4. On cylinders with reed valves, leave the intake port open because you will need to reach in through the port to push the piston-ring ends back in place.
5. The best way to slip the piston into the bottom of the cylinder, is to rotate the rings toward one side of the locating pins and squeeze the rings with your middle finger and thumb. That will leave your other hand free to position the cylinder.
6. Take care to align the exhaust valve control mechanism as the cylinder is bolted to the crankcases.

Gasket Hygiene

The oven cleaner you used to clean the cylinders will help loosen the old gasket material so you can remove it. Carefully scrape the gasket off with a gasket scraper. Never use a flat screwdriver to remove the old gaskets because the aluminum surfaces of the head, cylinder, and crankcases are easily gouged. If these surfaces are gouged on your engine, they should be draw-filed flat to prevent air or coolant leaks.

Never reuse paper gaskets; *always* replace them with new gaskets, and spray sealer on the paper gaskets, so they will seal better and will be easier to remove the next time. The new-style steel gaskets can be cleaned and reused a few times, but you'll need to spray the gasket with a sealer such as Permatex Spray-A-Gasket or copper-coat.

Keep a Logbook

Keep a logbook that tracks the number of riding days and the periodic maintenance. From reviewing the log, you will learn how often you need to service the top end if you record the measurements of the ring gap and the piston diameter. A logbook also gives you greater leverage when you try to sell your used bike for a premium price.

Household oven cleaner works great for removing carbon deposits on the exhaust valves.

Measure the ring gap by placing the ring in the top of the cylinder evenly and measuring the gap with a feeler gauge.

Electroplated Cylinders

Rather than having a steel sleeve lining their aluminum cylinder, some modern dirt bikes use an aluminum cylinder with a bore area electroplated with nickel and silicon particles that form a thin, hard, and brittle wear surface. If the engine overheats and the piston expands and transfers aluminum onto the cylinder wall, plated cylinders can chip. Aluminum from the piston can be removed from a cylinder bore by applying muriatic acid to the aluminum with an acid brush. These items are available from most hardware stores. Wash the cylinder in a bucket of soapy water and dry the cylinder bore before examining it for chips and cracks in the plating. Most chip marks are harmless unless they are located on the center exhaust bridge. If the plating is chipped on the bridge, it will always cause the piston to seize. The repair options are either to buy a new cylinder or have the plating reconditioned.

The high price ($300 to $400) of a new OEM cylinder makes plating services an inexpensive alternative at about half the cost.

Most damaged cylinders can be repaired, even if there are deep gouges in the bore from ring breakage or erosion from coolant leaks. There are three cylinder replating companies in the United States They repair a cylinder by chemically stripping off the old plating material (Nikasil on CRs, YZs, and KTMs; tungsten on KX; boron composite on RMs). After stripping, the cylinder can be welded to repair cracks, erosion, or gouges. Then, the cylinder is bored to size, electroplated, and diamond-honed. It's also possible to overbore and plate a cylinder for an oversize Wiseco piston kit (for about $200).

Big Bore Kits

One of the best ways to increase horsepower is to increase displacement by overboring the cylinder. This can be ideal for play or Vet Class riders, where the increased displacement won't be illegal for your race class. When done right, a big bore kit can give you more power everywhere rather than an increase in only the top or the bottom of the powerband. Such increases are typically more usable and give you more power where you need it.

Don't replace the piston if you don't have to! Instead, measure the diameter of the piston below the wrist pin and above the intake cutaway with a digital caliper or micrometer.

Piston manufacturers such as Wiseco, Niks, and Pro-X make oversize piston kits for popular model bikes. These kits boost the displacement of the cylinder to the limit of a racing class or to a larger displacement class, for example: 80cc to 100cc, 125cc to 145cc, 250cc to 265cc or 295cc, and 495cc to 550cc.

Riders competing in the AMA veteran class can ride a bike with any displacement. Riders competing in hare scrambles and enduro can race the 200cc class with a 125 converted to 145cc displacement. AMA motocross and enduro racers can make the 250cc bikes legal for open class by increasing the displacement a minimum of 15 percent (to 286cc). There are a number of pistons kits to convert the popular 250s to 295cc. In the hill-climbing and grass drag classes, a 500cc motocross bike can become legal for the open class (750cc maximum) with a displacement of 550cc. The motocross bikes have an advantage over the four-cylinder 750cc bikes when racing on the hills with jumps. The lightweight and excellent handling of the motocross bikes makes it possible to fly farther off the jumps or

even double one of the jumps, saving valuable time.

Be careful if you decide to go with a big bore kit, though. If the overbore is not performed properly, though, it can result in the wrong kind of power or, at worst, a ruined cylinder. When you change the displacement of the cylinder, there are so many factors to consider, such as port time-area, compression ratio, exhaust valves, carb jetting, silencer, and ignition timing. Here is an explanation of what you need to do when planning to overbore a cylinder.

Also, you should at least consult with an expert before tackling a big bore kit. To get the most from an overbored engine, you need to make sure the carburetion, exhaust, porting, and timing are all adjusted to suit the larger bore.

Port-Time Area

The term port-time area refers to the size and flow range of the intake and exhaust ports, relative to rpm. The ports enter the cylinder bore at angles. When the cylinder is overbored the transfer ports become lower and wider. The same thing happens to the exhaust port. This

A dial bore gauge is the best tool to use to measure the cylinder bore's taper and out-of-round wear.

squish clearance. The larger bore size will increase the squish turbulence, so the head's squish band may have to be narrowed. The volume of the head must be increased to suit the change in cylinder displacement. Otherwise, the engine will run flat at high rpm or ping in the midrange from detonation.

Exhaust Valves

When the bore size is increased, the exhaust valve-to-piston clearance must be checked and adjusted. This pertains to the types of exhaust valves that operate within close proximity of the piston. If the exhaust valves aren't modified, the piston could strike the valves and cause serious engine damage.

Carburetor

The larger the ratio between the piston's diameter and the carb's size, the higher the intake velocity. That makes the jetting richer—and that's what happens when you overbore your cylinder because you are making the piston's diameter larger while keeping the carb's size constant. Figure on leaning the jetting after an engine is overbored.

Ignition Timing

The ignition timing has a minimal effect on the powerband. Retarding the timing has the effect of reducing the hit of the powerband in the midrange and extending the top end overrev. "Overrev" is a slang term that describes the useable length of the powerband at high rpm.

The scientific reason for the shift of the powerband to extremely high rpm is because the temperature in the pipe increases with the retarded timing, and that enables the pipe's tuned length to be more synchronous with the piston speed and port timing of the cylinder.

Advancing the timing has the effect of increasing the midrange hit of the powerband, but makes the power flatten out at high rpm. The reason is that the relatively long spark lead time enables for a greater pressure rise in the cylinder before the piston reaches TDC. This produces more torque in the midrange but the high pressure contributes to pumping losses at extremly high rpm.

effectively retards the port timing and reduces the total degrees of duration. When the displacement of the engine increases, so does the demand for more port-time-area.

If you just overbored and plated a cylinder, it would have much more low-end power than stock but the top-end power would suffer. Normally tuners have to adjust the ports to suit the demands of the larger engine displacement. The proper dimensions for the ports can be calculated using a computer

program from Two-Stroke Racing (TSR). The program "PORTTIME" enables tuners with limited math skills to run strings of formulas for determining the optimum dimensions of the ports.

Cylinder Head

After overboring the cylinder, the head's dimensions must be changed to suit the larger piston. First, the head's bore must be enlarged to the finished bore size. Then, the squish-band deck height must be set to the proper installed

Pipe and Silencer

Because only the bore size is changed, you won't need a longer pipe—only one with a larger center section. FMF's line of Fatty pipes work great on engines that have been overbored. Some riders use silencers that are shorter with larger outlets to adjust the back-pressure in the pipe for the larger engine displacement.

Head Gasket

The head gasket will need to have the bore diameter increased to the dimension of the new piston. If the head gasket overlaps into the cylinder bore more than 1mm on each side, it could contact the piston or be susceptible to pressure blowouts.

Breaking In a New Top End

Electroplated top ends don't really need much in the way of break-in. On the other hand, you can't hurt a new top end by going easy on it for the first few minutes. If you want to be on the safe side with an electroplated top end or if you have a freshly bored steel-sleeved cylinder, use the following break-in routine.

Ride the bike for three 15-minute riding sessions with 15-minutes of cool down in between sessions. Don't use more than

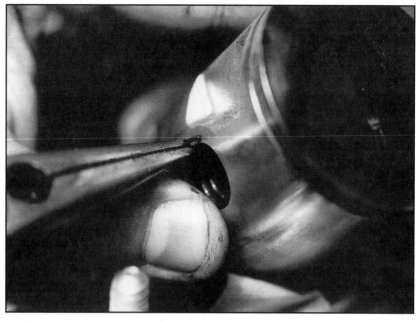

Use a small needle nose pliers to install the wrist pin circlips in the piston.

3/4 throttle, and keep engine loads light. One you've been through this procedure, your steel-sleeved cylinder is good to go.

Troubleshooting Piston Failures

Reading a piston is easier than reading a spark plug. The condition of the piston gives you clues to the condition of the crank, bearings, jetting, rider's style, and maintenance practices. This section is a guide to trouble-shooting chronic piston failures in two-stroke engines.

Scuffing

Description: Piston is seized at four points, with the majority of the seizure on the exhaust side.

Causes: Improper warm-up—You must warm an engine up slowly to allow the aluminum piston to expand to the proper tolerances. Scuffing occurs when the piston expands too fast and jams into the cylinder wall. The best way to warm up a bike is to ride for about five minutes in second gear, below half throttle. Scuffing can also occur if the mixture is too lean. If the main jet is too small, the piston will scuff or seize momentarily. Remember, when the temperature drops, the air becomes more dense and you need to richen your jetting. Remember also that a lean jetting condition can be created when you mix your fuel–oil ratio too rich.

Overheating

Description: Cooling system overheats and blows coolant out overflow. If left unchecked, this may cause the engine to seize.

The technique for installing the cylinder is to use your thumb and index finger to squeeze the rings and your other hand to lower the cylinder onto the piston assembly.

Causes: The head gasket may develop a leak at the headstay, causing the engine to ingest coolant. The combustion pressure will pressurize the cooling system, causing coolant to flow out the overflow vent tube. The engine will then overheat for lack of coolant.

Scouring

Description: The piston has deep vertical scratches on the skirt.

Causes: There are two main types of abrasives that scour pistons, dirt that enters the air box and "flashing" left over from the cylinder plating process. If you find any dirt inside the air boot, you must seal the air-boot-to-air-box flange with weather-strip adhesive. Do not use silicone seal because it is fuel soluble. On modern plated cylinders, a thin layer of the hard alloy material may adhere to the port edges. Occasionally this flashing breaks loose and falls into the cylinder bore. When it gets trapped between the cylinder wall and the piston, it scratches the soft aluminum piston. The best way to remove the loose flashing is by bead-blasting the ports before assembling the engine.

Shattered

Description: The intake skirt or the top edge of the exhaust side of the piston cracks off or shatters.

Causes: As the engine rotates, the inertia of the connecting rod loads the top exhaust side of the piston on the down stroke from TDC. On the upstroke from bottom dead center (BDC), the rod loads the lower intake side of the piston. The loads become greater where the cylinder-bore surface area is taken over by the intake and exhaust ports. That's why the cylinder bore and piston wear out faster near the intake and exhaust ports. When the piston or cylinder becomes worn, the excessive piston-to-cylinder-wall clearance causes the piston to eventually shatter. Whenever you re-ring your engine, always measure the piston diameter and the cylinder bore size. Check the sizes with the specifications in the service manual.

Shattered Top Edge, Exhaust Side

Description: The top edge of the piston has cracked off above the ring groove.

Although some OEM head and base gaskets are coated with gasket sealer, you should still spray a light coating of sealer on each side of the gaskets. To seal O-rings, use Vaseline petroleum jelly.

Causes: If the top edge of the exhaust side of the piston cracks off, the problem is either a leaky head gasket or the cylinder head was poorly designed so that squish-band velocities are too high. When there is a leaking head gasket, coolant hits the hot aluminum piston, making it brittle. Coolant leaks are most often the result of the top shock mount flexing the headstays and lifting up the head, allowing coolant to enter the combustion chamber. Another major cause of coolant leaks is erosion of the top edge of the cylinder. Kawasakis are notorious for this problem and they offer an extra-thick head gasket to eliminate this problem. Head gaskets should be sprayed with a gasket sealer prior to installation.

If the cylinder-head design causes too much squish velocity (squish-band turbulence), the piston will have some seizure marks all around the top of the piston but no erosion marks on the top edge of the cylinder. Many production cylinder heads have too much squish velocity because the squish bands are too wide or the clearance between the piston and cylinder head at TDC is too little. WR250s built from 1990 to 1995 YZ and are notorious for this problem. In the tuning-tips sections we recommend cylinder-head modifications to reduce the squish velocity

Exhaust-Side Seizure

Description: The exhaust side of the piston is melted from top to bottom. The intake side looks normal.

Causes: Air leaks. When the exhaust side of the piston melts, it is usually preceded by a steadily increasing low-speed bogging problem. This problem is caused by a crankcase air leak, and the extra oxygen that leaks in increases the engine temperature, causing the exhaust side of the piston to melt. Most likely, the magneto-side crank seal is blown. The cylinder base gasket or intake gasket may also be leaking.

Most base-gasket leaks are caused by gouges in the aluminum of the base that are made when the cylinder is removed by prying it up with a screwdriver or chisel. Do not pry off your cylinders! Use a plas-

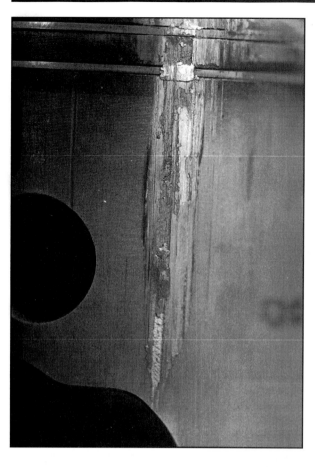

This is a close-up view of a four-corner seizure, caused by a combination of overheating and lean jetting.

The intake side of the piston is scoured from the dirt passing through the air filter.

tic mallet to rock the cylinder from side to side to remove it. Then grease the dowel pins to prevent them from corroding into the cylinder or cases.

Intake-Side Seizure

Description: The intake side of the piston is seized or scoured and the exhaust side looks normal.

Causes: The only reason a piston will seize on the intake side only is lack of lubrication. Either there was no oil mixed with the fuel, a castor-based oil was used and it separated from the fuel, or water passed through the air filter and washed the oil off the piston.

Holed Piston

Description: There is a hole burned through the top of the piston.

Causes: Fuel problems or black-box failure. If the fuel's octane rating is mismatched to the engine's needs, the engine may develop a detonation or pre-ignition problem. Before the piston fails, the rider will hear a loud pinging or knocking noise from inside the cylinder head.

The black box encases a series of zener diodes that control the ignition curve through the rpm range. All of the black boxes have a high-speed retard circuit that retards the ignition timing to cool the engine. Sometimes, one of the zener diodes will fail, causing the ignition-timing circuit to continue advancing the timing the higher you rev the engine. The engine will run great, until it melts a hole in the piston. The only way to check the black box is to warm up the engine, use a tachometer and a strobe timing light to check the ignition curve for high-speed retard. The service manual will list instructions on exactly how to check the black box for your particular model.

Two-Stroke Exhaust Valves

Three words sum up exhaust valve maintenance: grimy, gooey, and grungy. If two-stroke exhaust valves didn't have such a dramatic effect on the engine's powerband, I'm sure mechanics would remove them and beat them bits with a hammer in frustration because there is little information given by the manufacturers on how to diagnose and repair the exhaust valve systems on well-used dirt

This piston has a hole melted in it at the crown and the exhaust skirt is melted. This problem was caused by a bad black box that advanced the ignition timing too far. The engine was detonating under acceleration. When an engine is detonating, you will hear a "pinging" noise when you get on the gas. It is a distinct ticking rattle under load that tells you to stop running your bike and check for air leaks or rejet.

bikes. This section is a guide to the characteristic mechanical problems that occur to the exhaust valve systems of dirt bikes. Plus we'll give you some tips on how to re-time exhaust valve systems for late-model KXs and 1988–91 Honda CR250s.

How Exhaust Valves Work

An exhaust valve system is designed to increase the engine's low-range and mid-range power. There are three different designs of exhaust valve systems. The first-generation design uses a variable-volume chamber mounted to the head pipe to change the tuned length of the head pipe. A butterfly valve is used to separate the surge chamber and the head pipe. At low rpm, the valve is open to allow the pressure waves in the pipe to travel into the surge chamber and effectively lengthen the pipe and reduce the pressure wave's magnitude when it returns to the exhaust port. These systems were primitive and not very effective on 125cc dirt bikes. This type of exhaust valve system was used by Honda from 1985 to 1989.

The second-generation design features valves that control the effective stroke and the time-area of the exhaust port. These valves are fitted to the sub-exhaust ports and the main exhaust port. The main exhaust-port valves operate within close proximity to the piston to control the effective stroke of the engine. The effective stroke is defined as the distance from TDC to when the

These pistons shattered because the cylinder bores were worn and the connecting rods had too much side clearance. The rods broke on both engines.

This ring alignment pin fell out and became wedged between the piston and cylinder wall.

Advanced Piston Research *By H. Sean Hilbert*

H. Sean Hilbert is a mechanical engineer and partner in Red Cedar Engineering. RCE is a state-of-the-art dyno test cell for contracted high-performance development of two-stroke engines used for racing motor sports.

Recent improvements in temperature-measurement technology will have a profound effect on the design of future pistons. As two-stroke engine designs become more and more powerful, all types of stresses on internal moving components increase, and one of the stressed components is the piston. High engine rpms cause large mechanical stresses, and higher output can cause high thermal stresses. As everyone knows, the combination of these often leads to disaster.

Thermal stresses are especially troublesome in two-stroke engines because the two-stroke piston gets very little chance to cool. Since the engine fires on every crankshaft revolution, the heat from combustion is constantly being absorbed into the piston crown. Knowing how much and where the heat is absorbed is essential to designing durable pistons. For years, designers have approximated what kind of thermal stresses the piston would be under. This has been done through simple heat-transfer calculations and, mainly, a lot of guesswork.

Recently the power of the computer has allowed complex modeling of heat flow throughout the engine, but the results are still only approximations. Actual measurement of the piston temperatures in a running engine is an extremely difficult task. Monitoring temperatures electronically would require that the temperature signal would make it from the piston to a read-out device outside of the engine somehow. Obviously, running a wire to a piston that is moving up and down at 10,000 rpm is not going to work. The answer, then, is to devise a way to transmit a signal without any hard connections. A device invented at the Southwest Research Institute in San Antonio, Texas, does just that. Piston temperatures are monitored and then sent to an antenna located just outside the running engine. The key component to this system is the power generator. This device uses piston acceleration forces to move a tiny steel slug up and down through a magnetic field. This creates an alternating current that is used to power the measurement and signal generation units. The entire device is 40mms long and 12mms wide and tall.

So what does this mean in terms of racing? A lot! Any time that a piston can be made lighter, stronger, and more durable, beneficial effects on the race track will be noticed. A system such as this could be used to measure and improve piston-crown coatings (thermal barriers) or develop new piston designs such as the carbon-carbon (double-cured carbon fiber) type invented at NASA.

exhaust port opens. At low rpm, the engine needs a long effective stroke, which results in a high compression ratio. At high rpm, the engine needs a shorter effective stroke, longer exhaust duration, greater time-area, and a lower compression ratio. Yamaha used this system starting in 1982 on the YZ250. Honda's HPP system is similar and was used on the 1986–91 CR250 and 1990 to current model CR125.

The third generation of exhaust valve systems attempts to change the exhaust-port velocity, effective stroke, exhaust-gas temperature, and the pressure of the compression wave. Yamaha and Suzuki started using these systems on their 125s in 1995. Both companies employed a venting system to the outside atmosphere. This is very complex because they are attempting to affect the temperature and pressure of the returning compression wave to synchronize it with the piston speed. The exhaust-gas velocity and the effective stroke are controlled by two round wedge valves that enter the exhaust port at a 45-degree angle. The wedge valves partially block the exhaust port, thereby boosting the gas velocity. Kawasaki's KIPS system uses wedge valves in the main exhaust port to control the effective stroke, drum valves in the sub-exhaust ports to control the time-area, and a surge chamber to absorb the excess compression-wave pressure at low rpm.

The exhaust valves are opened and closed by a centrifugal governor mechanism. The governor is mounted under the right side cover and is gear-driven by

These three pistons have different carbon burn patterns on their crowns. Left: The black patches denote a right side crank seal leak, allowing oil to enter the crankcases and being burned in the combustion chamber. Center: The light gray color denotes that the engine was jetted lean. The crown was starting to melt. Right: This is the ideal piston crown color and carbon pattern. The color is a light brown and the carbon is spread evenly side to side which indicates that the transfer ports are of equal size and flow.

Look on the underside of the piston crown. A black spot denotes that the engine was running hot and some pre-mix oil burned on the piston.

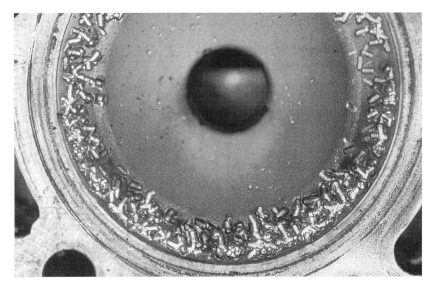

The piston detonated and broke apart on this engine. The bits of metal were smashed into the cylinder head.

This piston was treated with Teflon to reduce scuffing by an American company named Swain-Tech.

If the piston seizes it can tear the Nikasil plating off the cylinder wall. First remove the aluminum deposits with muriatic acid then inspect the cylinder walls for chipping.

the crankshaft. As the engine rpm increases, the governor spins, thereby increasing the angular momentum of the four steel balls encased in the governor. The steel balls fit into an angled ramp-and-cup arrangement. and a spring is used to provide tension on the steel balls. When the momentum of the steel balls overcomes the spring's tension, and the balls force their way up the

angled ramp. A spool attached to the ramp, enabling it to change its linear position with changes in rpm, and the spool is attached to a linkage system that operates the exhaust valves in the cylinder. Factory race teams have different combinations of springs, ramps, and balls to tune the exhaust valve operation and enhance the powerband.

Exhaust Valve Tips and Tuning

Although exhaust valves use the same essential principles, the implementation is different with each manufacturer. Also, each type has its own flaws and fixes. The list below gives you tips on how to install and service the most common exhaust valves, as well as some tuning tips.

Exhaust Valve FAQs

♦ 1987 Honda CR125 ATAC Test

Question: I have an older CR125 with an ATAC system. How can I test the system to be sure it is working properly?

Answer: To test any of the ATAC systems, remove the chamber cover and start the engine. The exhaust note should be very loud and exhaust gas should be coming out of the chamber. When you rev the throttle wide open, the valve should close off the chamber and the exhaust should only be coming out the pipe.

♦ 1995 KX125 Runs Flat

Question: My 1995 Kawasaki KX125 seems to run flat on top end. My friend's 1994 KX125 blows mine away in a drag race. Could there be something wrong with my engine's exhaust valves?

Answer: Yes, there is definitely something wrong with the exhaust valves. The 1995 model had a design defect in the governor control that prevents the KIPS valves from opening fully. Replace your governor's ramp cup with the one from the 1994 or 1996 model, both of which carry the same part number.

♦ Top-End Clicking Noise

Question: My 1989 Yamaha WR250 makes a clicking noise from the top end, until about half throttle. It's not a loud scary noise, just annoying because I can't figure out where it's coming from. Any ideas?

Answer: The power valve's stop tab is worn from slamming closed thousands of times. This enables the power valve to rotate further closed at low rpm. The clicking noise is probably from the piston rings striking the power valve. Disassemble the top end and look for shiny spots on corresponding areas of the power valve and the piston. You can use a file to relieve the power valve at the shiny area. This will provide a clearance gap so the power valve does not contact the piston. This same procedure should be performed to YZ and WR cylinders that use steel sleeves, and are overbored for larger pistons.

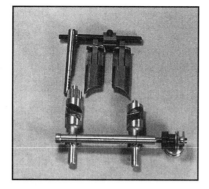

This is the late model KIPS, the exhaust valve system used on Kawasaki dirt bikes. It uses a precisely timed upper and lower rack and pinion system.

Kawasaki Exhaust Valve

Kawasaki's KIPS exhaust valve system uses a center wedge valve with two side drum valves engaged to a rack-and-gear actuating system. The KX125 and KDX200 models have drum valves made of aluminum. When the drum valve becomes carbon seized, the steel teeth on the rack shear off the aluminum teeth on the drum valve, rendering the drum valve inoperable. Check the condition on the gear teeth every time you do a top-end service.

The drum valves on the KX250 and 500 are also aluminum but have a hard-anodized coating that resists wear. However, the drum valves eventually wear at the drive channels for the center wedge valve, and the sloppy fit between the wedge and drum valves prevents the center valve from fully opening. That is why these bikes get noticeably slower as they get older. There is no preventative cure or aftermarket part. You just need to replace the drum valves when the drive channels wear out. On the late-model KXs that use the wedge valves, there is an upper gear and rack. A left-hand-thread nut retains the gear to the rod that actuates the wedge valve. Check the nut periodically; if the nut loosens, the wedge valves become inoperable.

The 1993–96 KX250 wedge valve tends to form burrs at the outer edges that face the piston. These burrs prevent the wedge valve from opening fully, and the thin flap that comprises the exhaust-port roof hangs out into the exhaust-gas stream, producing a shock

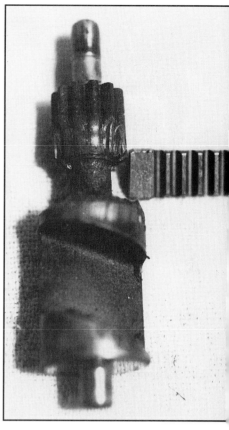

The steel rack teeth shear off the aluminum drum valve teeth when the valve becomes carbon seized.

wave that closes off the exhaust port. File the burrs smooth and check the wedge valve through the full range of movement. Another characteristic problem of the KX250 KIPS is broken governor levers. The lever that transmits the movement from the centrifugal governor to the right-side case lever tends to break in half. This piece is located under the right side cover.

1988–92 KX250 and KX500 KIPS Timing Procedure

The explanation of this procedure, written in the Kawasaki service manual, is confusing. It requires you to time the upper and lower racks at the same instant. My method of timing the exhaust valves is composed of simple steps that enable you to check your work as you go. The 1988–92 KX250 and KX500 use the drive-channel system to actuate the center valve. Here is the best way to time the KIPS on these models.

The drum valves on the 1988–92 KX250 and 500s wear at the drive channels.

1. Set the cylinder upside down on a bench.
2. Install the center valve, but don't bolt it in!
3. Install the side drum valves and align the drive channels on the drum valves with the center valve, but don't bolt it in!
4. Install the side drum valves and align the drive channels on the drum valves with the engagement pins on the center valve.
5. Lift up the drum valves so the bottoms of the gears are flush with the cylinder base. Take care not to disengage the center valve.
6. Slide in the rack from either side of the cylinder. Position the rack by installing the seal pack and pulling the rack out until it bottoms against the seal pack. This is the full-open position.
7. Drop the drum valves onto the rack so the valves are in the full-open position. Don't pay attention to alignment dots or marks on the valve or rack, just remember that the valves should be open when the rack is pulled out and closed when the rack is pushed in.

This actuator lever is located inside the right side engine cover of late model KX250s.

The center wedge valve on the 1993-95 KX250s develop a burr (right side) and that keeps the valve from opening. Polish the valve as shown on the left.

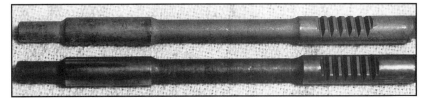

A common problem with the HPP is a broken rack. This happens because the cylinder is forced on to the cases with the rack in the wrong position.

1992–96 KX125 and
KX250 KIPS Timing Procedure

The system used on the 1992–96 KX125 and KX250 uses both wedge and drum valves with racks. This is the best exhaust valve system for performance but the most difficult to maintain. Here are some tips for retiming this KIPS system.

1. Install the wedge valves in the cylinder and the actuating rod and lever.
2. Pull the wedge valve into the full-open position, place the gear on the end of the rod, and rotate the gear counterclockwise until the rack butts against the stop plate. Thread the nut on the rod and tighten it counterclockwise because it is a left-hand-thread nut.
3. Place the drum valves into their respective cavities until the top of the gears are level with the cylinder base. Now push the lower rack into place, and bolt the seal pack on the rack into the cylinder.
4. Pull the rack out until it stops and push it in one millimeter; now it is in the correct position to install the drum valve. Before you push down the drum valves, make sure the wedge valve and drum valves are in the full-open position.
5. Push down the left drum valve first because it must engage the upper rack and lower rack. Then push down the right drum valve and install the idler gear. Now install the bushings and check the system. The valves will bind and stick if you try to move the valves without the bushings installed.

Suzuki Exhaust Valve

Suzuki's ATEV exhaust valve system works on a different principle than traditional exhaust valve systems. It is a simple and reliable exhaust valve system. The ATEV system is designed to regulate the exhaust-gas velocity through the exhaust port and into the pipe, whereas most exhaust valve systems control the effective stroke of the engine. The ATEV system is also self-cleaning in that the valves are scraped of carbon every time they move. Some of the early-model RMs suffered from broken exhaust valves when the stem would detach from the cylindrical wedge. That problem was cured in 1991 when the

If the HPP engagement bolt won't lock-in, use a pliers to squeeze the detent fork.

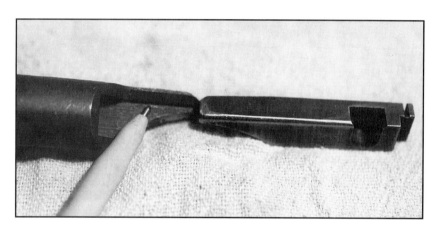

This is the valve guide. Carbon builds up in the sharp corner. Use a file to clean the carbon. Chamfer the edge of the valve to prevent the valve from carbon seizing.

radius between the stem and valve was increased. The only problems that occur with the ATEV are caused by the two following errors in assembling the system: Here are some of the common problems.

1. Too much preload on the spring. On the left side of the cylinder is a dial that controls the spring preload for the exhaust valve system. The preload doesn't have that great of an effect on the engine's powerband, but too much preload will prevent the valves from opening, which causes a lack of top-end power.

2. Crisscrossed spring. A centering spring on the right side of the cylinder, located on the rod, actuates the valves. This spring is commonly installed wrong. The spring tabs should be parallel when coupled to the lever and rod. If the spring tabs are crisscrossed, the valve travel will be limited and won't open fully.

This is the proper position of the pinion shaft slots when the HPP valves are closed.

Suzuki exhaust valves commonly break off at the shaft, as shown above. If your top-end power or low-end response suddenly disappears you can suspect this problem. If your powerband becomes erratic, you know you have an exhaust valve problem.

The Suzuki ATEV springs are easily damaged when you turn the tensioner knob too far counter-clockwise.

Honda Exhaust Valves

Honda's early model HPP system, used on CR250s from 1986 to 1991, is plagued with a mixture of design problems and misinformation on how to service and retime this complicated exhaust valve system. This section lists some common problems and some tips for timing the system, installing the cylinder, and engaging the HPP mechanism.

Common HPP Problems

Two main problems plague the HPP system: carbon fouling and rack-and-cam-spindle damage. The square shape of the valves contributes to the accumulation of carbon on one corner of the valve guide (stationary part), in the corner of the guide that is directly in the exhaust gas stream, and this carbon seizes the valve in place. Chamfering the corresponding edge (one millimeter) of the valve (moving part) will eliminate this problem. The rack and cam spindle are easily damaged when the cylinder is installed incorrectly, or the HPP mechanism is engaged incorrectly. See the photos for examples of damaged rack and cam spindle parts.

The spring on this RM Suzuki is crisscrossed and that is the wrong position. The spring ends should be parallel.

If you tighten the tensioner knob too far on the Suzuki RM, the exhaust valves won't open but the actuator lever will move.

How well you've done your engine work will be determined here, in that all-important drag race to the first turn. These 500cc Grand Prix racers are lining up for the first race of the 1993 season at Hawkstone Park.

This is a close-up view of the stop-tab on the late model YZ power valve. The tabs get worn and that allows the power valve to rotate so far that the piston hits the power valve.

This is an exhaust valve governor control. It is driven by the primary gear and fits in between the right side crankcase and side cover.

This is a governor control disassembled. Starting from the left, drive gear, spring, radial bearings and shims, ramp cup, ball weights, center shaft, and drive channels.

HPP Timing Procedure

Use the following procedure to time the HPP system:

1. Install the HPP valves and levers and tighten the pivot nuts. Place the washer on the stud first, then the lever (marked left and right), and then the flanged center bushing with the flange side facing up.

2. Turn the cylinder upside down. To position the rack correctly, slide it to the left until it stops; then move it right 2mm. Rotate the rack so the square notch faces you. Now the rack is in the correct position so you can install the pinion shafts. Carefully turn the cylinder right side up without changing the position of the rack.

3. Close the valves and install the left pinion shaft with the screwdriver slot facing the one o'clock position. Install the right pinion shaft with the screwdriver slot facing the eleven o'clock position (see photo for correct positions). A simple way to determine if the pinions are mis-timed to the rack is to look at the screwdriver slots. The wrong position is with both slots facing twelve o'clock.

Installing the Cylinder and Engaging the HPP Drive

After timing the HPP mechanism, the cylinder is ready to be installed on the crankcases. Here are some tips for installing the cylinder and engaging the HPP drive mechanism:

1. Make sure the reed valve is removed from the cylinder. CR250s have such large intake ports that the rings tend to slip out of the ring grooves during installation of the cylinder. This takes the spring pressure off the cam spindle. Now turn the engagement bolt 1/4 turn clockwise. You should feel it positively lock into a groove and stop. Remember that the HPP engagement bolt is a spring-loaded detent not a threaded bolt. Slide the cylinder down onto the piston and rings, use a screwdriver to push the rings back in the grooves until the rings clear the intake port.

2. The HPP mechanism should be engaged while the cylinder is being installed, just to keep the cam spindle in position. The cylinder will stop about 3mm from the crankcases because the cam spindle and the rack are misaligned. Now disengage the HPP mechanism by turning the engage bolt 1/4 turn counter-clockwise. Grasp the right-side valve lever and wiggle it; the cylinder should then drop evenly onto the crankcases.

3. Bolt the cylinder down tight. The best way to engage the HPP mechanism is to insert a screwdriver in the right-side pinion shaft and turn it counter-clockwise. Now turn the engagement bolt clockwise. You should feel the engagement bolt lock positively in position. If you try to rotate it too far, you will bend the cam spindle and the system won't work at all, so don't be a hammer-head! The best way to check the HPP system is to remove the left-side valve cover from the cylinder, start the engine and warm it up, then rev the engine. The valves should be fully closed at idle and fully open when the engine is revved.

Yamaha Exhaust Valves

Yamaha was the first motorcycle manufacturer to adapt exhaust valves to two-stroke motorcycle engines. Yamaha's simple design of a cylindrical valve that rotates one-quarter turn to vary the height of the exhaust port requires little maintenance. Occasionally, you have to replace the seals and O-rings to prevent exhaust oil from drooling out of the side of the cylinder. In 1989, Yamaha added a stop plate to limit the travel of the power valve, primarily so mechanics couldn't install the valve in the wrong position. The stop plate is located on the left side of the cylinder. The valve has a small tab that bumps up against the stop plate to limit the fully open and closed position of the valve. This design enabled Yamaha to position the valve closer to the piston to make it more effective at varying the exhaust-port timing. Unfortunately, the soft-aluminum tab on the valve gets worn, allowing the valve to rotate farther in the fully closed position. Eventually, (after about three years of use) the tab wears enough so the valve strikes the piston, causing damage to the piston. Yamaha's exhaust valve is cheap to replace. I recommend replacing the valve when the tab wears more than 0.030 inch (0.7mm). Yamaha's exhaust valve is also easy to tune for better performance. Look to the sections on tuning tips for Yamahas.

TWO-STROKE LOWER END

CHAPTER SIX

Rebuilding the lower end of a two-stroke engine is the procedure that is most often put off until next race/month/season. When you start hearing the engine make a strange knocking sound, it's time to shut it off and tear it down rather than pin the throttle wide open and hope it will just go away! The normal service interval for lower end rebuilding is once a year on engines under 200cc and once every two to three years for 250 and larger engines. While rebuilding the lower end you should replace the ball bearings that support the crankshaft and the transmission shafts, plus the rubber seals. In most cases, the crankshaft will need to have a new connecting rod, pin, bearing, and thrust washers installed. Some manufacturers (Honda) don't sell parts for their crankshafts, only the entire part. However, there are companies that offer higher-quality replacement parts (Hot Rods) to rebuild modern Japanese cranks and vintage Spanish cranks. Although some aspects of lower end rebuilding are very specific to a particular model engine, this section gives you an overview of the general process.

The Right Tools

Engine rebuilding is nearly impossible without the right tools. Some guys try to use the "caveman" method—big hammers and chisels. As a result, they usually do some stupid thing that ruins expensive engine components.

To properly rebuild your lower end, you will need the following tools from the manufacturer: a service manual for torque specs and disassembly/assembly techniques specific to your model engine, a flywheel puller, a clutch-hub holder, a crankcase splitting tool, and a crankshaft installation tool—but I'll show you techniques for removing the clutch and installing the crank so you can save money on those tools. You will also need an air- or electric-powered impact wrench to remove the nuts that retain the flywheel, clutch, countershaft sprocket, and primary gear; a parts washer with solvent to clean the engine parts; a hydraulic press to remove and install the bearings because a hammer will only damage them; a propane torch to heat and expand the aluminum crankcases to remove or install the bearings because they have an interference fit (meaning that the bearing is a slightly larger diameter than the hole that it fits into); a digital caliper to measure certain engine parts and compare them to the minimum wear specs listed in the service manual; a variety of tools such as wrenches and sockets; and soft tools such as brake cleaner, thread locking agent, penetrating oil, seal grease, and gasket sealer. A simple way to hold the engine while you work on it is to make an open square box from wood blocks. A universal box for any engine can be made from 2×4-inch blocks with the dimensions of the box being 5×10 inches. CC Specialty makes a ball-vise for $100 that is convenient if you plan to rebuild engines frequently. To permanently remove the temptation to use steel hammers when rebuilding engines, buy a plastic mallet. Snap-On makes a lead-filled plastic mallet that works excellently. The last thing you will need to rebuild an engine is several parts storage bins. I prefer to separate the engine's components into separate bins—top-end parts, electrical parts, clutch parts, shifter parts, transmission, and crankcase bolts. This enables me to keep the parts organized for quick assembly. I also puncture small holes in the bottom of the bin so I can pour parts cleaning solvent into the bins to clean the parts. Then there isn't any chance of the parts becoming lost in the bottom of the parts-washing tank.

Top End Disassembly and Inspection

Refer to the sections on top-end rebuilding and exhaust valve servicing for more information on this topic.

These are some of the tools you'll need to rebuild an engine: a propane torch, rubber bands, brake cleaner, and a wood-framed box to support the engine.

Electrical System Disassembly and Inspection

Use an impact wrench to remove the flywheel nut. Don't be tempted to jam a screwdriver in through one of the holes in the flywheel to prevent it from spinning. That will damage the coils under the flywheel. K&N makes a threaded flywheel puller that has left-hand threads to fasten to the flywheel and a right-hand-threaded bolt to push on the crankshaft. Put a dab of grease on the flywheel end to prevent the bolt from galling and damaging the machined center on the crankshaft end (if the center is damaged, it is much more difficult for a technician to true the crank). It's OK to tap on the end of the tightly threaded puller with a plastic mallet.

Here is a tip for removing stuck flywheels. Use a propane torch to heat the center hub of the flywheel. Take care not to shoot the flame through the holes in the flywheel. Then spray penetrating between the crankshaft end and the flywheel. This should loosen the flywheel enough for the puller to pop it off.

When the flywheel comes off, inspect the center-hub rivets and look for tiny cracks in the hub around the riv-

ets. Replace the flywheel if there are any cracks. Big-bore bikes may have problems with shearing flywheel Woodruff keys, especially on the KX500 and YZ490. The problem is that the flywheel is not matched to the crank at the taper, but that can be corrected, using the following procedure. Remove the Woodruff key and apply grinding paste to the crank's taper. Hand-press the flywheel onto the crank and turn it back and forth for five minutes. This will hone down the high spots on the surfaces of each part so the flywheel won't ever loosen up and shear the Woodruff key. After matching, clean the parts thoroughly with contact cleaner.

Clutch Disassembly and Inspection

There are a number of things to check on the clutch, and you will need a factory service manual for specifications on the wear limit of the clutch parts. Some of the things you want to inspect include the clutch springs for free length, the clutch plates for thickness or for any broken plates, the outer pressure plate for a sizable worn-in ridge that would indicate the plate is too thin, the

▶ Bike Blows White Smoke

Question: My old YZ250 smokes so much that I'm embarrassed to ride it. The front of the pipe drools oil out the manifold, and the engine fouls plugs fast. What could be causing this problem, and how can I fix it?

Answer: Your bike may be drawing trans oil into the crankcases and burning it in the combustion chamber. You should monitor the trans oil level to confirm this suspicion. The crankshaft main bearings are probably worn out and the crank is wobbling at high rpm, allowing oil from the trans to slip past the right-side crank seal. Eventually, the crank will be stressed so hard that it will seize the lower end. The average labor charge for a lower end rebuild (assuming you take the engine out of the frame) is $100 plus parts, and crank rebuilding is about $45. Average parts tickets range from $75 to $275.

▶ Locked Clutch

Question: I trail ride a 1987 KX125. When the engine gets hot, the bike keeps pulling after I pull in the clutch lever. I tightened the cable, and I watch the lever on the engine move when I pull in the clutch, but it still won't disengage. What's happening to my clutch?

Answer: The clutch basket is probably worn out. That means that the fiber plates have worn grooves into the fingers of the clutch basket. The plates get locked into the grooves, and even if you pull in the clutch lever, the plates still won't pull apart from each other so the power is still transferred into the transmission. The clutch basket is an expensive part at about $130. It is a common problem on that model and year of KX125. Kawasaki has since updated the clutch baskets on the 1987–92 models with a better design that resists grooving.

inner hub and outer basket for chatter marks, the clutch basket's aluminum housing and the primary gear for excessive free-play between the two, and the center bushing (measure its diameter). A worn bushing will cause a variety of problems, including broken clutch plates. See the section on clutch rebuilding for more details.

Shifter, Kickstarter, and Primary Gear Disassembly and Inspection

You will have to remove the shift shaft, power-valve governor cartridge, and the primary gear that is bolted to the end of the crankshaft. The best way to remove the primary-gear bolt is with an impact wrench. There is no factory holding tool for this gear; it's just an accepted practice to use an impact wrench. If you are only going to change the main bearings, you don't need to remove the kick-start cartridge or the shift drum and spring-loaded shifting mechanism.

Splitting the Crankcases

Remove all the case bolts, and install the case-splitting tool onto the left-side crankcase. The puller's two bolts thread into the stator-plate mounts. The center bolt of the puller threads up against the crankshaft end. Apply some grease to the end of the crankshaft so the puller's tapered bolt doesn't gall the end of the crankshaft. Slowly tighten the puller bolt and tap around the outside of the cases with a plastic mallet. This will help break the bond of the case alignment pins. If the cases start to split apart with an uneven gap from front to rear, then tap on a part of the right-side crankcase with a plastic mallet. You may also have to tap on the countershaft, but be careful because you could break the bearing support ring that is cast into the case.

To remove the transmission shafts, you need to first remove the shift forks. Pull the rods that hold the forks, and then pull out the forks. Place the forks onto the rods, and set them in a parts bin in the order that they fit in the engine. The rod with the outside of the right countershaft bearing is very vulnerable on Hondas. Pay attention to the placement of shims on the ends of the transmission shafts; sometimes they will

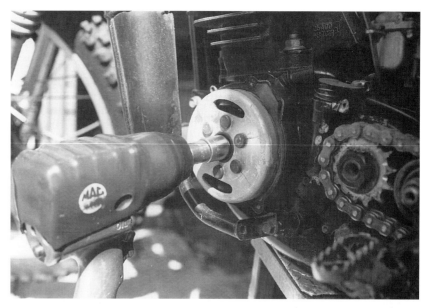

Use an impact wrench to remove the flywheel nut. As an alternative, stuff a sock into the combustion chamber and use a breaker bar, BUT be gentle. An impact wrench is a much better solution.

This is a K&N flywheel puller. Apply some grease to the crank end so the puller doesn't gall the crank's machined center.

The crankcase halves are being separated with a special tool. The tool threads into the stator plate mounting holes and a center bolt presses on the crankshaft. Its possible to modify a universal bearing puller tool to fit most Japanese dirt bikes. The motorcycle manufacturers offer special tools to separate the crankcase halves, at a premium price.

Crankshaft Removal and Inspection

Sometimes, the crank will be difficult to remove from the right-side main bearing (on all engines except Suzukis). Never strike the end of the crank with a metal hammer; try a plastic mallet first. If that doesn't work, then thread the primary-gear nut on to protect the threads and use a hydraulic press to remove the crank. Measure the rod clearance to determine if it needs to be rebuilt. Check the crankshaft run-out and true it if necessary before installation. See the section on crankshaft repair if your inspection reveals a problem.

Bearing Removal and Installation

The best way to remove or install bearings is by heating the aluminum crankcases with a propane torch and then using a hydraulic press to gently push them out. Never pound the bearings out with a hammer and punch. The outer race of the bearing is the only part of the bearing where a press slug should be placed. Large sockets or discs work well as press slugs. Placing the new bearings in the freezer for two hours and heating the cases with the torch will enable you to install the bearings without a press. Fit the bearings into position with as little stress as possible exerted on the crank ends. Some manufacturers make special tools that wedge in between the flyweights so you can press the crank into place (Kawasaki). Other manufacturers use a threaded tool that draws the crank into the bearing.

Crankshaft Installation

Here is a simple way to install the crank. Place the crank in a freezer for two hours so it contracts in size. Get a cylindrical piece of aluminum with the same diameter as the inner bearing race. Heat and expand the bearing's inner race by heating the aluminum slug with a propane torch for five minutes while it rests on the inner race of the right-side main bearing. Drop the cold crank into the hot right main bearing. Now repeat the procedure for the left main bearing and prepare to assemble the cases.

stick to the bearings and fall out later when you are washing the cases.

Transmission Disassembly and Inspection

There are three shift forks in the transmission, and they are marked "L" for left and "R" for right. They each have a different radius, so you can't install them in the wrong position. Visually check the sides of the shift forks for blue marks. That would indicate that the forks are bent and need to

be replaced (RM250s and KX500s are notorious for bending shift forks). Now remove the transmission shafts, paying close attention to shims that may be stuck to the case bearings. Visually inspect the gear engagement dogs for wear. The female and male dogs will have shiny spots on the corners if they are worn. Also, the bike will have the tendency to jump out of gear during acceleration. The best way to keep the gears and shims on the transmission shafts is with rubber bands.

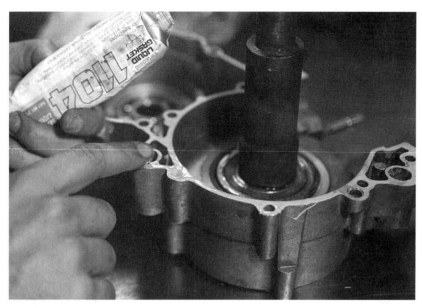

A steel slug is placed on the inner race of the main bearing and heated with a propane torch. This serves to expand the race so the crank can be installed easily. Nondrying liquid gasket sealer is used to seal the cases on Yamahas and Kawasakis.

Assembling the Crankcases

With the crank and transmission fitted into the right crankcase, you're ready to assemble the cases. Kawasaki and Yamaha use nondrying sealer as a center gasket between the crankcases. Apply the sealer to one side of the case. Spread it evenly with a business card and let it set-up for about 10 minutes. Next, place the left case over the crank and transmission cases, press the cases toward each other to within 5mm of sealing, install the bolts that fasten the cases together, and slowly tighten them while maintaining an equal gap between the cases. You may need to tap the case lightly because you are trying to align eight different cylindrical pieces all together (crank, transmission shafts, shift-fork rods, shift drum, and case alignment pins. Once the case bolts are snugly tightened, try to turn the crankshaft and the transmission shafts. The transmission should turn easily, and the crankshaft should turn with some resistance. Using the plastic mallet, tap lightly on the transmission shafts while spinning them. Do the same with the crankshaft, tapping on both ends. The crankshaft may make a sharp cracking sound. That is good because it means that the crankshaft has centered between the main bearings. Now torque the bolts on the cases.

Bench Testing

When you get the lower end together and the cases are sealed tight, install the shifting mechanism and turn the clutch shaft while clicking through the gears. The transmission is your main consideration when bench testing.

Final Assembly

Assemble the rest of the engine components, mount the engine in the frame, hook up all electrical wires, control cables, and linkages. Torque all the mounting bolts, and then you're ready to break in your rebuilt engine.

Breaking In a New Bottom End

The new lower end will need some patient break-in time. The best way is to let the engine idle for three separate 10-minute sessions with a 20-minute rest period between sessions. You don't need any extra pre-mix oil because the engine load is minimal when the engine is idling.

Crankshaft Repair

Crankshaft-related problems can cause the most expensive engine damage. Consider that at 10,000 rpm, the piston moves up and down in the cylinder 166 times per second. The reciprocating mass of the piston and rod are supported by the rod bearing and the crankcase main bearings. If you don't keep your air filter clean, the dirt will wear out the bearings causing the crank and piston to whip around unsupported and destroy the inside of the engine. All of this can happen in a matter of seconds in a 125cc engine. There are several ways for you to check the condition of the engine bearings, and you should do so, frequently, to prevent catastrophic engine damage. Here are some tips for monitoring the condition of the crankshaft.

Checking for Crankshaft and Bearing Damage

Use these techniques for checking the condition of lower end parts such as the connecting-rod bearing, main bearings, and flywheel rotor.

Flywheel Movement

Grasp the flywheel with your hand and try to move it up and down and in and out. If you feel any movement, the main bearings are worn out. Remove the flywheel and the stator plate. Check the left crank seal for fuel leakage. This seal is blown, and dirt was drawn into the engine past the seal. Usually a bike will bog at low speed or heat-seize the piston on the exhaust skirt when the left crank seal leaks.

Connecting-Rod Movement

Grasp the connecting rod and try to pull it straight up and push it down. It is normal to feel some radial play because the rod bearing is a needle bearing. You shouldn't feel any up and down play. If you do, rebuild the crank. The side clearance between the rod and the thrust washers is a good indicator of rod-bearing wear. Use a feeler gauge to measure the side clearance. The factory service manual lists the maximum side-clearance specification for your model of bike.

Shattered Flywheel

Flywheels can occasionally come apart. The reason for this is worn main bearings. The crank is supported by the primary drive gear on the right side of the engine. When the main bearings wear, the crank deflects more on the left side where the electrical components are mounted. When the flywheel is allowed to gyrate, the flywheel rivets will eventually shear.

These are the factory crank tools. The Kawasaki "wedge" tool is on the left and the Suzuki "draw-through" tool is on the right.

Crankshaft Rebuilding Techniques

Before you decide to have your crankshaft rebuilt, do a survey on the exact cost of buying a new crank assembly as opposed to the parts and labor for rebuilding. Check the crankshaft ends for hammer marks or peening. When the machined centers of the crankshaft ends are distorted or marred, the crank cannot be set in a truing jig and is nearly impossible to align. If the ends of your crank are marred, you should buy a new crank. You must also evaluate the technician who will perform the rebuilding service. If he doesn't have the proper training or special tools, then he can't do the job! Use this section as a guide to evaluating the quality of a crankshaft rebuilding company. If you have a Suzuki or Yamaha, you will find that it is must cheaper to rebuild the crank than to buy a new one. In contrast, Kawasaki and Honda crankshaft assemblies are relatively inexpensive.

The Right Tools

To rebuild a crankshaft, you need special tools. The two most important and expensive tools are a 30-ton hydraulic press (about $500) and a truing jig (about $750). It is possible to use a lathe as a truing jig but only when the crank is set between two live centers. You cannot clamp one side of the crank in the chuck and one end in the center and expect to get an accurate deflection measurement; the deflection of the

The Kawasaki wedge tool fits into the crank to prevent it from being tweaked when the crank is installed in the cases.

crank is redirected, and the crank reads true when it is far out of true. Other tools needed are a small square, a scribe, a dial indicator and stand, a brass hammer, a steel wedge such as a chisel, and a variety of rectangular steel blocks and pins so you can secure the crank in the press during assembly. RCE makes a great tool ($750) that allows you to assemble the crankshaft in perfect alignment; no additional truing is needed. The tool uses bushings to align the crank journals as the crank is pressed together.

Honda CR Crankshafts

Honda cranks have thin, bell-shaped sheet-metal covers pressed onto flyweights. About one-third of the crank periphery (around the crankpin) is hollow, so you cannot use the impact method to align a Honda crank. You must use the RCE tool to align the crank. Honda doesn't offer OEM replacement connecting rods, but Hot Rods are an aftermarket rod kit available for late-model Japanese dirt bikes, including Honda CRs.

Suzuki cranks easily fit into the right side case but have a tight fit into the left case half. The draw-through tool threads onto the crank and pulls the crank into the bearing.

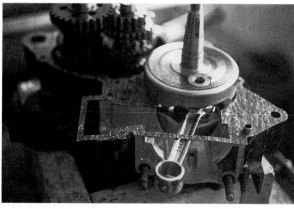

Honda and Suzuki center case gaskets. Take care aligning the gasket around the top and reed port.

Once you have pushed the cases down to within 5mm, install the case bolts and tighten them evenly.

Once the cases are tight, tap the crank with a plastic mallet on each side. You will hear a sharp cracking noise when the crank centers on the ball bearings.

Step-By-Step Crank Rebuilding

The following step-by-step procedure tells how a technician would rebuild a crank using conventional jigs and a truing stand:

1. Before disassembling the crank, the technician places a square against the side of the flyweights and scribes two parallel lines, 180 degrees apart, across the face of the flyweight. These alignment marks will help the technician align the crank upon assembly. Now the crankpin can be pressed out of the flyweights and all of the old parts should be discarded. Never reuse the old connecting rod, bearing, pin, or thrust washers.

2. The technician then applies a thin layer of assembly grease to the bearing surfaces of the crankpin, bearing, thrust washers, and rod. After the grease has been applied, the crankpin can be pressed into one of the flyweights. The washers, bearing, and rod are then placed onto the crankpin.

3. The technician heats the other flyweight's pin-hole with a propane torch for about three minutes. This will expand the diameter of the pinhole and reduce the need for excessive pressure to assemble the crank. He then uses the square to align the scribe lines on each flyweight so the crank is assembled very close to true.

4. As the crank is pressed together, the technician uses a feeler gauge to monitor the clearance between the connecting rod and the thrust washer. The proper clearance is listed in the service manual. The manual also lists an overall crank width spec that can be measured with a caliper.

Check the rod by trying to move it up or down. Radial play is normal because all connecting rods use needle bearings.

Check the side clearance of the rod by inserting a feeler gauge between the rod and thrust washers.

In this photo, the technician is rebuilding a crankshaft. He starts by pressing a new pin into one of the crank weights. Lithe grease is applied to the pin as a lubricant for the connecting rod bearing.

In this photo the technician prepares to press the other crank weight on to the pin. He uses a steel ruler to sight the alignment marks so the crank is pressed together fairly close to true before the final truing process.

A feeler gauge is inserted between the rod and thrust washer to monitor the side clearance while the crank weights are pressed together.

This is an example of how to true a crank on a lathe. Live centers are installed into the three-jaw chuck and the tail-stock to support the crank. Three dial indicators are positioned on the two crank journals and the side of one of the crank weights.

Truing the Crank

1. During the truing process, the technician supports the crank between live centers.

2. Knife-edged bearings must be used if the machined centers of the crank ends are damaged. Dial indicators are used to measure the run-out of each crank end and the side run-out of the flyweights.

3. If the crank has side run-out, then the flyweights aren't parallel and must be adjusted before the crank ends can be trued. This is accomplished by hitting the wide side of the flyweights with a large brass hammer, and then wedging the flyweights apart at the narrow side with a large tapered chisel and hammer. It sounds very caveman-like, but this is the way the pros do it. Of course, the crank must be removed from the jig before the run-out can be adjusted; otherwise the dial indicators and jig centers will be damaged. The crank ends have run-out because the flyweights aren't parallel and must be rotated about the crankpin. This is accomplished by striking the flyweight at the exact point of the greatest run-out, with a brass hammer, while holding the opposite flyweight in hand. It doesn't take must force to rotate the flyweight into true.

4. Now you may understand why we must be careful how the crank is installed into the crankcases during engine assembly. It is very easy to throw the crank out of true if you beat the hell out of it and the cases during assembly!

This is the RCE crank assembly jig. The pin is pressed into one crank weight, the rod and bearing assembly is installed and the two crank weights are installed into the two sides of the jig, then the whole crank assembly is pressed together true. This jig doesn't require any additional truing.

If the threads of the crank ever become damaged, you can repair them with a thread file rather than a die. This thread file is available from Race Tools and fits eight popular metric and American standard thread pitches.

BASIC TWO-STROKE TUNING

CHAPTER SEVEN

Changing the powerband of your dirt bike engine is simple when you know the basics. A myriad of aftermarket accessories are available for you to tune your bike to better suit your needs. The most common mistake is to choose the wrong combination of engine components, making the engine run worse than a stock engine. Use this section as a guide to inform yourself on how changes in engine components can alter the powerband of your bike's engine. Use the guide at the end of the chapter to map out your strategy for changing engine components to create the perfect powerband.

Two-Stroke Principles

Although a two-stroke engine has fewer moving parts than a four-stroke engine, a two-stroke is a complex engine with different phases taking place in the crankcase and in the cylinder bore at the same time. This is necessary because a two-stroke engine completes a power cycle in only 360 degrees of crankshaft rotation, compared to a four-stroke engine, which requires 720 degrees of crankshaft rotation to complete one power cycle. The following explains the basic operation of the two-stroke engine.

1. Starting with the piston at top dead center (TDC 0 degrees) ignition has occurred and the gasses in the combustion chamber are expanding and pushing down the piston. This pressurizes the crankcase causing the reed valve to close. At about 90 degrees after TDC the exhaust port opens ending the power stroke. A pressure wave of hot expanding gases flows down the exhaust pipe. The blow-down phase has started and will end when the transfer ports open. The pressure in the cylinder must blow-down to below the pressure in the crankcase in order for the unburned mixture gases to flow out the transfer ports during the scavenging phase.

2. Now the transfer ports are uncovered at about 120 degrees after TDC. The scavenging phase has begun. Meaning that the unburned mixture gases are flowing out of the transfers and merging together to form a loop. The gases travel up the back side of the cylinder and loop around in the cylinder head to scavenge out the burnt mixture gases from the previous power stroke. It is critical that the burnt gases are scavenged from the combustion chamber to make room for as much unburned gases as possible. That is the key to making more power in a two-stroke engine. The more unburned gases you can squeeze into the combustion chamber, the more the engine will produce. Now the loop of unburned mixture gases have traveled into the exhaust pipe's header section. The gases aren't lost because a compression pressure wave has reflected from the end of the exhaust pipe, to pack the unburned gases back into the cylinder before the piston closes off the port. This is the unique supercharging effect of two-stroke engines. The main advantage of two-stroke engines is that they can combust more volume of fuel/air mixture than the swept volume of the engine. Example: A 125cc four-stroke engine combusts about 110cc of F/A gasses, but a 125cc two-stroke engine combusts about 180cc of F/A gasses.

3. Now the crankshaft has rotated past bottom dead center (BDC 180 degrees) and the piston is on the upstroke. The compression wave reflected from the exhaust pipe is packing the unburned gases back in through the exhaust port as the piston closes off the port to start the compression phase. In the crankcase the pressure is below atmospheric, producing a vacuum and a fresh charge of unburned mixture gases is flowing through the reed valve into the crankcase.

4. The unburned mixture gases are compressed, and just before the piston reaches TDC, the ignition system discharges a spark causing the gases to ignite and start the process all over again.

How to Choose a Powerband

By making changes in engine components, nearly every Japanese dirt bike has the potential for two types of power. The engine can be tuned for midrange and high-rpm power or for low-end and midrange power. The midrange and high-rpm bike will have little or no low-end, hit explosively in the midrange, and have an abundance of top-end power that can be overrevved. This kind of power can put you out front in the straights, but it is harder to control and will tire out the rider more quickly. Expert outdoor riders tend to use engines tuned for high-rpm power.

An engine can also be tuned for low-end and midrange. Such an engine will have plenty of power down low, a beefy midrange, and a flat top-end. Supercross riders and enduro riders favor this kind of power. It is easy to use and gives the rider confidence. Most riders can see faster times or just have more fun with more low-end and midrange.

With tuning, you can change your motorcycle's powerband to somewhere between one of these extremes. Only a few riders use the extremes. Professionals on outdoor tracks—especially 125cc European Grand Prix bikes—use engines that are almost all high-rpm power. These machines are extremely fast and require highly talented professionals to make the most of them. Enduro riders in extremely slippery, technical conditions use bikes tuned for lots of low-end. Trials riders use bikes that are tuned for nothing but low-end.

For most of us, though, the ideal solution is somewhere in between. A rider should choose a powerband according to their skill level, terrain obstacles, and maintenance practices. Here are some tips on how to select the right powerband for you using these criteria.

Skill Level

Generally speaking, beginning riders need low- to midrange powerbands, whiles expert riders can benefit from top-end powerbands. There are exceptions, though. Supercross bikes have low- to midrange powerbands because the steep far-spaced jumps are positioned so close to the turns. Keep in mind that low-end to midrange powerbands are typically easier to use. In conditions where traction is minimal and the terrain is particularly technical, low-end power will allow you to keep the bike under control and ultimately go faster. Also, torquey bikes are more fun to ride casually. Expert and top-level riders need high-end power to be competitive, but the extra juice can easily slow down lesser riders even in good conditions and is a handicap in slippery, difficult conditions.

Terrain Obstacles

This term describes a wide variety of things ranging from the soil content to the elevation changes and the frequency of jumps and turns on a race course. Low- to midrange powerbands work well on soil such as mud and sand. Tight tracks with lots of off-camber or difficult corners will favor low-end to midrange power. Smoother broader powerbands work well for enduro or trail riding over a wide variety of terrain and soil conditions. Midrange to top-end powerbands work best on terrain with loamy soil, long fast uphills, and fast sweeping turns.

Maintenance Practices

Generally speaking, powerbands designed for low- to midrange require less engine maintenance than powerbands designed for high rpm. High-rpm powerbands usually require frequent use of the clutch in order to get the engine up into the rev range where the powerband is most effective. An engine that sustains high rpm requires more frequent replacement of parts, such as, piston and rings, reeds, crankshaft bearings, and clutch plates. Also the carb jetting becomes more critical. If the main jet is one size too lean, the piston can seize. High-rpm powerbands have high compression ratios so fuel selection is critical. Most tuners recommend racing fuel because the specific gravity of fuels such as these doesn't vary with the season like super unleaded pump fuel.

Basic Tuning FAQs

◗ Powerband Questions

Question: I have a couple of questions about powerbands for you to answer. What exactly are they and where on the bike are they located? How do powerbands work?

Answer: The powerband of a motorcycle is a term that describes the usable power produced over an rpm band. The rpm band is about 3,000 rpm wide on a mini or 125cc bikes and as much as 5,000 rpm on a 250cc engine. In magazine test articles, powerbands are usually described in one of the following terms: wide, narrow, pipey, torquey, or over rev.

◗ Flywheel Weights on a 125cc Bike

Question: I have a 1994 CR125 that I use to race motocross. I have a question. What advantages would I get from putting on a heavier flywheel? I understand it helps with wheel spin (the main reason I'm considering one), but will it affect my throttle response in areas where it's important like, say, in whoops? Also, will it affect my top-end power? I want to have less wheel spin to drive out of corners faster, but I don't want to lose throttle response over lips of jumps and in whoops. Is the flywheel weight my dream come true?

Another question, are there any advantages to weld-on models or bolt-ons?

Answer: A flywheel weight can only be effective if the engine has enough torque to control it. If you are having problems with too much wheel spin, then install a flywheel weight. The advantage to a thread-on flywheel weight is that if it doesn't work, you can just remove it. Weld-on flywheel weights are permanent.

Tuning for Specific Powerbands

This chart is designed to give you some general guidelines on different powerbands and the changes required to the individual engine components. For specific recommendations on your model bike, refer to the chapters on tuning tips.

Cylinder Head

Low- to Midrange: 8:1 compression ratio, squish band 60% of bore area
Midrange and High-Rpm: 8.6:1 compression ratio, 40% squish

Cylinder Ports

Low- to Midrange: Exhaust port 90 ATDC, transfer ports 118 ATDC
Midrange and High-Rpm: Exhaust port 85 ATDC, transfer ports 116 ATDC

Reeds

Low- to Midrange: Dual-stage or .4mm fiberglass petals.
Compromise: Thick carbon fiber petals
Midrange and High-Rpm: Large area 30-degree valve

Carburetor

Low- to Midrange: Smaller diameter or sleeved down carb (26mm for 80cc, 34mm for 125cc, 36mm for 250cc)
Midrange and High-Rpm: Larger carb (28mm for 80cc, 38mm for 125cc, 39.5mm for 250cc)

Pipe

Low- to Midrange: Fatty or Torque
Midrange and High-Rpm: Desert or Rpm

Silencer or Spark Arrestor

Low- to Midrange: Long, small diameter
Midrange and High-Rpm: Short, large diameter

Ignition Timing and Advance Timing

Low- to Midrange: Stock timing
Midrange and High-Rpm: Retard timing

Flywheel

Low- to Midrange: Add weight
Compromise: Stock flywheel
Midrange and High-Rpm: PVL internal

Fuel

Low- to Midrange: Super unleaded 93 octane
Midrange and High-Rpm: Racing fuel 105 octane

Tuning Guide to Performance Modifications

When deciding what to do to your engine, you first need to decide what you want. What kind of riding do you do? What level of rider are you? How much money do you have to spend? Also, remember that you need to bring the bike to peak stock condition before you add aftermarket equipment.

This section lists each performance mod and describes how to modify each system for the performance you want.

Cylinder Porting

The cylinder ports are designed to produce a certain power characteristic over a fairly narrow rpm band. Porting or tuning is a metal-machining process performed to the cylinder ports (exhaust and transfers) that alters the timing, area size, and angles of the ports to adjust the powerband to better suit the rider's demands. For example, a veteran trail rider riding an RM250 in the Rocky Mountain region of the United States will need to adjust the powerband for more low-end power because of the steep hill climbs and the lower air density of higher altitudes. The only way to determine what changes will be needed to the engine is by measuring and calculating the stock engine's specifications.

The most critical measurement is the port's time-area. A port's time-area is a calculation of a port opening's area and timing in relation to the displacement of the engine and the rpm. Experienced tuners know what exhaust- and transfer-port time-area values work best for different purposes (motocross versus enduro, for example).

In general, if a tuner wants to adjust the engine's powerband for more low to midrange, he would do the following two things:

1. Turn down the cylinder base on a lathe to increase the effective stroke (distance from TDC to exhaust-port opening). This also retards the exhaust-port timing, shortens the exhaust-port duration, and increases the compression ratio.
2. Narrow the transfer ports and re-angle them with epoxy to reduce the port's time-area for an rpm peak of 7,000. The rear transfer ports need

to be re-angled so they oppose each other rather than pointing forward to the exhaust port. This changes the flow pattern of the transfer ports to improve scavenging efficiency at 2,000 to 5,000 rpm.

For both of these types of cylinder porting changes to be effective, other engine components would need to be changed as well.

Cylinder Head Modification

Cylinder-head shape also affects the powerband. Generally speaking, a cylinder head with a small-diameter, deep combustion chamber and a wide squish band combined with a high compression ratio is suited for low-end and midrange power. A cylinder head with a wide, shallow chamber and a narrow squish band and a lower compression ratio is suited for high-rpm power.

Cylinder heads with wide squish bands and high compression ratios will generate high turbulence in the combustion chamber. This turbulence is termed maximum squish velocity (MSV) and is rated in meters per second (m/s). A cylinder head designed for Supercross should have an MSV rating of 35m/s, whereas a head designed for motocross should have an MSV rating of 25m/s. The only way to accurately determine the MSV rating of a head is by measuring some basic engine dimensions and inputting the numbers into a TSR computer program called SQUISH.

In the model-tuning-tips sections of this book, the SQUISH program was used to calculate the modified head dimensions.

Aftermarket companies also offer variable-shape cylinder heads, which have different cartridges to give different cylinder head shapes. The various head cartridges have different combustion bowl shapes, compression ratios, and MSV ratings. The head cartridges are incrementally different, corresponding from powerbands ranging from extreme low-end to high rpm.

Crankshaft Modification

There are two popular mods hop-up companies are doing to crankshafts: stroking and turbo-vaning.

Stroking increases the stroke of the crankshaft, which boosts the midrange power but decreases the engine's rpm

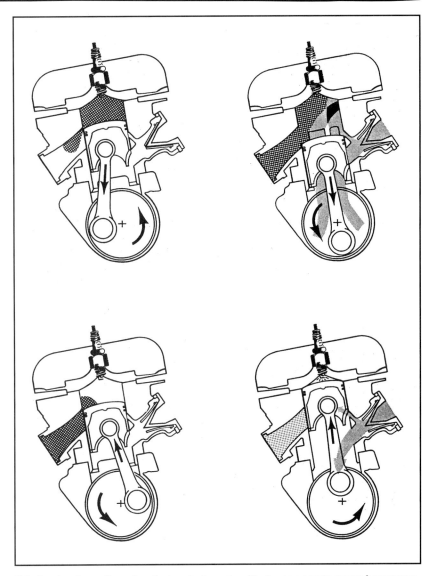

This drawing shows the cycles of a two-stroke engine. The key to extracting more horsepower from a two-stroke is simple—more flow. The basic principle is also quite simple, but the techniques for increasing horsepower output are a bit more complex.

peak. Two techniques are commonly used to stroke two-stroke crankshafts: welding closed the old big-end hole and redrilling a new big-end hole or installing an offset big-end pin. The method of welding and redrilling is labor intensive, more expensive, and permanent. The offset pin is cheap, nonpermanent, and can be changed quickly.

Turbo-vaning a crankshaft is an old, discredited technique used to improve the volumetric efficiency of the engine by fastening scoops to the crank. Every decade some hop-up shop revives this old idea and gives it a trendy name

with product promises that it can't live up to. These crank modifications cause oil to be directed away from the connecting rod, and often the vanes will detach from the crank at high rpm, causing catastrophic engine damage. My advice: Don't waste the $750!

Carburetor Modification

In general, a small-diameter carburetor will provide high air-mass velocity and good flow characteristics for a low- to mid-rpm powerband. A large diameter carburetor works better for high-rpm powerbands. For 125cc engines, a 34mm carburetor works well for Supercross and enduro and a 36- or 38mm carburetor works best for fast motocross tracks. For 250cc engines, a 36mm carburetor works best for low- to mid-rpm powerbands, and a 39.5mm carburetor works best for high-rpm powerbands. Recently, there has been a trend in the use of airfoils and rifle-boring for carbs. These innovations are designed to improve air flow at low throttle openings. Some companies sell carb inserts to change the diameter of a carb. Typically a set of inserts is sold with a service of overboring the carb. For example, a 38mm carb for a 250cc bike will be bored to 39.5mms and two inserts will be supplied. The carb can then be restricted to a diameter of 36 or 38mm.

Aftermarket Reed Valves

Like large-bore carburetors, bigger reed valves with large flow areas work best for high-rpm powerbands. In general, reed valves with six or more petals are used for high-rpm engines. Reed valves with four petals are used for dirt bikes that need strong low-end and midrange power. Three other factors must be considered when choosing a reed valve: the angle of the reed valve,

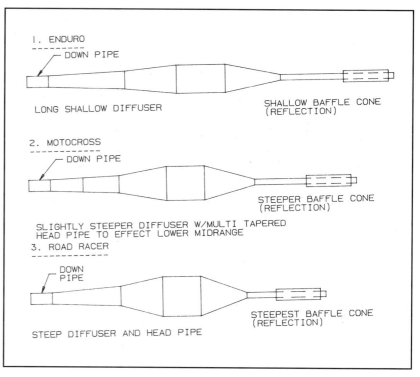

These three different exhaust pipe configurations are tuned for different types of power. A shallow diffuser and long silencer tube gives torquey, smooth power. By opening the diffuser a bit more and shortening the silencer tube, you get more horsepower in a shorter, more explosive powerband. The bottom pipe is tuned for upper-rpm power only, with a steep diffuser and short silencer tube.

The cylinder base of this KTM440 cylinder is being turned down on a lathe in order to boost the low-end power.

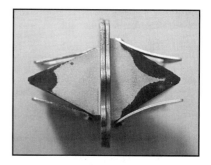

These are two different reed valves for the same model bike. The valve on the left is from a 1994 KX125 and the one on the right is from the 1993 model. The valve on the left has four petals set at a 30-degree angle. It works good for low- to midrange powerbands used for enduro or Supercross riding. The valve on the right has six petals set at a 45-degree angle. It is best suited for a high-rpm powerband.

the type of reed material, and the petal thickness. The two common reed valve angles are 30 and 45 degrees. The 30-degree valve is designed for low-end to midrange power and the 45-degree valve is designed for high-rpm power. Two types of reed-petal materials are commonly used, carbon fiber and fiberglass. Carbon fiber reeds are lightweight but relatively stiff (spring tension) and are designed to resist fluttering at high rpm. Fiberglass reeds have relatively low spring tension so they instantly respond to pressure changes in the crankcase; however, the low spring tension makes them flutter at high rpm, thereby limiting the amount of power. Fiberglass reed petals are good for low-end to midrange powerbands, and carbon fiber reeds are better for high-rpm engines.

Some aftermarket reeds, such as the Boyesen dual-stage reeds, have a large thick base reed with a smaller thinner reed mounted on top. This setup widens the rpm range where the reed valve flows best. The thin reeds respond to low rpm and low-frequency pressure pulses. The thick reeds respond to higher pressure pulses and resist fluttering at high rpm. The Boyesen RAD valve is different than a traditional reed valve. Bikes with single rear shocks have offset carbs. The RAD valve is designed to evenly redistribute the gas flow from the offset carb to the crankcases. A RAD valve will give an overall improvement to the powerband. Polini of Italy makes a

These composite pipe guards protect the pipe from rock dents and also help contain the heat in the pipe for more top-end overrev. This guard is distributed by CRE in America and Pro-Racing in England.

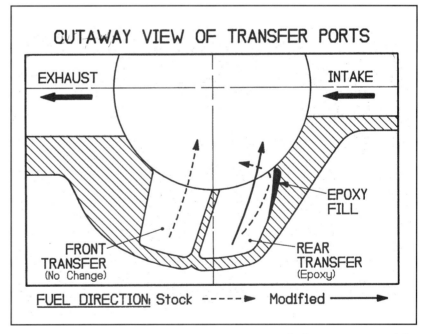

This diagram shows how the epoxy improves flow at lower rpms by directing gases toward the exhaust port.

Epoxy can be applied to the transfer port bridges to raise the crankcase compression ratio and change the flow characteristic of the cylinder for more low- to midrange power.

This German-made PVL ignition has an internal flywheel that gives it less flywheel inertia and makes the engine quicker revving.

reed valve called the Supervalve. It features several mini sets of reeds positioned vertically instead of horizontally (as on conventional reed valves). These valves are excellent for enduro riding because they improve throttle response. In addition, tests on an inertia-chassis dyno show the Supervalve to be superior when power-shifting. However, these valves don't generate greater peak power than conventional reed valves. Supervalves are imported to America and sold by Moto Italia in Maine.

Aftermarket Exhaust Pipes

The exhaust pipes of high-performance two-stroke engines are designed to harness the energy of the pressure waves from combustion. The diameter and length of the five main sections of the pipe—head pipe, diffuser cone, dwell, baf-

fle cone, and stinger—are critical to producing the desired powerband. In general, aftermarket exhaust pipes shift the powerband up the rpm scale. Most pipes are designed for original cylinders not tuned cylinders. Companies such as Motowerks custom computer design and fabricate pipes based on the cylinder specifications and the type of powerband targeted.

There are two reasons for buying an aftermarket pipe: to replace a damaged pipe or to gain performance. The stock exhaust pipes of most late model Japanese dirt bikes offer excellent performance. In fact, many aftermarket pipes are just copies of OEM pipes. The reason nobody buys OEM pipes is because they are way too expensive. There are several different manufacturers of pipes in the world. Generally speaking, the pipes manufactured in Europe (SPES, DEP Sport, MESSICO, HGS) offer greater high-

rpm performance at a much higher price ($350) than the American pipes (FMF, PC, Dyno-Port, Bill's, R&D). The European pipes are designed to work in conjunction with ported cylinders whereas the American pipes are designed to work with stock cylinders.

Most pipes are available in bare metal and plated finishes. Plated pipes require no maintenance whereas bare metal pipes require constant maintenance to prevent corrosion. There is no performance difference between the two finishes. The energy of the finite amplitude waves reflecting through the pipe is not affected by surface finish. However, the fuel/air particles carried by the waves are affected by sharp edges and abrupt transitions between sections of the pipe.

There is no way to look at a pipe and make a determination of how the design will affect the performance of

This is a close-up view of the stator plate. The plate has index marks so you advance or retard the ignition timing to affect the powerband. Turning the stator plate clockwise advances the ignition timing and improves the midrange hit in the powerband. Turning the plate counterclockwise reduces the powerband hit but extends the top end overrev.

your bike. The pipe manufacturers label their pipes with terms that describe the pipe's effect on the powerband. Terms like "Fatty, Supercross, and Torque" are associated with enhancements in the low to midrange of the powerband. Terms like "Desert, motocross, or RPM" are associated with enhancements in the upper midrange and top end of the powerband. Generally speaking, pipes with designations such as these work well with cylinders and heads tuned for the same type of powerband. It is unusual for a "RPM" pipe to work well with a "torque" cylinder.

Aftermarket Silencers

Silencers come in all sorts of shapes and sizes. What they do is affect the powerband. A long silencer with a small diameter enhance the low-range and midrange power because it increases the bleed-down pressure in

the pipe. A silencer with a short length and a large core diameter provides the best bleed-down pressure for a high-rpm engine. Too much pressure in the pipe at high rpm will radically increase the temperature of the piston crown and could cause the piston to seize in the cylinder.

Flywheel Weights

A heavier flywheel will smooth out power delivery. The flywheel is weighted to improve the engine's tractability at low to mid-rpm. Flywheel weights are best for powerful bikes with decent low-end and an explosive hit. The weight will smooth out the hit and reduce wheel-spin, which will improve your drive out of corners.

Two different types of flywheel weights are available: weld-on and thread-on. A-Loop performs the weld-on flywheel weight service. Steahly

makes thread-on flywheel weights. This product threads onto the fine left-hand threads that are on the center hub of most Japanese magneto rotors. Thread-on flywheel weights can only be used if the threads on the flywheel are in perfect condition. The advantage to weld-on weights is they can't possibly come off.

Modern bikes use external rotor flywheels. They have a larger diameter than internal rotor flywheels so they have greater flywheel inertia. PVL makes an internal rotor flywheel that gives quicker throttle response.

Ignition Timing

The ignition timing has a minimal effect on the powerband. Retarding the timing has the effect of reducing the hit of the powerband in the midrange and extending the top-end overrev. Overrev is a slang term that describes the useable length of the powerband at high rpm.

The scientific reason for the shift of the powerband to extremely high rpm is because the temperature in the pipe increases with the retarded timing and that enables the pipe's tuned length to be more synchronous with the piston speed and port timing of the cylinder.

Advancing the timing has the affect of increasing the midrange hit of the powerband, but makes the power flatten-out at high rpm. The reason is that the relatively long spark lead time enables for a greater pressure rise in the cylinder before the piston reaches TDC. This produces more torque in the midrange but the high pressure contributes to pumping losses at extremly high rpm.

Aftermarket Ignitions

The latest innovation in ignition systems is the internal rotor with bolt-on discs that function as flywheel weights. PVL of Germany makes these ignitions for modern Japanese dirt bikes. Another advantage to the PVL ignition is that they make a variety of disc weights so you can tune the flywheel inertia to suit racetrack conditions.

MSD makes ignition systems for CR and RM 125s and 250s. MSD's ignition system features the ability to control the number of degrees of advance and retard. These aftermarket ignition systems sell for less than the OEM equivalent.

FOUR-STROKE ENGINES

Four-stroke engines are very reliable, but when they finally break down, there are so many engine components that problems can be hard to diagnose. A four-stroke engine has more moving parts than a two-stroke engine, especially in the top end of the engine. Components such as the valves, guides, piston, and rings wear at different rates based on service intervals and riding use. For example, if you run the engine with a dirty air filter, the piston and rings will wear faster than the valves. Conversely, if the valve-to-tappet clearance is too tight and the valves hang slightly open from the valve seats, the valves are subject to being overheated by the high combustion temperature and pressure. So how are you supposed to diagnose top-end engine components without totally disassembling the engine?

There is a simple diagnostic test that can be performed to any four-stroke engine that enables you to determine the condition of the top-end components. That test is the leak-down test.

Leak-Down Testing

A leak-down tester is a device that provides a regulated pressurized air source to the cylinder through a hose threaded into the spark plug hole. A leak-down tester has two pressure gauges, one for controlling the test pressure and one for monitoring the percent of air flow that leaks past the worn engine components. These types of testers are available from Snap-On tool dealers or auto parts stores. You will also need an air tank with 100 psi or an air compressor. Leak-down testers come with a variety of adapters that thread into any size of spark plug hole. Leak-down testers sell for $50 to $150.

How to Test

First, attach your compressed-air source to the tester and set the regulator control so the gauge needle reads 100 percent. Thread the adapter hose into the spark plug hole. Turn the crankshaft so the piston is at TDC on the compression stroke. Attach the adapter hose to the leak-down tester. The compressed air will fill the combustion chamber. If there is a pressure leak, then the leak-down tester's gauge will show the percentage of loss.

The normal amount of pressure leakage is 1 to 8 percent. If the percent of leakage exceeds 10 percent, then you need to find and repair the leak. The most apparent places to track down a leak is at the crankcase breather, the carb, and the exhaust pipe. The following are some tips on diagnosing leaks for the top-end engine components.

Piston Rings

If the piston and rings are worn, pressure will seep past the rings and into the crankcases. When the pressure is too great it pushes crankcase oil out at two places, the rubber crank seal and the breather hose that connects to the air box. An oil leak at the crankshaft seal (behind the ignition rotor) is a tell-tale sign of worn rings. Excessive oil in the air box is another sign. Check the air box and filter for oil residue. With the leak-down tester installed and pressure in the cylinder, remove the breather vent hose from the air box. Cap your thumb over the end of the hose and feel for leaking air pressure.

Valve-to-Seat Leaks

Most pressure leaks are the result of carbon build-up on the valves. This occurs when oil leaks past the valve-stem seals, burns, and accumulates on the valve seat. This wedges the valve open slightly, causing the leak. When this happens to the intake valves, the engine may make a coughing sound at idle. The coughing noise indicates that a small amount of combustion gasses are flowing backwards in the intake port and into the carburetor. The back flow of gasses causes a surge in the carb and momentarily stops the fuel from flowing. Remove the air box and the exhaust pipes, and then connect the leak-down tester to the engine and pressurize the cylinder. Then, cup your hand over the end of the carburetor or exhaust port and feel for leaking air. You will probably be able to hear the sound of the leaking air quite easily.

Fixing the Leaks
Piston, Rings, and Cylinder Bore

The average service interval for a dirt bike's piston and rings is about 3,000 miles. After 3,000 miles, you probably will need to overbore the cylinder for an oversize piston because cylinder bores become worn in a taper, or slightly out-of-round pattern. Some tuners prefer to overbore cylinders to boost the engine's displacement or compression ratio. If the rings are leaking on a relatively new bike (less than 1,000 miles) it's probably due to improper break-in procedure. If an engine isn't broken in properly, oil will burn into the cross-hatch grooves in the cylinder walls. This forms a glazing that prevents the rings from sealing properly. The best fix for this problem is to replace the rings and hone the cylinder bore with a Flex-Hone. Flex-Hones are made by Brush Research in Los Angeles, California. Flex-Hones are made of hundreds of silicone-carbide balls mounted to plastic stems and fastened to a center shaft. They don't remove metal like a mandrel hone, but Flex-Hones remove the burned-oil glaze and polish down the surface of the bore so the rings can seal properly.

Valves and Seats

Fixing this problem can be as easy as replacing the stem seals and cleaning the valves with a wire brush. However, if the valve has been wedged open by the carbon for many engine running hours, then the valve and seat surfaces are probably burnt and pitted. In this case, the valve-seat angles will need to be re-cut and the valves replaced. Whenever the valves are removed, I recommend lapping the valve to the valve seat with fine lapping compound. Auto parts stores sell kits with fine lapping compound and a suction-type valve-lapping tool. The tool looks like a round rubber tentacle. You just put a dab of lapping compound on the valve seat and squish the lapping tool onto the valve face. Then turn the tool back and forth for about two minutes until the lapping compound polishes the valve-to-seat interface.

This is a Snap-On Blue-Point tester. You'll need a compressed air source to supply the tester.

Get Help Fast!

If you don't have the specialized knowledge or the tools to perform a leak-down test on your bike, then bring it to a motorcycle shop. A leak-down test takes about an hour and shops charge between $30 and $60. A leak-down test is much less expensive to do during a tune-up because the technician will already have the valve cover removed to set the tappet clearance. Performing a leak-down test once a year will keep you informed on the condition of your bike's engine.

Common Problems

A word of caution to all of you slackers who refuse to work on your bike until it breaks down. Here are some examples of what can happen when simple mechanical problems manifest into catastrophic engine damage.

Tight Valves

If the tappet clearance is inadequate, the valves may hang open when the engine is running at peak temperatures. The exhaust valves may get so hot that they break apart, causing cata-

◗ Advanced Cam Timing

Question: I'm having a problem with my KLX250. I rebuilt the top end, and the bike was slower. I performed a leak-down test, and the pressure was leaking past the exhaust valves. Is it possible that I could have bent both of the exhaust valves but not the intake valves? If not, what could be the problem?

Answer: Its likely that the cam timing is advanced one tooth. That would make the engine sluggish. Another reason why I think it's a timing problem is this, when you perform a leak-down test you set the crankshaft to TDC on the compression stroke. If the cams were mistimed, then the exhaust valves would be cracked open causing the pressure leak.

◗ Motor-Oil Question

Question: I bought a brand-new bike and broke it in with a synthetic motor oil. Now, the bike has less than 1,000 miles, and it leaks oil at the crankshaft seal and it runs like it's jetted rich. I thought I was being careful with my new engine's break in, but obviously I did something wrong. Any clues?

Answer: Synthetic oil is not for breaking in engines. The extreme "slipperiness" of synthetic oil prevents the rings from seating and allows the combustion gasses to pressurize the crankcase. The pressure escapes through the crankcase vents and drags some oil with it. The crankcase vent is attached to the air box, so the excess oil coats the air filter and effectively makes the engine run richer. To this problem, hone the cylinder with a Flex-Hone and replace the rings. Clean the air filter of the excess oil and break in the engine with petroleum-based motor oil.

◗ Four-Stroke Choke System

Question: I just bought a Yamaha XT225. When I first start the bike with the choke engaged, the engine idle is very high, and if I put the bike in gear it bogs and stalls easily. After a few minutes, it works fine. Does my bike have a problem, and should I worry about it?

Answer: Your XT225 is a street-legal bike with a four-stroke engine. These bikes are often jetted leaner than two-stroke dirt bikes because street-legal bikes have to meet EPA pollution standards. When you first start your bike, you must engage the choke to provide the engine with a rich fuel-air mixture. That is why the engine idle is so high. The engine must be allowed to warm up to operating temperature before you can try to ride it. If the engine is too cold, it will bog or stall, and the piston could expand too fast and temporarily seize to the cylinder bore. Spend the extra time to warm up your bike properly. Once the engine comes up to operating temperature, you must disengage the choke or the engine will cough and sputter from the excess fuel.

◗ Black Smoke Exhaust

Question: I have a 1987 XR250R that has suddenly started to run rich in the midrange. The bike was running fine one day, and the next weekend it started running badly. If I hammer the throttle it screams until it levels off, then it spits, sputters, and blows black smoke out the pipe. It idles smoothly, though. Your help would be appreciated.

Answer: The black smoke that comes out the pipe is partially burned fuel. Your bike is running very rich for one or more reasons. Check these parts of the fuel system:
1. Check for clogged carb vent hoses. Clogged hoses will restrict fuel flow.
2. Remove the float bowl and check to see if the main jet is threaded into the needle jet. If the jet unthreaded due to vibration, the engine would run rich.
3. Check the air filter. If the filter is clogged with dirt, that would also cause a rich condition.
4. Check the choke mechanism. If it is a butterfly type, the actuating mechanism could be faulty. That might allow the choke to be engaged, causing the rich running condition.

These are the four most common problems with fuel delivery systems that cause rich running conditions. If you don't think you have the tools or special knowledge to carry out these mechanical tasks, then look to a dirt bike mechanic in your area or to a Honda dealer.

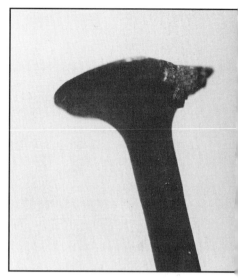

When the exhaust valve clearance is too tight, the valve can burn and crack.

This intake valve had a leaky seal at the valve guide, causing oil to run down the valve stem and burn on the valve. These carbon deposits can have a dramatic affect on the engine performance because they reduce the low lift flow past the intake valve.

Never use a hammer and chisel on the top-end parts. Use a plastic mallet instead.

Check the alignment of the cam sprocket's markings with the gasket surface when the crank is at TDC.

strophic engine damage. Leaky intake valves may cause a back-fire that ignites unburned mixture gasses in the air boot and air box, thereby starting a fire!

Worn Spark Plug

Over time, the spark plug gap will increase due to erosion of the electrode and ground arm. The greater the spark plug gap the greater the voltage required to arc across the gap. This raises the temperature of the electrode and ground arm, eventually causing the metal to fracture. If the spark plug's tiny ground arm breaks off, it could wedge itself between the valve and valve seat, causing the valve to break apart. Spark plugs last as long as 60,000 miles on some automobiles, but only a fraction of that in a motorcycle. Modern motorcycle engines have high compression, high-turbulence combustion chambers that produce spark plug temperatures between 1,800 and 2,300 degrees Fahrenheit. Most manufacturers recommend changing the plugs every 1,000 miles.

The cam chain tensioner is located on the lower rear side of the cylinder.

Worn Piston

A worn piston has excessive clearance to the cylinder wall. This causes an increase in crankcase pressure, which forces some oil out the breather vent. When too much oil is lost, the remaining oil's temperature will rise, causing a breakdown in lubrication. Eventually, the piston will shatter from the vibration. The shattered fragments of the piston fall into the crankcase and can damage the crankshaft and gearbox.

Four-Stroke Top-End Rebuilding

A four-stroke engine is more difficult to rebuild than a two-stroke engine because there are more moving parts in the engine's top end. Here is a guide to rebuilding the top ends of single-cylinder four-stroke engines.

Before you disassemble the engine, you need to do a pressure leak-down test to determine what top-end parts are

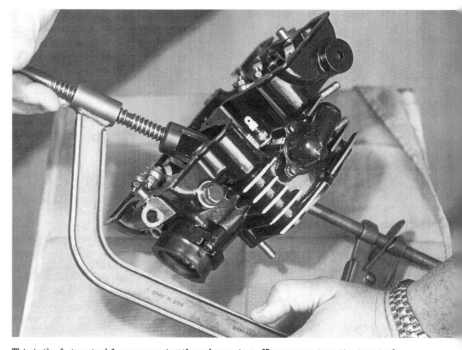

This is the factory tool for compressing the valve springs. Never use automotive type tools because they could damage the head.

worn. See the previous section for detailed instructions.

Before you attempt to disassemble the engine, you should remove the fuel tank and pressure-wash the engine and upper frame. This will help prevent dirt from falling into the disassembled engine. The following section details the procedures for rebuilding the top end of a single-cylinder four-stroke engine.

Tools and Materials

You should have the following tools and materials before you begin: new top-end gasket kit, service manual, torque wrench, oil drain pan, spray penetrating oil, spray cleaner, plastic mallet, assorted wrenches and sockets, parts bins, clean towels, measuring caliper, Flex-Hone, and drill.

Check the valve guide clearance by rocking the valve back and forth in the guide. There should be hardly any movement.

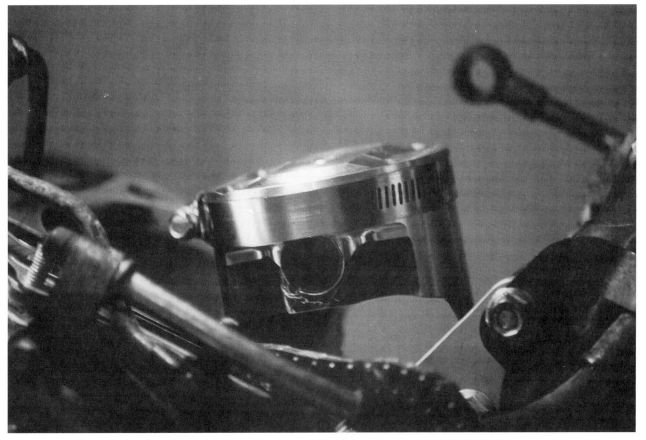

Use a hose clamp or ring compression tool to compress the piston rings prior to installation in the cylinder.

Flex-Hones come in many sizes. They work great for deglazing the cylinder bore prior to installing new rings.

Tear Down

Start the engine disassembly by removing the inspection caps from the left-side engine cover. One is located in the middle of the cover, which allows access to the crankshaft bolt. This bolt retains the flywheel and will be used to rotate the crankshaft to get the piston in the proper positions while rebuilding the top end and timing the camshaft. The crankshaft should only be turned in the normal direction of rotation; otherwise, the cam-chain tensioner could be damaged. The other inspection cap is mounted in the front of the engine cover, and it allows you to see the TDC stamping mark on the side of the flywheel. This is an important reference mark when

The proper technique for installing the cylinder is to support the piston from underneath and use your other hand to lower the cylinder evenly on to the piston assembly.

timing the camshaft during top-end assembly. Then, remove the spark plug, exhaust pipe, carburetor, cam cover, and oil lines.

Camshaft Removal and Reference Marks

After removing the cam cover, rotate the crankshaft so the TDC mark on the flywheel aligns in the center of the inspection window. The camshaft should not be depressing the valves; if it is, rotate the crankshaft another revolution, and the piston will be at TDC on the compression stroke. All Japanese four-stroke single-cylinder engines are designed for camshaft installation at this crankshaft position. Look at the reference marks on the right side of the camshaft drive sprocket. Compare these marks with the ones in the service manual or make a drawing for your own reference. Normally, there is a straight line on the sprocket that aligns

with the gasket surface of the cam cover. Pay close attention to these marks because you will have to align the camshaft upon assembly and to synchronize the crankshaft to the camshaft. Failure to do this properly will cause engine damage! To remove the camshaft, you may have to remove the sprocket from the camshaft, depending on your model engine. If you do remove the sprocket, take care not to drop the sprocket alignment pin into the crankcases.

Head Removal

Now, you can remove the cam-chain tensioner, head, and cylinder. The head and cylinder are fitted with alignment pins, so it may be difficult to remove these parts. Never use a screwdriver or chisel to split the head and cylinder apart because that will damage the gasket surfaces. Instead, use a dead-shot plastic mallet to split the engine

This is an air flow-bench. A flow-bench simulates and measures the air flow that passes through the intake and exhaust ports of a four-stroke cylinder head. In this photo, a Honda CBR900 head is being tested on a Superflow 110 model flow-bench.

components apart. The cam-chain guides are just plastic bars that either fasten or are wedged into place. Tie a piece of wire around the cam chain to prevent it from falling into the crankcases.

Cleaning and Inspection

Clean the engine parts in mineral-spirits solvent to remove the oil. Carbon build-up can be removed with spray oven cleaner. After cleaning, rinse the parts with detergent and water. If you don't have the proper tool to compress the valve springs, bring the head to your local franchised dealer and pay them to remove the valve springs. Warning: Automotive-type valve-spring compressors may not fit the tiny valve retainers of motorcycle engines and may damage the cylinder head. Take care to keep the sets of valve springs and retainers together, matched to the sides they were removed from. To check the valve-to-guide clearance, extend the valve from the seat 10mms, grasp the valve head, and try to move it side to side. If you feel excessive movement and the backside of the valve is covered with carbon deposits, then the valve guide and seal are worn and must be replaced.

Next, clean the valve with a wire brush and check the valve seat for pitting or a sharp edge. The pitting indicates that the Stellite coating on the valve is destroyed, and a sharp edge indicates that the engine was over revved and the valve springs floated, causing the valve to hammer up against the seat (common on KTM 400LCs). Stellite valves cannot be re-faced on a valve grinding machine because that would remove the Stellite coating. The only option is to replace the valve. All Japanese four-stroke engines use Stellite-coated valves, but European bikes do not.

Measuring the Piston and Cylinder

An easy way to measure the piston and bore diameters is with a digital caliper. Calipers cost about $125 and are very accurate. Measure the piston at its widest point, near the bottom of the skirt, and compare the measurement to the minimum-diameter spec listed in the service manual. Measure the bore at the bottom of the cylinder because bores tend to wear fastest at that point. Some

mechanics prefer to measure the cylinder bore with a dial-bore gauge. This is a precision measurement device that enables you to check the out-of-round and taper of the cylinder. Most motorcycle machine shops will do this service for free in an effort to get your business for overboring. If you have the tool, it only takes 10 seconds to check the size. The piston rings can be measured by inserting them into the cylinder bore evenly, then measuring the end-gap with a feeler gauge. If you go through the trouble to disassemble your engine, you may as well replace the rings.

Cylinder Honing

If the cylinder does not require boring, you should hone it before reassembling the engine. The best tool for de-glazing a cylinder bore is a ball-hone. The flexible aluminum-oxide balls remove burnt oil and refinish the cross-hatch marks that are so important for proper ring sealing. Ball-hones are available from Brush Research Co. under the product name Flex-Hone. These hones work great for both two- and four-stroke engines. Cylinder honing is performed by chucking the hone in a drill, coating the cylinder with penetrating oil, and spinning the hone in the cylinder while rapidly moving it up and down in the cylinder for 30 seconds. Clean the cylinder in detergent and water, dry it, and spray it with penetrating oil.

Ready for Assembly

There are several different methods for installing the piston and rings into the cylinder. The Japanese motorcycle manufacturers make a special tool for squeezing the rings, but it is expensive and cumbersome. My method is as follows: Install the piston onto the connecting rod and lock in the circlips. Align the end gaps of the rings so they don't overlap each other and cause a loss of compression or oil. Buy a hose clamp that is slightly larger than the piston diameter from an auto parts store. Clamp it snugly around the piston rings. Make sure that some part of the piston is exposed above the hose clamp. This will act as a pilot to guide the piston into the bottom of the cylinder evenly so the rings don't break upon installation. Grasp the cylinder with one hand and

center it above the piston. Use your other hand to support the underside of the piston. Push the cylinder down onto the piston until the hose clamp slides down past the rings. Now, remove the hose clamp. Bolt down the cylinder head and install the cam-chain guides.

Timing the Camshaft and Crankshaft

The cam chain may have some slacking links below the sprocket on the crankshaft, so grasp the chain and pull it taught while turning the crankshaft until the TDC mark on the flywheel is centered in the inspection window of the left-side engine cover. Install the cam, paying attention to the alignment marks. The cam shouldn't be depressing the valves. Install the sprocket but don't lock the tabs on the bolts yet. Install the cam-chain tensioner and release it so it tightens the chain. Now, rotate the crankshaft two revolutions and check the alignment marks. You may find that the marks are slightly off, indicating that the cam sprocket must be moved one tooth on the cam chain. This is a common problem because the cam-chain tension was loose when the cam sprocket was installed because the tensioner wasn't installed yet (it is impossible to get the cam sprocket on to the cam with the tensioner installed). To realign the cam chain to the sprocket in the proper position, you must remove the cam-chain tensioner and repeat the process. After the camshaft and crankshaft are aligned properly, apply a locking agent to the threads of the bolts that fasten the sprocket to the camshaft, then lock the tabs over the bolts.

Break-In Procedure

If you ball-honed the cylinder, no special ring break-in procedure is necessary. Just go easy on the throttle for the first ride. If the cylinder was overbored you will need to break in engine in three separate sessions of 20 minutes each, with a 20-minute rest period between each session. In the first session, never exceed one-half throttle and third gear. In the second and third sessions, never exceed three-quarter throttle and fourth gear. Rev the engine up and down while shifting gears. Ride the bike on flat, hard ground (mud and sand exert too much of a load on the engine and can make it overheat easily).

WHEELS, TIRES, AND BRAKES

CHAPTER NINE

Wheels, tires, and brakes make our bikes roll, stick, and stop. How effectively these things happen depends on how true you keep the wheels, the types of tires you choose, and how often you service the brakes. This chapter gives you helpful tips that will save you money on catastrophic failures and reduce the time spent working on your bike so you can spend more time riding it!

How to Fix Wheels

Your bike's wheels are your safety net. When you land from a big jump and the suspension bottoms, the wheels are the only thing that keeps you and your bike from smashing into the ground. Yet hardly anyone checks the spoke tension between rides. That is the only way you can prevent catastrophic damage to the wheels. This section is a comprehensive wheel maintenance guide that covers the spectrum from routine spoke tensioning to total lacing and truing. The information presented is applicable to the older-style, angle-head spokes and modern straight-pull spokes.

Right and Wrong Tools

Tools such as vise grips and adjustable wrenches are the wrong tools to use on spokes because they will deform the flats on the spoke. Spoke wrenches are the right tools to use; they are designed to tightly fit the spoke flats, so you can tighten the spoke without the chance of stripping the flats.

Basic Tensioning Tips

If you overtighten the spokes, the rim could crack at the weld line. Take care when tensioning spokes. A little loose is better than too tight.

Apply penetrating oil to the threads of the spoke before attempting to tighten the spokes. Power-washing a bike can cause the threads to corrode. The penetrating oil breaks down the corrosion on the threads.

Tighten every third spoke one-quarter turn, starting with the spoke nearest the air valve. After three revolutions you will have tensioned the spokes equally. The spoke threads on from the inner-tube side of the tire, so when you look at the spokes from the rim center, you need to turn the spoke nipple counterclockwise to tighten it.

Lacing and Truing Wheels

The following wheel-lacing procedure is for wheels with inner and outer spokes. Wheels with inner and outer spokes are more difficult to service than the straight pull spokes. The inner/outer spoked wheels require you to remove four spokes just to install one new one. Inner/outer spoked wheels have two different styles of angled heads, one for the inner spokes and one for the outer spokes. Straight pull spokes do not have angled heads, so they are easy to remove and replace individually. However, the truing process is the same for either type of wheel.

1. Wrap a piece of masking tape around the crossed spokes before you remove the spoke nipples. This will make it easier to relace the spokes into the proper rim holes. The spoke with the 110-degree bend is an inner spoke. The spoke with the tighter, 90-degree bend is an outer spoke. Wheels with modern straight pull spokes, have only one type of spoke.
2. Place the spokes in the hub and swing them into position. Spokes next to each other cross four other spokes. This is called a "cross-four" pattern and is the standard spoke pattern for dirt bike wheels.
3. Place the rim over the top of the hub and spokes. Start by installing one inner spoke into position and lace all the inner spokes around the rim. Take care that you lace the spoke through the spoke hole on the correct side of the rim. Do the initial spoke tightening with a screwdriver. Thread all the nipples onto the spokes an equal number of threads. Repeat the process for the outer spokes.
4. Mount the wheel in a truing stand, and then fix a dial indicator stand onto the truing stand and against one side of the rim. Tighten the spokes one-quarter turn, alternating every third spoke, until all the spokes are tight. Use the dial indicator to check for run-out; adjust the spoke tension so the rim has no more than 0.020- to 0.050-inch run-out.

If you have to change the rims but not the spokes, wrap tape around the spokes at the cross point. That way they won't rotate out of position when the spoke nipples are removed.

Modern wheels use straight-pull spokes that are all the same length and shape. Older dirt bikes use inner and outer spokes with different head angles. The spoke on the left is an inner spoke and the one on the right is an outer spoke.

For wheels with angled head spokes, start by lacing the inner spokes first.

This is a wheel truing stand. There are two types of indicators shown: a fixed pointer and a dial indicator. The fixed pointer can be used for initial truing, but the dial indicator should be used for final truing. The dial indicator will enable you to true the wheel to within .040 inch (1mm).

Use a straight-blade screw driver to tighten all the spoke nipples to an equal number of threads.

Use a pry bar to remove the wheel bearing seal. Be sure to grease the seal before you put it back in place.

Check the wheel bearing by trying to turn it with your finger. If it is hard to turn or exceptionally loose, it is time to replace the bearing.

What to Do About Dented Rims

There is no way for you to remove the dents from your rims; you will have to replace them. Excel rims are much stronger than OEM rims. Perhaps the reason that you are stripping the flats on the spoke nipples is because of your spoke wrench. I use a Rowe spoke wrench. That brand has wide flats that are case-hardened. Tallon Engineering of England offers stainless steel spoke nipples for all popular brands.

Wheel Bearing Repair

Top GP mechanics replace the wheel bearings after every race. In racing, you need every small advantage. Less demanding riders might only need to replace their bike's wheel bearings once a race season. This section's tips show you how to check and change your wheel bearings the easy way.

Basic Cleaning and Inspection

1. The seals in the hubs can be removed, cleaned, and greased many times before replacement is needed. You should also clean out the area between the seal and the sealed bearing. Now you can check the condition of the bearing.
2. Place your finger on the inside race and try to spin it. If the bearing is worn out, it will be hard to turn. Check for excessive movement in the race. A wheel bearing should never have any movement!
3. Wheel bearings have an interference fit into the hubs. That means that the bearing is larger than the hole it fits into in the hub. The hub must be heated with a propane torch in the area around the bearing so that the hub will expand enough to allow the race to be removed.
4. After the hub has been heated with a propane torch for about three minutes, use the following procedure to remove the bearings: From the back

The best way to remove the first wheel bearing is with a round drift rod that is shaped like this. The reason you need to shape the drift rod is because you have to reach the backside of the bearing from the opposite side of the hub.

To remove the wheel bearings, put a drift rod through the bearing from the opposite side and rest the drift rod on the inner race of the bearing.

This is what is inside a typical wheel: outside seals, bearings, and a center spacer. Rear wheels (shown) use double sets of bearings; front wheels just use a single set.

side, position a long drift-rod onto the inner race of the bearing and strike it with a hammer; rotate the position of the drift-rod around the circumference of the race so you push the bearing out of the hub evenly.

5. The wheel-bearing assembly consists of two seals on each end, two wheel bearings, and one axle spacer. After removing one bearing, pull out the axle spacer. Then remove the second bearing. Notice how dirty and corroded the bearings and spacer become when the seals fail.

6. Clean the inside of the hub, and then heat it with a propane torch for about three minutes, just prior to installing the bearing.

7. One side of the bearing is sealed (the side that faces out). Before installing the bearings, pack the open side with high temperature wheel bearing grease such as white-lithe or moly grease.

8. Use a hammer and a bearing driver to install one bearing. Universal bearing/seal driver kits are available from auto parts or industrial-supply stores. Drive the bearing until it's completely bottomed into the hub. Now install the seal with a dab of grease to prevent water from penetrating the bearing. Install the axle spacer, and then install the second bearing until it is fully seated. Install the second bearing's seal with a dab of grease, and you're done!

Damage Control

Imagine that your wheels have the most catastrophic bearing failure and the bearing cups in the hub get damaged. That would mean that the bearing cup is worn oblong and won't retain the bearing tightly in the hub. Normally, you would have to buy a new hub, but a company in New England offers a service to repair worn bearing cups. Rapid Precision Machining bores and sleeves a bearing cup for only $50. This process also works for repairing swingarms and linkage systems.

Tires

The tires of a dirt bike are so important because of the terrain that we ride upon. You can have a bike with the most expensive suspension revalving and a powerful engine, but if the knobs are all rounded off, you'll still end up on your butt. In the European motocross GPs, riders and mechanics regard tires as a suspension component. They are constantly fiddling with different tire patterns, compounds, and hybrid mousse inserts, all this just to get a slight competitive edge. I try not to let tires dominate too much of my mechanical duties, and I refuse to be intimidated by a chunk of rubber. This section gives you information that will make tire selection and tire changing a lot less stressful.

Tools for Home and Trail

You will need the following tools to change a tire: a 12mm wrench for the rim lock and the Schraeder valve, a valve-stem tool, an air pressure gauge, a set of short and long tire irons, a compressed air source, and a bottle of spray detergent. If you want to put together a collection of tools that fit into your trail-riding tool kit, get two short tire irons, a valve-stem tool, pressure gauge, a bar of soap, and Moose Racing's compressed air cartridges.

Changing Tires

Changing tires without tearing the bead or pinching the inner tube is just a matter of technique. You can struggle with the task, or you can use your head and stay patient. Here are some tips that I've learned over the years.

You will need the following tools: a 12mm wrench, valve stem tool, air pressure gauge, long and short tire irons, and spray detergent (warm, soapy water

This is the technique I use for breaking the tire's bead from the rim. Place the wheel on a flat surface and put one foot on the rim while using the other foot to press down on the sidewall of the tire.

This is the proper technique for removing one side of the tire. The curved end of the tire iron is inserted between the tire and rim and pulled back at a 45 degree angle to the rim while another iron is inserted about three inches away. The first iron is then pulled back to the rim while the second iron is set at a 45-degree angle. Then the first iron is removed and inserted three inches away from the second iron and the process is repeated.

in a spray bottle works just fine).

First, loosen the rim lock and remove the valve-stem nut. Then break the bead using the following technique: place the wheel on a flat surface, and put one foot on the rim while using the other foot to press down on the sidewall of the tire. Remember to protect the disc rotor with a piece of cardboard, so it doesn't get scratched by the ground.

The proper technique for removing one side of the tire, goes like this. Insert the curved end of the tire iron between the tire and rim and pulled back at a 45-degree angle to the rim while inserting another iron about three inches away. Then pull back the first iron to the rim while setting the second iron at a 45-degree angle. Remove the first iron and insert it again, three inches away from the second iron, and the process is repeated. At some point you will be able to use your hands to remove the tire. The fewer times you insert the tire irons, the less the chance of pinching the tube. I prefer to use the shorter tire irons for the front tire because the sidewall of the tire is thinner and requires less force to lift it off the rim.

After you have lifted one side of the tire over the rim, reach inside the tire and remove the tube and rim lock. Then, you can use the long tire irons to remove the tire. This is the proper technique: grasp the rim with one hand and cross your other hand over and insert the flat side of the iron between the tire and rim. Once you bend the iron over as far as it will go, you can usually grasp the tire with your hand and push it downward to remove the tire all at once.

Before you try to install the tire, elevate the wheel by putting it on top of a rigid plastic or steel bucket. To install the tire, first put the rim lock into the rim and the rim band over the lock to hold it in position. Spray detergent on the inner side of the tube to prevent it from being pinched by the rim and irons. Spray some detergent on the inside of the tire's bead. This will help it slide on to the rim. Use the short irons to carefully install the tire over the rim. Then rest both irons on each side of the rim lock and push it up into the tire past the bead. Remember to thread the lock nut on a few threads to the rim lock before popping the rim lock past the

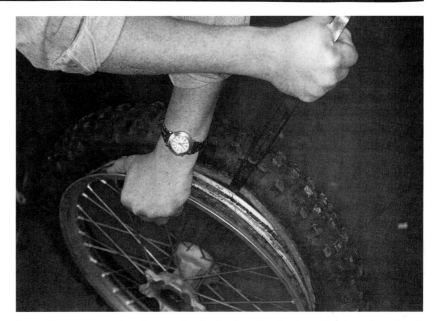

This is the proper technique for removing the tire from the rim. Grasp the rim with one hand and cross your other hand over and insert the flat side of the iron between the tire and rim. Once you bend the iron over as far as it will go, you can usually grasp the tire with your hand and push it downward to remove the tire all at once.

Use the short irons to carefully install the tire over the rim. Then rest both irons on each side of the rim lock and push it up into the tire past the bead. Remember to thread the lock nut on a few threads to the rim lock before popping the rim lock past the bead.

bead. Otherwise the rim lock could fall into the tire, making it difficult to install in the hole of the rim. Start at the rim lock and work over to the air valve, then around the rest of the tire. Try to roll the tire's bead on with your hand before using the tire irons. Every time you use the tire irons you run the risk of puncturing the inner tube. When I first started working in motorcycle shops in the early 1970s, motorcycle tire machines had not yet been invented. The service manager wouldn't let the mechanics use tire irons to install tires. We had to roll the entire bead of a street tire or knobby with our hands. It's possible but only with the right technique.

Tread Patterns, Compounds, and Pressure

There are many different tread patterns and compounds for off-road tires. In general, hard compounds are better for soft terrain such as mud and sand, and soft compounds are better for hard terrain such as clay. Regarding tire patterns, the best patterns for hard-packed surfaces are ones with tightly spaced low-profile knobs. That way the soft compound short knobs can conform to the terrain surface without breaking loose. In the 1995 Supercross season, Jeremy McGrath had great success using Dunlop's dual sport tire (K940) on the tracks with hard-packed clay surfaces. The best tire patterns for soft terrain are ones with tall knobs that are widely spaced. That way the hard compound knobs can penetrate the terrain surface and resist becoming clogged-up, due to the open area between the knobs.

A tire's air pressure can be adjusted to take advantage of the tire's tread pattern and compound. In general lower pressure is used for soft terrain because that allows the tire to conform to the ground for maximum traction. On a muddy surface there aren't as many sharp-edged bumps and it's difficult to get big air over jumps, so it isn't necessary to use high air pressure to prevent the tube from being punctured. However, on hard-packed or rocky surfaces, it's necessary to run higher pressure for three reasons: to resist punctures from hard landings, to keep the tire from spinning on the rim lock, and to make the soft-compound tire conform to proper profile.

This is an example of a Pirelli tire machine. It has a gear-driven tire iron that is hand-cranked to multiply the technician's leverage and reduce the chance of pinching the tube. This machine makes it easy to install a mousse insert or tube into a tire. Most of the GP racers use either a mousse insert with a heavy duty tube or a mousse inner tube. That is because most of the GP tracks in Europe have sharp rocks that can cause punctures.

Here are some guidelines for selecting the proper models of the two most popular brands of tires—Dunlop and Bridgestone—along with some recommendations on air pressure.

Puncture Protection

There are some precautions that you can take to ensure against punctures. Heavy-duty inner tubes should be used on every bike except mini 125s that are raced competitively in motocross. The reason is that the tubes are heavy and pose a bit of drag on these small engines. In some forms of racing such as desert events held in rocky terrain, the risk of puncture is great, even with heavy-duty tubes. For this situation you may want to use either a mousse tube or a combination mousse and inflatable tube such as the Dunlop Crescent mousse. Many off-road racers riding large-displacement bikes choose to install mousse in the tires. The mousse is a dense, closed-cell-foam tube that does not deflate when punctured. Mousse also gives the tire some extra protection from rock impacts. The mousse enables the tire to absorb the impacts of rocks instead of bottoming and deflecting in a random manner. Mousse tubes do have

some disadvantages, however. They are prone to shrinkage, and they have a high cost per usage ($175 each for about 1,000 miles). The Dunlop Crescent mousse product sells for about $120 and is available for both front and rear tires.

Snow and Ice Tires

Riding in snow and ice can be as much (if not more) fun than riding typical terrain. It also can be a way for riders in northern climates to stay sane during the winter. With good tires, the effect is not all that different from riding on loose sand.

Winter conditions can vary drastically. Off-road bikes can't handle extremely deep snow, but studded tires allow the bike to navigate 12 inches of snow and less with ease (not to mention throwing huge amounts of roost). Also, ice riding and racing is generally good as long as the ice is safe, and is basically flat-tracking (although you can find heaved ice to jump under the right conditions).

Ice Studs

There are several different ways to get good traction in frozen conditions. The most common is to screw ice studs

Tire Chart

Hard	Intermediate	Soft
Clay, Churt, Dry Dirt	Loamy Soil, Some Rocks	Sand, Mud, Rocks
K490/K695	K755/K737	K752/K752 DUNLOP
M23/M22	M57/M58	M25/M26 BRIDGESTONE
14–16 psi	12–14 psi	10–12 psi

The first set of numbers is for the front tire and the second set is for the rear tire. The same follows for the recommended tire pressure.

Jeff Fredette demonstrates how he installs the tread of a street tire into the Kenda Ice Master tire for a liner. Note that the sidewall and bead are stripped off of the street tire. When Fredette adds 800 5/8-inch Kold Kutter ice studs, they will screw through the Kenda and into the street tire.

This is an example of the screw pattern that Jeff uses (front on left, rear on right). The alignment of the screw heads are critical because it is the edges and corners of the screws that help the tire gain traction on the ice. The edges of the screw are used for a paddle effect and the corners are positioned to bite when the tire is leaned over in a turn.

into your tires. The aftermarket studs are better than regular sheet metal screws for several reasons. For one, they are actually unfinished sheet metal screws. The finishing process smoothes the surface of the screws, which reduces the traction they give. Also, the aftermarket screws are coated, making them more durable than regular sheet metal screws. Use the pattern shown in the photos to install these screws.

Keep in mind that screws will eventually round off and will pull out of the tire on occasion. Replace the screws regularly as you ride.

Trelleborg Ice Tires

Former national enduro champ Kevin Hines recommends Trelleborg tires for winter trail riding. He says Trellys have the best compound and stud arrangement. The studs are carbide-tipped points molded into the knobs. Trellys are very durable and cost about the same as a tire and liner with 800 screws (under $200 each).

Ice Racing Tires

Jeff Fredette is an avid ice racer, besides being the "King of KDXs." Fredette was one of the first racers to use a

Japanese dirt bikes use Allen head brake pins to retain the brake pads. Make sure you clean out the recess in the Allen head screws before you attempt to unthread them. Otherwise the Allen socket or wrench won't fit all the way into the screw and may strip the screw head.

21-inch front wheel for ice racing. I remember when he showed up for a race at a popular circuit outside the Chicago area back in 1980. That circuit attracted the local hard-core dirt-track racers. People thought Fredette was lazy because he just studded-up the stock tires of his Suzuki PE175. He left the lights on the bike and everything. People weren't laughing much when he kicked their asses by holding the inside line!

Fredette's reasoning was that the wide spaced knobs of the 21-inch tire are ideal for penetrating the top layer of snow and ice debris that covers the corners of an ice-racing track. Since then, he has

become a well-known ice tire expert.

Fredette sets up his own tires for oval-track ice racing. He lines his tires with old street tires. He first strips the sidewalls and bead off these street tires with a carpet knife. He lines the rear with an 18-inch street tire and uses a 21-inch Harley-Davidson tire to line the tire up front. The lining keeps the points of the screws from rupturing the tube.

He places only the tread of the street tire into the a Kenda Ice Master trials tire. The tread pattern and compound of the Kenda tire are excellent for holding the 800 5/8-inch Kold Kutter brand screws that provide the traction on ice and fasten

the Kenda and street tire liner together.

You might think, "Hey what's the big deal? You just get a screw gun and jam a bunch of sheet-metal screws into a set of tires." You might be able to get away with that for donkeying around the cow pasture, but to be competitive in ice racing, you'll need to do more. The alignment of the screw heads are critical because it is the edges and corners of the screws that help the tire gain traction on the ice. The edges of the screw are used for a paddle effect and the corners are positioned to bite when the tire is leaned over in a turn. Each of the 800-

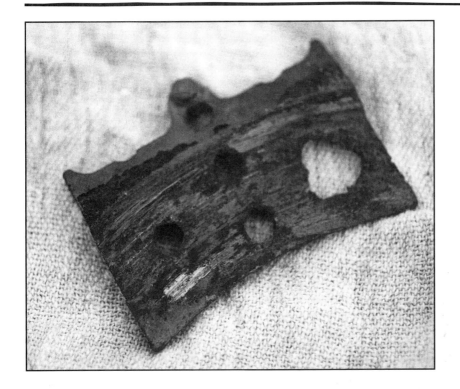

This is an example of a brake pad that was left in the caliper too long. The pad material has worn off completely, allowing the steel backing plate to rub against the disc. The disc was ruined because the steel backing plate wore grooves in the disc.

odd screws must be threaded into the tire perpendicular to the knob with a screw gun (see photograph).

Brake Systems

The brakes of a dirt bike are punished by the elements and the laws of physics. The disc brake pads push against a disc that is sometimes covered with water, mud, and sand. Consequently, dirt bike brake systems wear much faster and need much more maintenance than the brake systems on cars or street bikes.

In racing, the front brake is primarily used to slow the motorcycle. The rear brake is used to change a bike's attitude over jumps by creating a torque reaction. The rear brakes can also be applied lightly to keep the rear end of the bike tracking straight through whoops sections. Dragging the brakes quickly wears out the pads, so you should check them often. The friction from dragging the brakes also creates a lot of heat, and that heat transfers through the caliper piston and into the brake fluid. This heat rapidly breaks down the fluid, so it, too, must be checked often.

In addition to normal maintenance, you can also tune your brakes in a number of ways. Manufacturers make different pad material to improve longevity in various riding conditions. Metallic pads work best in sandy conditions, and composite pads offer superior braking power. There are different types of discs, too. This section will give you all the basics of brake-system repair, maintenance, and tuning, along with some tips on troubleshooting braking problems.

Basic Cleaning and Pad Replacement

The following are some basic tips on checking and changing brake pads. If you are having a specific problem with your brakes, see the troubleshooting

Once the brake pins are removed, you can just slip the pads out the rear of the caliper.

Brake FAQs

▶ Brakes Get Hot and Lock Up

Question: The disc brakes on my bike start to get hot and lock up. The pads get wedged against the disc and I can't even turn the wheel until the brakes cool down. I have to bleed out some brake fluid when it gets real bad. What do you think is wrong with my bike's brakes?

Answer: This is a common problem. The two brake pins that the pads slide on become grooved and prevent the pads from moving away from the disc, when the brake lever is released. Try replacing the pads and pins and changing the brake fluid to a DOT 4. The best fix for preventing the problem of grooved brake pins are stainless-steel pins made by WER (Works Enduro Rider). They make these pins with hex heads too, so they are easy to remove when changing brake pads.

▶ Kevlar Brakes Pads Wear Too Fast

Question: I put a set of expensive Kevlar brake pads on my bike and they are shot after only a few rides. The material is still on the pad, but I have to pull in the lever really hard just to get them to lock up. What gives?

Answer: I'm guessing that you are a real power-washing freak. That is a sure way to damage Kevlar pads. The strong detergents that the commercial power-washing systems use can damage the Kevlar material used on the pads. The detergent bonds to the pad and causes them to form a low-friction glaze. That is why the pad material has not worn down, but the pad won't grip the disc. Don't try to file or sand the pad; just get a new set, and wash your bike with water only!

guide listed at the end of this chapter. Always review the factory service manual for your model bike before attempting any service procedures.

1. Before you attempt to change the brake pads, first power-wash the brakes clean with water (no soap). The high-strength detergents used in power-washers can damage the caliper seals, disc surface, and even attack the bond used on the pad, so avoid spraying the brakes when you wash your bike. Next, clean the dirt from the inside of the Allen-head caliper screws with a pick or brake cleaner. This will ensure that the Allen wrench gets a rigid grip and doesn't strip the screw when you go to remove it.

2. Remove the brake pins and check the pin's surface for divots, dents, and corrosion. These surface blemishes can cause the pads to drag when the brakes get hot. Replace the pins at least once per year, and never apply grease to the pins!

3. After you have removed the brake pins, you can remove the caliper and pull out the pads. Check the pads for glazing or wear. If the pads are worn out, replace them.

4. Reinstall the pads, calipers, and pins, and tighten all the screws. Always depress the brake lever several times after you have installed the wheels. This will enable the brake pistons to pump up to the pads.

Fluid Replacement

The brake fluid should be changed at least two times a year. Race mechanics change the fluid on their bikes every two races. There are two methods for replacing the brake fluid and bleeding the brakes: pump-and-purge with a hand-operated vacuum pump.

The Pump-and-Purge Method

If you don't have a brake bleeder tool, this is the best method to change brake fluid.

1. Remove the master-cylinder cap, and top the cylinder with brake fluid.

2. Put a six-point box-end wrench on the bleeder valve located on the caliper. Slip a 10-inch-long piece of clear plastic tubing over the end of the bleeder valve.

3. Slowly pump the brake lever and hold it fully engaged; then loosen the bleeder valve a quarter of a turn for one second before tightening the valve.

4. While frequently checking fluid level in the master cylinder and topping it off as necessary, repeat Step 3 until the fluid is coming out of the tube is clean and clear and without bubbles.

5. Remove the hose, snug down the bleeder valve, top off the master cylinder, and replace the master-cylinder cap.

The Hand-Pump Method

A brake bleeder tool will speed up your brake fluid change. Use the following method to change your oil with the tool.

1. Connect a collection tank between the pump and a hose attached to the bleeder valve.

2. Remove the master-cylinder cap. Be prepared to constantly replenish the master cylinder with brake fluid during the bleeding process.

3. Loosen the bleeder valve a half-turn and use the vacuum pump to slowly pump the fluid through the brake system. Don't forget to replenish the master cylinder!

4. When the fluid coming out of the bleeder valve looks clean, clear, and free of bubbles, stop pumping and snug down the bleeder valve.

5. Detach the pump from the bleeder valve, replenish the master cylinder, and replace the master-cylinder cap.

Troubleshooting

Problem: The brakes drag when they get hot.

Solution: The brake fluid could be saturated with water. It's best to change the brake fluid twice a year.

Problem: After only 15 minutes of riding, the rear brake pedal has no free movement and the brakes are very sensitive.

Solution: The brake pins could be bent or have divots that cause the pads to drag against the disc. The heat is transferred through the caliper piston and into the brake fluid. The water in the fluid boils and expands, and that causes a lack of free movement at the brake pedal. Check the brake pins and change the fluid.

Problem: The brake lever or pedal pulsates when the brakes are applied.

Solution: The disc is bent and is pushing the piston back into the caliper. This force is transferred into the pedal/lever, making a pulsation for every revolution of the wheel. Replace the disc because it cannot be repaired.

Problem: The front brake pads wear on an angle.

Solution: The front caliper carrier bracket is bent; replace it.

Problem: The brakes make a squealing noise.

Solution: The discs and pads have a thin film of glazing on their surfaces. The glazing could have occurred from leaking fork seals, power-wash detergent, or chain lube accidentally sprayed on the disc. Medium-grit sandpaper can be used to remove the glazing off the surface of the discs and pads. Afterward, clean the discs with brake cleaner—never with a detergent!

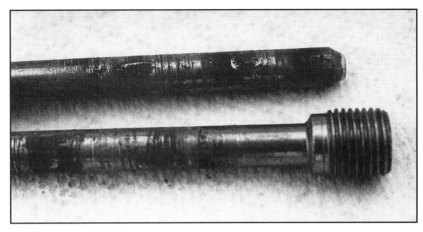

This is an example of brake pins that were damaged from the pads. There are divots worn in the pins. That allowed the pads to rest in the divots and rub against the pad, thereby accelerating the wear on the pads. These pins should be replaced.

Jorgen Nilsson winning his first 500cc Grand Prix race.

TUNING TIPS FOR SPECIFIC DIRT BIKES

CHAPTER TEN

When tuning your bike for more performance, the place to start is to fix the flaws inherent to the model. The flaws may not be obvious to you, and the fixes can be cheaper than you think. The 1990 CR250 forks are a good example. As with most CR forks, they are the weakest link on the bike, but one of the major problems is that the coating on the stock springs flakes off and clogs the system. By simply cleaning out the forks, changing the oil, and adding aftermarket springs, the fork will work world's better. They'll still be CR forks—which means mediocre—but the improvement will give a front suspension that is decent rather than nearly useless. In cases where the flaw is expensive to fix—as with early KX500's tendency to round out the cases around the main bearing—more economical fixes are listed.

The tuning tips in this chapter will be especially beneficial to home-based mechanics who work on many different dirt bikes. The flaws and fixes portion of each model tuning section will help you zero in on mechanical problems that are hard to diagnose. The best value mods portion will give you recommendations on the high-performance services and aftermarket accessories that make the biggest difference.

Note that this section is also useful when buying a used dirt bike. You can pinpoint typical flaws on a bike you are looking at, and perhaps save yourself some money.

1992–96 Honda CR125

Flaws: carb jetting off, clutch fades, rims dent easily

Fixes: richen jetting, install steel clutch plates, lace-up Excel rims

The CR is regarded as the best 125 of the early to mid-1990s. These models had their share of problems, but overall this was the most reliable 125cc motocross bike. Simple problems such as carb jetting can be adjusted with just a needle and main jet change. The clutch performs better with steel plates and frequent oil changes. The stock rims are very soft and dent easily when riding in rocky conditions. It's best to replace them with Excel rims once they are dented.

The CR engine can be modified to be a better enduro bike, or have the raging top-end power for GP motocross. Whatever type of dirt riding you do, the CR125 can be modified to suit your riding demands.

Best Value Mods

Engine: 1468 Needle for carb, RAD Valve, 53-tooth rear sprocket

Suspension: stiffer fork springs

Supercross or Enduro Powerband

If you want to increase the low-end and midrange power of your CR125, these following modifications are the hot ticket. These are great for Supercross, where you need quick bursts of power, or enduro riding, where mellower power is better for navigating snotty trails. Also, these modifications are well-suited to lower level riders. The bike will be easier to ride, with the sacrifice of some top-end power.

HPP Valves

The exhaust valve guides of the 1993 and later models, are manufactured with such a high opening, that when the valves are closed the exhaust gases can bypass over the top of the valves. For more low-range to mid-range power, install the exhaust valve assemblies from the 1992 CR125. These parts are very expensive! Honda part numbers: Left 14700-KZ4-860 and Right 14600-KZ4-860.

Head Mod

The 1990 and 1991 models had domed pistons and hemi-shaped combustion chambers. The 1992 model was the first year of the flat-top piston design. Never mix heads and pistons on the earlier and later CRs, or engine damage can occur. The 1990 and 1991 cylinder head can be improved by turning down the face of the head 0.028 inch or 0.7mm. Then the squish angle must be cut at a 10-degree angle, with a deck height of 0.020 inch or 0.5mm. On

This is a view of the exhaust port of a 1993–96 CR125. Notice the light passing through the gap between the top of the exhaust valves and the valve guides? Install the valve guides from the 1992 CR125 if you want more low-end power.

the 1992 and later models, the spark plug doesn't thread in flush to the combustion chamber. The top of the spark plug lug should be turned down on a lathe 1mm. The compression ratio and squish band width are good so no other mods are needed.

Reed Valve

The Boyesen RAD Valve makes a tremendous difference in the low- and midrange of the powerband and is a must for enduro riding.

Exhaust Pipe

The best pipe for these engine mods is a Dyno-Port low-end pipe.

High Rev Powerband

The stock engine peaks at about 10,500 rpm. To be competitive in the national championships or GPs, the engine must have a powerband that starts at 9,500 and peaks at 12,500 rpm. Modifying the CR for that extra elusive 2,000 rpm is very expensive and requires total engine disassembly and special machining. This is a parts list of the engine components and an explanation of how they are tuned to work together: 1992 CR125 cylinder #12110-KZ4-860, 1991 Head #12200-KZ4-730 38mm PJ Keihin carb, aftermarket pipe and silencer, and carbon fiber reeds.

The 1992 CR125 cylinder has more aggressive exhaust and transfer port timing than the 1993 and 1994 models. You can use the 1993–96 HPP valves, but you need to switch to the domed piston and head. The domed set up enables more efficient cylinder scavenging at high rpm. The carbon fiber reeds are less prone to fluttering and the larger carb is needed to boost the rpm peak of the engine.

Crankcase Mods

The cases must be machined for a larger intake port with better flow up to the transfer ports.

Reeds

Carbon fiber reeds should be used because the stock reeds start to flutter at about 10,700 rpm. The carbon fiber reeds produce excellent top-end power without fluttering at high rpm.

Head and Piston

The domed piston has a slight advantage at extremely high rpm. Use a Wiseco Pro-Lite and the 1991 head.

Honda FAQs

◆ Retro Honda Cartridge Forks

Question: I have a question about an older bike. I have a 1985 CR250 and I'm looking for better performance from the forks. Is there a cartridge-fork kit for these older bikes?

Answer: The Race-Tech Emulator Valve is well known as a fork kit for modern mini-cycles, and it fits into the older noncartridge forks. The kit is easy to install because it just slides in from the top of the fork and is held in place by the fork spring. When you install the Emulator Valve, clean the fork's internal parts. Check and replace the fork bushings and seals and add new fork oil. New fork springs will reduce front-end diving and headshake at the end of fast straightaways. All fork-spring manufacturers have recommendations for the correct spring rate for your model bike and your riding weight. Guides such as these are published and printed in catalogs.

◆ 1995 CR Fork Recall

Question: I heard that Honda issued a recall on the 1995 CR's forks, in March of that year. What is the problem with the forks? Did Kawasaki and Yamaha be issuing similar recalls on their Kayaba forks? I just bought a used 1995 CR250 and I want to find out if the forks were ever fixed.

Answer: The problem with the 1995 Honda Kayaba forks, is a possibility that a limited number of fork tubes weren't heat treated properly. The defective fork tubes can crack near the bottom of the tube where the axle clamp is fastened. If you have a 1995 dirt bike with Kayaba forks, check with your local franchised dealer. Your bike's serial number is registered with the manufacturer. Dealers have access to a computer record of what factory-directed recalls or updates need to be performed with your bike.

CR125 Carb Jetting

Here are some specs on a starting point for carb jetting. The specific gravity is different from North America and Europe so European jetting specs will need to be slightly richer. American carb jetting for 36mm PJ Keihin using 93 octane pump gas with a premix ratio of 40 to 1 is as follows: air screw 1.5 turns, slow-jet #58, needle #1468, main jet #168 European specs for unleaded premium petrol, 40 to 1 premix. Air screw 1.5 turns, slow jet #62, needle #1468, main jet #178.

Baseline carb specs for a 38mm PJ Keihin are one step richer on the slow and main jets using the 1468 needle.

CR Clutch Tips

Never install stiffer clutch springs in a CR125. The clutch is designed to slip when the gears engage on up-shifting. This helps reduce the impact on the transmission. Stiffer clutch springs could accelerate wear on the transmission because of the increased load. Steel clutch plates wear slower and don't contaminate the gear oil. However, they do increase the drivetrain inertia, just like a flywheel weight. The effect of the heavier steel clutch plates will help you hook and stay in control in slippery hard-packed tracks, but the bike will feel a bit slower to respond in deep sand or where you have good traction. The additional weight of steel clutch plates can make the bike a bit easier to ride, as well.

1985-91 Honda CR125

Flaws: left-side crankshaft seal leaks, clutch plates wear out

Fixes: replace seal often, install Barnett steel plates

Honda really perfected the 125 in the late 1980s. Here are some general things to pay close attention to or modify for better performance.

Best Value Mods

Engine: 53-tooth sprocket, 1468 carb needle

Suspension: shock revalving, stiffer fork springs

Gearing

A good baseline for gearing on all models should be 13/53 for motocross and 12/52 for Supercross and enduro. Ideally, adjust by single teeth on the rear for slightly different tracks and conditions.

Carburetor

A 36mm works best. Use these jetting specs: 58 slow jet, 6 slide, 1468 needle, and 168 main jet (vary slightly according to elevation and extreme air temperature differences).

Crankshaft

The left-side crankshaft seals wear out quickly because the left side cover is flimsy. Replace the seal often; otherwise,

This is the view of the intake sleeve that protrudes from the bottom of cylinders like the ones used on KX125s and CR125s. On the left is the original sharp edge of the sleeve. On the right is the rounded sleeve. The rounded edge enables mixture gases to flow around the sleeve with minimal turbulence.

the piston could overheat and seize on the exhaust skirt. The 1987 model's crankshaft was updated to a stronger design. The new connecting rod uses a 15mm pin, so you must change the piston with the crankshaft. Both parts are standard on the 1988 model.

Cylinder Interchange

The 1989 cylinder is Nikasil plated and it will fit the 1987 and 1988 models (which are not plated).

Clutch

Replacing the aluminum clutch plates with steel plates makes the clutch last longer and doesn't hurt performance. Never install stiffer springs in the clutch of a CR125 because it will cause first gear drive to fail. That gear wears quickly on these bikes normally,

and it is part of the clutch shaft so it is expensive to replace.

Reeds

Honda doesn't make replacement reeds for their bikes, so use Boyesen reeds.

ATAC System

The exhaust valve on the 1987–97 models can be damaged on installation. The right-side valve end has a flat machined on it, and if you tighten the actuator lever too tight, it can round the flat edge. This causes the valve to hang open and raise the exhaust-gas temperature at high rpm, eventually causing the piston to seize.

Shock

The rear shock can be modified for better handling on the 1985–88 models.

These types of shocks use the straight shims. The rebound-valve stack has two transition shims, one in the middle and one closest to the piston. Put both transitions shims between the number 26 and 27 shim from the piston. After this, the shock will handle square-edged bumps much better.

1992–96 Honda CR250

Flaws: chain and sprockets wear, cylinders break, rear suspension kicks

Fixes: loosen chain tension, use 1995 cylinder, install Devol link kit

There is hardly any difference between the 1992–96 engines, so the mods listed will apply to the previous models. The focus of our engine mods will be to make the CR easier to ride for motocross riders and especially great for enduro riders.

This is a view of the outside of a right side crankcase from a 1992 CR250. These bikes had chronic problems of burning clutch plates due to the lack of oil flow. The arrows mark the positions of three holes that were added to the 1992 model cases. This enables the oil to flow through the right side cover and trans.

Best Value Mods

Engine: carb jetting, flywheel weight
Suspension: DeVol link set

Crankcase Mods

The 1992 CR250 has a problem of poor oil flow between the trans and clutch cavity. On any dirt bike, when the clutch is spinning it forces the oil into the transmission. There has to be passageways that link the trans and clutch cavities so the oil can circulate and cool the clutch. Starting in 1993 Honda bored two more oil flow passages in the right side crankcase, linking the two cavities. If your 1992 CR is burning up clutch plates frequently, then you need to drill two 8mm holes in the crankcase as shown in the photo.

Carburetor

The jetting needs to be richened to a #1368 needle and a #185 main jet.

Cylinder Head Modification

Index the spark plug depth by turning down on a lathe. The spark plug lug must be turned down .040 inch. If the cylinder base hasn't been turned yet, then 0.5mm can be turned off the cylinder head gasket surface. This will reduce the minimum clearance space from between the piston and head, increase the compression ratio, and give a stronger pulling powerband for more torque.

Cylinder Tuning

The original Honda castings are excellent and the port timing is consistent. However, a big increase in low-end torque can be gained with the proper use of epoxy and a right-angle hand-grinding tool. This work is better left to professional tuners. The cylinders are interchangeable between the 1992–96 models. The 1995 and later cylinders are the best because of the smaller exhaust and intake ports. These cylinders have the best timing combination and the most sealing surface area for the rings. The smaller intake port doesn't hinder performance and is stronger to reduce piston skirt wear. The cylinders with the smaller intake port is easier to install because the rings are less likely to pop out of the grooves when sliding the cylinder down on the piston. More crankcase compression is gained by applying the epoxy on alternate sides of the separating bridge. This also changes the flow-pattern up through the transfer ports and into the cylinder bore. Flow-shaping is also performed on the rear transfer port window exit angles. This cylinder will peak at 7,500 rpm and work great with the stock pipe, stock or spark arrestor silencer, and intake system. To attain the optimum compression ratio and exhaust port's time-area, the cylinder base must be turned down (0.5mm) on a lathe. Now the transfer ports must be raised to a dimension of 58mm measured from the top of the cylinder.

CR250s and CR125s need to have the top of the spark plug lug turned down on a lathe. This will allow the spark plug to thread flush into the combustion chamber. For CR125s with flat top pistons, turn it down .040 inch (1mm); for 1990–91 CR250s, turn it down .120 inch (3mm); and for 1992–96 CR250s, turn it down .040 inch (1mm).

Flywheel Weight

The final component for tuning is the flywheel weight. This component is normally overlooked by tuners. Dave Watson teaches riding schools in England. Dave thinks that flywheel weights make the power delivery easier for most riders to handle. Especially junior and vet motocross riders or trail riders.

Rear Suspension

In 1996 DeVol Racing designed a linkage kit with a modified ratio. The DeVol kit is a replacement linkage set that greatly improves the rear suspension of the CR250s. This kit fits the 1992 and newer CR250s. This mod is especially beneficial to 1995 CR250s. Those models handled poorly when accelerating out of turns, over sharp-edged bumps. The DeVol linkage set has a more linear ratio than the stock Honda linkage. This makes the suspension perform smoother while riding over a series of small sharp-edged bumps, such as those found at the exit of turns.

1990–91 Honda CR250

Flaws: leaky air boot, carbon seized HPP valves, fork debris

Fixes: seal boot, chamfer HPP valves, Eibach springs, and Pro-Action preload cones

These bikes were very reliable but had some handling problems that are easily fixed. The engines produced good torque but the exhaust valve system is a nightmare to service. Here are some fix-it and tuning tips for these models of CR250s.

Best Value Mods

Engine: carb jetting, flywheel weight

Suspension: aftermarket springs, Pro-Action cones

HPP Valve Mods

The HPP valves are prone to carbon seizing. See the recommendations listed in the chapter on exhaust valve servicing.

Carb Jetting

Here are some jetting specs when using a 40 to 1 premix ratio with 93 octane unleaded fuel and an NGK BP7ES spark plug: 55 slow jet, 1369 needle in the third position, and a 175 main jet.

Air Box Sealing

The air-boot-to-air-box flange must be sealed on the older CRs. The best sealer to use is weather-strip adhesive because it isn't fuel soluble. Never use silicone sealer because the fuel will deteriorate the sealer and allow water and dirt to enter the air box.

Cylinder Tuning

There are some simple mods that can be performed to the cylinder with just a file. The casting flaws around the boost ports can be removed for smoother flow through the intake and the HPP valve guides should be matched to the exhaust port. This is a critical area of the cylinder because even a small mismatch can cause a shock wave that effectively blocks the exhaust port. Other more difficult mods include raising the transfer ports to 58mm from the top of the cylinder, turning down the cylinder base 0.5mm, and narrowing the rear transfer ports as listed in the paragraph for the late-model CRs.

Head Mods

The top of the spark plug lug must be turned down on a lathe 3mm to allow the spark plug to thread down flush into the combustion chamber. This mod improves throttle response and reduces spark plug cold fouling.

Flywheel Weight

The CRs benefit from a flywheel weight. Sixteen ounces is the standard size that companies such as A-Loop or Steahly use for their products, although they will have several options available. In general, heavier weights are better for enduro and off-road, while lighter weights are geared toward motocross or Supercross. For novice and intermediate riders, the heavier weights can work very well. Power delivery is a just a bit more manageable and low-end is greatly improved. The result is the bike is easier to control yet delivers the same amount of horsepower.

There are two different types of flywheel weights, weld-on and thread-on. A-Loop performs the weld-on flywheel weight service. Steahly makes thread-on flywheel weights. This product threads onto the fine left-hand threads that are on the center hub of most Japanese mag-

neto rotors. normally the threads are used for the flywheel remover tool. Thread-on flywheel weights can only be used if the threads on the flywheel are in perfect condition. The advantage to weld-on weights is they can't possibly come off.

Big Displacement Kits

If your cylinder's plating is worn and needs to be repaired, consider a Wiseco big oversize piston kit. Wiseco offers pistons in the size 265cc for AMA legal competition in the 250 class. To make a 250cc bike legal for open class competition, the displacement size is 295cc. Wiseco offers a piston kit with head gasket for the CR250s from the model years of 1986 to 1996. Both of these piston kits require modifications to the head and exhaust valves. These mods include increasing the diameter of the cylinder head and grinding the exhaust valve for more clearance.

Ignition Timing

Advancing the ignition timing gives the CR more midrange hit in the powerband. Normally Honda stator plates aren't adjustable. To make the plate adjustable you need to file the plate 1mm at the lower bolt hole. This will enable you to rotate the stator plate clockwise to advance the ignition timing.

Crankshaft Seal

The left side crankshaft seal is prone to failure. Honda redesigned the seal in 1992. The main reason that the seal fails is due to dirt and water entering the ignition cover Boyesen Engineering makes an aluminum cover that seals properly. If your CR bogs at low rpm, the seal is probably blown and needs to be replaced.

Fuel Tank Insert Nuts

The fuel tank insert nuts are square and pressed into reliefs in the plastic fuel tank. When the scoop bolts are overtightened, the insert nuts tend to spin in the tank when the bolt is removed. That makes it impossible to remove the radiator scoop. The solution is to remove the insert nut and epoxy bond it back in place. Removing the nut will be difficult. I use an air impact wrench to spin the bolt fast, while using a large flat screwdriver to pry off the scoop, just behind the insert nut. Take care not to puncture the fuel tank. Once you remove the scoop and insert nut, you can grasp the square insert nut with a wrench or channel-lock pliers and remove the bolt. Apply a dab of Duro Master-Mend epoxy to the insert nut and the relief in the fuel tank. Press the insert nut in place for about 15 minutes.

Forks

These cartridge forks have the early model valve design with the small diameter piston. They are prone to clogging with metal debris. These forks have to be disassembled and cleaned often. The main sources for the metal debris are the springs and the spring preload cones. The springs have a coating that flakes off. The preload cones are made of steel with sharp machined edges. That cone fits into the spring and aggravates the flaking problem. The solution is to use Eibach brand fork springs. They are powder coated with a flexible material that doesn't flake off. Pro-Action makes an aluminum preload cone that doesn't wear or vibrate like the stock steel cone. Performing these two mods will save you money in fork oil changes and improve the bike's handling.

Some suspension companies offer the service of hard anodizing for the fork parts. On bikes produced after 1989, most of the fork parts are hard-anodized from the manufacturer. Hard anodizing prevents the aluminum parts from wearing prematurely. This service is used for repair of the slider tubes on the 1990 and later CR250 models.

Many companies make aftermarket base valve kits for cartridge forks. These products offer improvements in performance because of changes to the piston design and the valve shim stacks. If you are going through the expense of installing a base valve kit, make sure that the fork springs are matched to your riding weight, skill level, and the base valve kit. Companies such as Race Tech provide a tuning manual with their Gold Valve products. The tuning manual provides guidelines on spring rates and valving changes for a variety of different rider profiles.

1985–89 Honda CR250 and CR500

Flaws: soft fork springs, magneto covers leak, air boot leaks

Fixes: stiffer fork springs, factory racing cover, seal air boot

The big CRs went through an amazing design evolution in the late 1980s. The suspension on them went from drilled passageways and squirting fork oil to upside down cartridge forks and a rear shock with technology rivaling an Ohlins. The CRs changed more in 5 years than they did in the previous 12 years since their inception. There are many innovative products built by European and American companies to bring the mid-1980s CRs into the 1990s. The CR250s can be improved greatly. The 1986 and 1987 models shared the same exhaust valve system, and this was a very controllable motorcycle. However, the HPP system requires frequent service. Here is a survey of the products and mods for these timeless motorcycles.

Best Value Mods

Engine: 1369 carb needle, chamfer HPP valves, T-vents in carburetor

Suspension: fork springs, check linkage bolts

CR250 Exhaust Valves

The earlier models (1984–85) have a butterfly valve linked to a can at the exhaust manifold to increase the volume of the header pipe at low rpm and boost the low-end power. The butterfly valves are prone to carbon build-up, which locks the valve in the open position and reduces the top-end power of the engine.

Suspension

Steve Simons, the motorcycle suspension tuner and prolific inventor, designed two excellent products for the noncartridge CR forks. The Anti-Cavitation fork kit is the only product you can use to simulate the benefits of a cartridge fork in earlier CRs. The kit includes a damper rod with a valve similar to the modern-day Race-Tech Emulator Valve, and a spring cone that prevents cavitation. Simons also invented a fork cap that was vented to bleed off pressure the forks built up after hard usage. Later, he invented a fork cap that was vented and

made the rebound circuit adjustable. This product is available for 1987–88 CR250s and CR500s. Also, base-valve kits are available for all the CRs with conventional or cartridge forks. These products are available from Pro-Racing in England. Honda had problems determining the proper fork-spring preload on the early cartridge forks. They used too much on production bikes, sometimes as much as 30mms! The proper amount is 5–15mms. The best fork spring rates to use are 0.40–0.41 kilograms for the CR250 and 0.44 kilograms for the CR500.

Linkage

Other trouble points include the suspension linkage and the floating rear drum brakes of the 1985 and 1986 models. The 1988 CR250 had chronic problems with bent rear-shock-linkage bolts, until Honda redesigned the parts and added flanges to the heads of the bolts. The part numbers for the new bolts are H/C 2976678 and H/C 2976686. The CR linkage requires careful attention and frequent lubing. A seized linkage can put an enormous strain on the frame, causing everything from cracks in the frame to leaks at the head gasket.

Rear Wheel

In 1989 Honda redesigned the rear hub to be lighter. It was too weak and shattered. Honda had a recall campaign in Europe but not in America. The 1990 hubs looked similar to the 1987 hubs, with a conical taper compared to the straight diameter hub of the 1989 model. Tallon makes an excellent replacement hub that is far stronger than the stock hub.

Ergonomic Changes

Some simple bolt-on parts for the rest of the chassis include wider foot pegs, stiffer seat foam, a skid plate to protect the frame, and a cable to prevent the rear brake lever from tearing off in berms.

Engine

The only real change to the CR500 in the late 1980s was the addition of water-cooling. The air-cooled models suffered from detonation, and the cylinder head had to be modified to lower the compression ratio and narrow the width of the squish band.

Spark Plug

The best spark plug heat range is an NGK BP7ES.

Carb Problems

The carb's fuel-inlet needle and seat wear out quickly because of the vibration, causing the engine to flood when the bike is dropped. Change them every season.

Silencer

The later model CR500s suffered from chronic breakage of the silencer core. The silencer needs to be packed often otherwise there is nothing to protect the core tube from vibration.

Reed Valve

In 1986, Honda put a plastic insert in the reed valve to boost the velocity by stuffing the dead-air space. Aftermarket "reed stuffers" are available from FMF. Boyesen reeds are a good investment because the reed stop plates block the cylinder's rear boost port. Boyesen reeds are more responsive than original Honda reeds and they don't require the stop plates.

Carburetor

Jetting for the 1986–91 models burning 93-octane pump gas and a pre-mix ratio of 40:1 should be 55 slow jet, 1369 needle, and 172 main jet. Take care setting the float level and replace the inlet needle and seat every year. Changing to a modern T-vent system for the carb is also beneficial. In this way, if you ride through mud your bike won't vapor lock because the carb's float bowl vents are blocked by the mud splattered up under the bike.

Ignition System

The ignition systems require frequent maintenance in the form of cleaning the inside of the flywheel. The dirt and water that get drawn in from the plastic side cover cause the coils to break down, the flywheel to get corroded, and the left-side crankshaft seal to wear. Boyesen Engineering makes aluminum side covers that seal better than the stock plastic ones, plus they function as a heat-sink to transfer damaging engine heat away from the ignition. Ignition coils and spark plug caps tend to break down on the CRs.

Air Box

The air-boot flanges on the CRs tend to leak after you pressure-wash the bike with strong detergents. Reseal the air boot with weather-strip adhesive, available from auto parts stores.

1990–96 Honda CR500

Flaws: abrupt powerband, headshaking
Fixes: lower compression ratio, stiffer fork springs

The CR500 hasn't changed much in the past five years and there is a lot you can do to this bike. The engine hits abruptly and riders complain that it is hard to ride on slippery surfaces. Here are some mods that will help the engine pull smoothly from low-end and rev out further.

Best Value Mods

Engine: DEP Sport pipe and silencer
Suspension: fork springs

Carb

A 39.5mm Keihin PWK carb will add 3 horsepower to the top end and make the engine pull cleanly off the low-end. Sudco sells an aftermarket PWK or you can use a carb from a KX500 1992 and later.

Cylinder Head

Reshaping the transition between the combustion chamber and the squish band can be accomplished by turning the head on a lathe. Set the tool angle to 25 degrees and cut into the squish band starting 15mm from the edge of the chamber. Install a projected nose spark plug such as an NGK BP6ES.

Cylinder

The hook angles of the rear transfer ports should be filled with epoxy so the transfers are aimed at each other instead of toward the exhaust port. The width of the rear transfer ports can be narrowed up to 15mms. The narrower the port, the sooner the powerband will begin. The minimum chordal width of each rear transfer port is 10mm. Raise the exhaust port 1.5mm and widen the two ports 1.5mm on each outer edge. The steel sleeve should be matched to the aluminum casting because it is very rough from the original manufacturing process. Polish the port edges with fine grit sanding paper. That will improve piston and ring life.

The bore of the cylinder should be monitored for out-of-round wear and taper wear. I have had the best luck running oversize Wiseco pistons, set to 0.035-inch piston to bore clearance.

Exhaust System

Jorgen Nilsson tested many different exhausts in the 1992 and 1993 seasons and found that the DEP Sport pipe and Kevlar silencer had the best power spread.

Fork Springs

Riders who weigh over 170 pounds may want to switch to a stiffer spring rate (23–25 pounds). If bottoming and headshake occurs frequently, that is a sign that you need stiffer fork springs and raise the fork oil level. The highest fork oil level is 120mms, for the minimum air space and highest pressure.

1990–96 Honda CR80

Flaws: fork damping
Fixes: emulator valve

This bike hardly changed from 1987 to 1995. The engine is excellent, a design far ahead of its time, but the chassis and the suspension were archaic. The swingarm is stamped sheet metal and clipped together. The forks are simple oil-orifice, damper rod type. This suspension set-up is the single biggest hindrance to an aspiring mini racer. The biggest problem with the CR is the spring rates of the forks and shock. WP makes a selection of different springs, calibrated accurately. Ask a suspension tuner for his recommendations on both front and rear spring choices, based on the rider's weight, height, and ability. Heavier or especially tall riders will need stiffer springs, for obvious reasons.

Forks

Riders who use the front brakes hard will need stiffer fork springs to prevent the front end from diving abruptly in braking bumps. These forks are damper rod, not cartridge, forks. There are two ways to change the damping rate: change the viscosity of the oil or vary the diameter of the hole in the damping rod. Changing the oil height will only change the

The Summers Racing Concepts XR600.

bottoming characteristics of the fork but not the damping. In 1994 a new product became available for CR forks. It's called the Emulator valve, and it's made by Race Tech. This valve improves the damping of the compression and rebound circuits, emulating the effect of cartridge forks. The valve costs just over $100 and is easy to install. The Emulator valve fits between the fork spring and the damper rod of each fork leg.

Engine

Honda has detuned the CR80 engine over the years. Simple mods such as turning down the cylinder head 0.020 inch or 0.5mm and matching the exhaust-port outlet to the manifold will boost the top-end. Matching the cylinder ports in width and height (from the top edge of the cylinder) will help the midrange power. Several manufacturers make exhaust pipes that work better than stock. Generally they shift the powerband up in the rpm range.

1987–95 Honda CR80 Big-Wheel and 100cc Conversions

The big-wheel CR80 became available in 1996. Before then, if you wanted to build a super mini, you had to buy special parts for the chassis that were available only in England.

Dave Watson of Race Spec in England makes a big-wheel kit for all CR80s prior to 1996. The kit consists of rims, spokes, Bridgestone tires, swingarm, and fork caps. The fork caps extend the fork tubes to accommodate the 19-inch front wheel. If you use this kit, consider using stiffer springs. The longer swingarm places greater leverage on the shock spring.

Wiseco makes a Pro-Lite piston kit to convert the 82cc cylinder to 99cc. This kit is designed for use with overboring and electroplating. Cometic makes a steel head gasket to fit the larger 51 millimeter bore size. This 100cc conversion also requires a modification to the cylinder head.

Honda XR Tuning
with Scott Summers and Fred Bramblett

Honda XRs are used for everything from play riding to hare scrambles to desert racing. They are perhaps the most bulletproof and widely used dirt bikes on the planet. Although enduro and trail riders have been using XRs for decades, Scott Summers, one of the best off-road riders in the sport, has put a number one plate on the flanks of an XR600 for several times in the 1990s and has demonstrated that XRs are capable of much more than just plonking down trails or crawling through the woods. He and his mechanic, Fred Bramblett, are not your typical rider mechanic duo. They are motorcycle innovators. They've devised some interesting innovations for the XR line of Hondas. They've tested just about everything possible for XRs. Whether they are racing the Baja 1000, the ISDE, or cow-trailing through the

This is a special chain guard that allows the chain to derail downward if the chain is forced off the sprockets or breaks.

deep woods of Kentucky, they know the setup that works best. Here are some of their tips on products to improve the longevity and performance of the XR line of motorcycles.

Routine Maintenance

These are some of the maintenance tasks that you will need to perform after every hare scrambles race or long trail riding weekend.

Engine
Air Filter

Clean the air filter and the air box after every ride. Check the filter for excess oil build-up near the point where the crankcase vent enters the air box. If the rings are worn, crankcase oil will flow up the vent and into the air box and coat the filter. This can cause a rich fuel jetting condition.

Oil and Filter

Change the crankcase oil after every two rides and the filter on every other oil change. Check the wire mesh screens that are mounted in the bottom of the frame and in the crankcase. If you ride a mud race and have to fan the clutch often, the fiber clutch plates can start to

disintegrate and pollute the crankcase oil. These particles will become trapped in the wire mesh filters. You should clean these filters at least twice each year.

Lube the Cables

Lube and adjust the clutch and throttle cables. Remember that the clutch cable free-play will be reduced as the clutch plates wear.

Valve Adjustment

The XRs don't need frequent valve adjustment, but keep in mind that the valve lash will be reduced as the valve and seat wear. Check and adjust the valve lash every 200 miles or after every fifth riding weekend.

Chassis
Chain and Sprockets

Clean the chain and sprockets after every ride, then lube the chain and check the free-play. Inspect the sprockets for chipped teeth, caused by rocks. Check the alignment of the rear chain guide. Sometimes the guide can get bent by rocks or ruts, causing the guide to push the chain out of alignment with the rear sprocket. This problem can cause the chain to derail.

Keep It Greased

The XRs have grease zerks mounted in the swingarm and linkage pivots. You should grease the zerks after every other ride for two reasons: to force water and dirt from the bearing cavity and to lube the bearing. Fred Bramblett fits grease zerks to the neck of the XR frame, to provide grease to the steering head bearings. The zerks are mounted to the frame and the races are notched to allow the grease to enter the bearing. The service interval for greasing the steering head bearings is every four rides. That may seem frequent but consider that the XR holds the crankcase oil in the frame. When the oil gets hot the frame temperature rises and the grease in the steering head bearings can melt from the bearing.

Spokes

Because the XR is a fairly heavy dirt bike, the spokes require frequent attention. Check the spokes after every ride and don't be tempted to overtighten the spokes. That can cause the rims to crack.

Brake Fluid

Change the brake fluid after every four rides. Use Dot 4 fluid.

Damage Control

The XR models are well-developed bikes that are extremely reliable. The one fault that even great bikes can't escape is their ability to survive a crash. Crashing is one thing that all dirt bikers do from time to time. The rider mechanic team of Summers and Bramblett have bumped their heads together to come up with a line of products that help make the XR more resistant to crash damage. They've come up with some interesting innovations to improve the XRs. Their products are available through Summers Racing Products, 800-221-9752.

Foot Levers

This shift and brake levers are reinforced to prevent them from bending but also designed so they break off clean to minimize damage to more expensive components. For example, the shift lever is designed to break clean at the shift shaft during really hard impacts. In that way the shift shaft doesn't bend or damage the crankcases. A stainless steel cable wraps around the end of the levers and connects to the frame, to prevent tree branches from becoming wedged between the side covers and the levers. The cables also serve to prevent the levers from snaring when riding through deep ruts.

Wire Protectors

The Summers team noticed a common problem with XRs. It is common for the wires and rubber plug that exit from the right side engine cover to get snared by branches and yanked out of the side cover. This allows the crankcase oil to leak out of the side cover and eventually cause catastrophic engine damage. The guys developed an aluminum guard to protect the wires from tree branches. The guard just bolts on to a few of the side cover's mounting screws, and silicone seal is applied to further insulate the wires.

Chain Guard

The original chain guard should be modified to allow the chain to derail downward, if the chain is forced off the sprockets or breaks. It is possible for the chain to bunch-up and break the crankcases with the original guard design.

Fork Brace

A special fork brace was developed for the conventional cartridge forks used on the XR650L, XR600, and the new XR400. The brace reduces the front wheel deflection when riding over ruts or over large rocks.

XR Performance Options

If you are considering bolt-on performance parts or high-performance services for your XR, you need to consider your riding demands and the type of terrain that you ride on. There are a myriad of products available for the XR. Products designed to suit a wide variety of different applications. Here is a survey of the different engine components and how certain products are designed for either high-speed off-road or slow-speed woods riding.

Cooling Systems

There are two ways to improve the cooling systems of air-cooled engines: welding additional fins to the head and cylinder or installing an oil cooler. The

This is an SRC fork brace designed to fit all XRs with conventional cartridge forks.

oil cooler is the most efficient setup for reducing the engine temperature. The weld-on fin setups are commonly used on desert racers that run at high speeds where there is more free air available to take advantage of the additional fins. XR's Only and Ballard Cycles sell the weld-on fin kits. Lockhart makes an aftermarket oil cooler, or you can adapt the OEM oil cooler from the XR250 to the XR600.

High Compression Piston

Wiseco makes an optional high-compression piston for the XR600.

Higher compression pistons are generally more beneficial for slow-speed woods riding or high-altitude riding.

Carburetor

The stock carb works great for woods riding and many riders prefer a larger 41mm carb for desert racing. The White Brothers 41mm carb kit gives an increase of about 4 horsepower and 6 mph. However, this larger carb sacrifices slow-speed throttle response that is important for woods riding over muddy or rocky terrain.

Head Pipe

There are three types of head pipes: straight, tapered, and oversized. All OEM head pipes are straight. The XR head pipes are two different lengths. This effectively widens the powerband at low rpm with a sacrifice in peak power. The Summers team uses the tapered head pipe marketed by Yoshimura. A tapered head pipe improves scavenging efficiency and reduces pumping losses because the pipe draws out the exhaust gases rather than relying on the piston to pump out the cylinder. Typically tapered head pipes can cause odd jetting problems, but Fred Bramblett says that he hasn't experienced any jetting problems with the Yoshimura pipe. Tapered head pipes work best with OEM cams or ones with slightly retarded exhaust timing. Oversize head pipes are generally used in conjunction with big bore kits, or for high rpm applications such as desert racing or DTX.

Tail Pipe

There are two types of tail pipes: straight through silencers and spark arrestors. Some riding areas and racing organizations require the use of spark arrestors on off-road motorcycles. Check with the rules before you purchase an expensive aftermarket tailpipe. Straight-through silencers provide the right flow characteristic and resultant back pressure to produce maximum power over a wide rpm band. Spark arrestors have a series of baffles that prevent particles of combustible gasses from exiting the tail pipe. The Summers team uses the Yoshimura tail pipe for closed course racing.

Cam

The Summers team uses the stock XR cam for hare scrambles and enduro racing and the HRC cam for desert racing. The HRC cam has a higher lift and longer duration. Most aftermarket cams offer 2 to 4 degrees of duration over OEM cams. Increasing the duration generally improves peak power but changing the overlap of the intake and exhaust has a more dramatic effect on the powerband. Decreasing the overlap improves low-end torque with a sacrifice of peak power, while increasing the overlap improves peak power with a sacrifice of low-end power.

This is a tapered header pipe designed by Yoshimura Racing for the XR Hondas.

Big Bore Kit

The highest performance top-end kit for the XR600 consists of a 102.5mm piston used in conjunction with a special sleeve. The steel sleeve is replaced with a lightweight forged aluminum sleeve that is electroplated with nickel and silicon-carbide. The displacement of the engine is increased to 660cc and the heat transfer is greatly increased. This mod requires that the crankcases be overbored to accept the larger diameter aluminum sleeve. The sleeve is forged from 6061 aluminum by Advanced Sleeve and the piston kit is made by Wiseco. This setup is designed for desert racing and is used by Australian desert ace Geoff Ballard.

1993–96 Kawasaki KX125

Flaws: stiff rear suspension
Fixes: revalve softer

The KX125 peaked in 1994. The 1996 model used the same linkage ratio and power-valve governor. The 1996 model was the first to use the new Keihin carb with airfoils. The 1993 model had the best top-end power, but the later models had much wider powerbands. The good thing about Kawasakis is that you can mix and match OEM engine

components to change your bike's powerband. For example, when converting a 1993 model for enduro riding, use the 1995 cylinder, head, piston, and wedge valves. The following are some tips on changing the KX125s engine for different types of powerbands.

Best Value Mods

Engine: cylinder porting
Suspension: Pro Circuit link rods, shock revalving

Supercross/Enduro Powerband

The stock 1994 and newer intake parts and pipe are ideal for Supercross, enduro riding, or novice motocross. These tuning components have a peak of about 9,600 rpm. The 1993 and older intakes were designed for a 13,000rpm peak. However, the 1993 cylinder and head can be greatly improved. Using TSR design software, I examined the 1993 cylinder and found that the rear transfer ports are too big. Also, the exhaust-port timing is very radical. The solution is to turn down 0.7mm from the base of the cylinder. This will retard the port timing and boost the compression ratio. Then remove the same amount of metal from the cylinder head's squish band to maintain the proper piston-to-head clearance of 1mm.

Next, use epoxy to re-shape and narrow the two rear transfer ports. The width of each rear transfer port should be 14mms, and they should be aimed directly at each other. This will improve the gas flow between 3,000 and 8,000 rpm and make the engine pull strong in the midrange. You won't have to fan the clutch with this little tractor!

Cylinder Interchange

The cylinders of the 1993 and 1994 models interchange. The 1993 cylinder is best for high rpm because of the size of the transfer and exhaust ports. Also, the exhaust duct on those cylinders is round instead of the smaller oval diameter of the 1994 cylinders. The 1994 cylinder is best for low-range to midrange, plus there is greater sealing surface for the piston and rings, so they last longer. The cylinder heads do not interchange because of flat versus domed pistons and water spigot positions of the different model years of KX125s. The 1995 KX125 cylinder will not interchange with earlier models because the center wedge exhaust valves are thicker.

Hi-Rpm Motocross Powerband 1994–96 KX125

The biggest improvement you can make in the top-end power of the 1994–96 KX is to switch to some engine parts from the 1993 KX. Parts such as the intake system will enable the 1994–96 models to rev to 12,500 rpm. The 1995 model needs different power valve governor parts because that year's design was faulty and prevented the KIPS valves from opening fully. Here are some tips on modifying the KX125s for more top end.

Carburetor

Use a 38mm Keihin PWK. The carb's air-boot spigot will need to be turned down and cut shorter to fit into the 1994–96 air boot. The 1994 model uses a small-body (35mm) Keihin PWK carb, and it can be bored to a maximum of 37mm.

Intake System

The reed valve from the 1993 KX is designed for better flow at high rpm, much better than the four-petal reed valve introduced in 1994. Install the 1993 reed valve and intake manifold (Kawasaki part numbers 12021-1085 and 16065-1246) in later-model KXs. The crankcases will need to be modified to accept the larger reed valve.

Crankcase Mods

The engine must be disassembled to modify the crankcases. It is necessary to remove about 0.080 inch or 2mm from the top and bottom of the reed valve cavity in the crankcases.

Air Box

The side panel ducts must be cut away with a hacksaw to enlarge the air ducts to the air box. You can also remove the clear-plastic splash shield from the front, top edge of the air box; this will also improve air flow.

Cylinder Head Mods

The squish band in the cylinder head is too wide to be revved to 12,800 rpm! Narrow the squish band's width to 5mms using a lathe.

Ignition

The igniter box from the 1996 model should be installed on earlier models because the timing curve is better suited to a high-revved engine.

Power-Valve Governor

The governor is a spring-loaded centrifugal device that controls the KIPS exhaust valve position in relation to engine rpm. When the engine gets to 8,000 rpm, the power-valve governor's steel balls develop enough centrifugal force to overcome the tension of the spring. The 1995 model had a two-stage ramp cup, designed to widen the powerband. Unfortunately the second angle of the ramp cup was too steep, so the governor never fully shifted. This prevented the exhaust valves from opening fully. The 1994 and 1996 models use ramp cup #49111-1051 It's best to switch to that part on the 1995 KX125.

Link Stay Bars

Pro-Circuit makes link stay bars for the 1993–96 bikes. This changes the rear ride height and transfers the weight differently, so the bike turns tighter. Caution: Because of the wide production tolerances on Japanese dirt bikes, you need to check the clearance between the aftermarket stay bars and the swingarm through the total rear-wheel travel. You have to do this with the shock removed and file the stay bars or swingarm if either part contacts the other.

Rear Shock

The original shock compression valving is too stiff. It must be revalved softer. Not only does this mod improve the bike's handling, but it also reduces shock fade. Shock fade is less likely because the velocity of the shock fluid is lowered by revalving the shock for softer/faster compression damping. Enzo Racing in America sells a thick foam bottoming cone and an extended reservoir cap for Kayaba shocks. The foam cone helps prevent the shock from bottoming hard and causing damage to the shock's internal parts. The reservoir cap allows for more oil volume, which will extend the amount of time before the shock fades.

1992 Kawasaki KX125

Flaws: chronic connecting-rod failure, carb bogging, shattered pistons
Fixes: install a Hot Rod kit, change carb jetting, fix crankshaft problem

This model featured a redesigned engine and chassis. As with most first-year bikes, it was plagued with mechanical problems. The following is a guide to fixing the common problems of the 1992 KX125.

Best Value Mods

Engine: 1990 igniter, porting
Suspension: fork springs, better fork bushings

Carb Jetting

Team Green recommends to switch to a 162 main jet and a NORH needle #16009-1707.

Crankshaft

The original connecting rods are sensitive to breakage if the engine is over-revved. The original rods didn't have enough torsional stiffness. Kawasaki later produced a better-quality connecting rod and bearing, but the Hot Rod kit is a better design.

Cylinder and Head

The 1992 model cylinder and head won't interchange with any other models. The best tuning mods are to turn down 0.5mm from the cylinder base and narrow the width of the rear transfer ports with epoxy, to a total width of 16mms. This gives more low-end power and reduces the need to over-rev the engine.

Gearing

Gear up to a 51-tooth sprocket.

Forks

The fork spring rate should be at least 0.38 kilograms. The bushing in the forks that support the piston rod in the top of the damping rod wears out fast and causes a loss of rebound damping. The forks top out fast and hard, often making a clunking noise. The bushings can be replaced with accessory parts. See the cartridge-fork section for information on how to change the bushings.

1990-91 Kawasaki KX125

Flaws: water and air leaks, frame breakage, rough acceleration

Fixes: lap crankcases and epoxy casting imperfections, gusset frame, jet carb

If you could combine the best parts of each of these models you'd have a great bike. The following are some tips on how to prevent mechanical failures and improve performance with Kawasaki parts.

Best Value Mods

Engine: Boyesen RAD valve, carb jetting

Suspension: frame gusseting

Carb Jetting

Stock pilot jet, 1.5 turns out on the air screw, CA6 slide #16025-1164, an N84C needle #16025-1164, stock or one size larger main jet.

Ignition

The igniter box from the 1990 KX125 has a timing curve designed for high rpm, while the 1991 model is designed for an enduro-type of powerband. If your 1991 KX coughs and sputters when you accelerate out of a turn or pops at high rpm, then the 1990 igniter will work best for you. The Mitsubishi

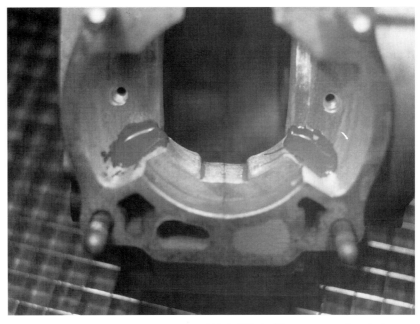

This is a photo of a set of crankcases from a 1990–91 KX125. The gray material applied to each side of the crankcases is epoxy. The crankcases on these models tend to have casting porosity in the front edges of the transfer ports.

stator-plate coils suffer from moisture build-up and break-down. Look to a service company to repair the coils. The best method for insulating the wires to protect them from moisture damage is a process called "wet wrapping." The copper wire is fed through a bath of resin and then wrapped onto the coil. Shoup Enterprises in Colorado specializes in repairing coils.

Ignition Timing

Here is a simple way to fine-tune your ignition timing without buying expensive measuring gauges. Remove the magneto cover from the left side of the engine. Looking directly at the stator plate from the left side of the bike, imagine that the stator plate is a clock. If you turn the stator plate clockwise you will advance the ignition timing. This makes the engine hit hard in the midrange but fall flat on top end. If you turn the stator plate counterclockwise you will retard the ignition timing. This makes the bike smoother in the midrange and rev higher before falling flat. Kawasaki has provided reference marks on the crankcases and the stator plate so you can gauge how far to rotate the stator plate without damaging the engine. Nor-

mally, enduro and Supercross riders prefer to advance the ignition timing and motocross; grass track, and kart racers prefer to retard the ignition timing.

Interchanging Top End Parts

The major difference between the KX125 models from year to year is the piston and head design. Never mismatch pistons and cylinder heads from 1990 and 1991 models. The concave design of the 1990 model offers better performance but suffers from head gasket leaks. The 1991 model used an alignment pin between the cylinder and head. All the 1991 KX parts will fit the 1990 model and offer greatly improved reliability.

Reed Valve

Boyesen's RAD valve makes a big difference on these models because the stock reed valve has too much flow area and a high-rpm peak. The RAD valve gives more torque before coming on the pipe, so the bike gets better traction out of corners. It will also save you money in clutch plates!

Clutch Tips

For best longevity, use steel clutch plates and springs from the KDX 200. EBC and Barnett make accessory clutch

Kawasaki's factory race mechanics at work on Damon Huffman's 1996 KX250. *Joe Bonnello*

Team Kawasaki mechanics prep Damon Huffman's KX250.

1994 KX250 Frame Cracks

Question: I have a 1994 KX250. I'm a heavy rider and I jump my bike high and bottom hard. My bike's frame has developed several small hair-line cracks in areas such as the foot pegs, top shock mount, and the link stay mounts. I've never had the suspension serviced. Would shock revalving help remedy this problem? Does anyone offer a frame repair service for Kawasakis?

Answer: Considering that you are a big guy and rode the wheels off that bike for two seasons, I'd say your KX held up pretty good. When the suspension bottoms, that puts a greater stress on the frame, so factory race teams employ professional fabricators to improve the strength of production frames—and you can, too. Many plates are welded to key areas of the frame to form gussets. The areas of the KX frame to gusset include footpeg mounts, upper shock mounting bracket, and the bottom cradle of frame. TUF Racing can gusset your KX frame.

Regarding the revalving question, yes, your shock could be tuned to prevent the hard-bottoming problem. Be prepared to buy a different shock spring (about $100) to match your riding weight. Since your shock has never been serviced, it will need a new seal pack and perhaps a piston seal (about $75). A professional suspension tuner will require your input to determine the best valving changes to complement your riding style.

♦ KX Chain Slapping

Question: I have a 1992 KX125 and when the chain gets too loose it slaps up against the inside edge of the sub-frame. I'm afraid it's going to wear through and weaken the expensive sub-frame. What can I do to protect the sub-frame from chain wear?

Answer: Go to your local hardware store and buy a short piece (6 inches long by 1/2 inch wide and 1/8th inch thick) of aluminum corner stock. Rivet the aluminum piece to the inside edge of the sub-frame. That way the chain will rub against the aluminum stock rather than your sub-frame. However if the sub-frame is already damaged, don't rely on the aluminum stock to act as a patch. Instead replace the sub-frame with an OEM part or a Pro-Circuit accessory sub-frame.

♦ KX Sloppy Pipe Fit

Question: My KX250 has a lot of oil drooling out from the point where the pipe fits into the cylinder, and when I rev the bike you can see exhaust smoke seeping from the manifold. I've tried sealing it with RTV orange silicone, but it keeps blowing out. I've replaced the O-rings on the exhaust pipe twice. Could the cylinder be worn out, and if so, is there an inexpensive way for me to fix this?

Answer: It is common for the steel exhaust pipe manifold to wear the aluminum spigot on the cylinder, causing the pipe to seal poorly and drool out unburned exhaust gasses. And yes, there is an inexpensive way to fix the problem. Innovation Sports makes a special nonhardening putty sealer that you can wrap around the manifold to improve the seal. The putty withstands the high exhaust gas temperatures and is reusable. This product can be ordered from your local dirt bike dealer through Parts Unlimited or White Brothers distributors.

♦ KX500 Gear Popper

Question: My 1992 KX500 pops out of gear after I shift into third and nail the throttle. I know it's not the way I'm shifting it, because it only happens in third gear.

Answer: Hey pal, transmissions don't last forever, especially on a bike with man-sized power! This is actually a common problem with KX500s. The shift fork that controls the third gear cluster gets worn or slightly bent before the other two shift forks. The reason is you shift up and down past third gear more often than the other gears. Replacing the shift fork requires that the crankcases be split. If the engine has never been rebuilt, then you should at least replace the crankshaft main bearings and the four bearings that support the two gear shafts in the crankcases. Replace the entire set of three shift forks because the others are probably worn out too. The average labor cost from a dealer would between $90 and 150. Parts would be about $250

♦ KX Loose Clutch Parts

Question: I just took apart the clutch on my 1982 KX80, and all the bolts were loose. The center nut that holds the clutch to the main shaft was ready to fall off. I just rebuilt the clutch two weeks ago; how could everything come loose so soon?

Answer: The manufacturer recommends applying a thread-locking agent (such as Loctite blue) to all the nuts and bolts in the clutch. There is a lot of vibration and sudden movements in a clutch, so a worn out clutch will just rattle apart. Sometimes, the center bearing and clutch hubs get deep wear marks in their moving surfaces, and that can also cause a clutch to fail. It's best to have a technician examine your clutch basket, hub, spring length, and the clutch plates' thickness. Change the oil every month of riding, and use a good hypoid gear oil such as Bel Ray or Spectro.

♦ KDX Electrical Problem

Question: My 1989 KDX200 cuts out at high rpm on flat ground or at lower rpm when I try to take a hill. The spark plugs tend to foul quickly too. What could it be?

Answer: The problem might be that the spark plug is too cold of a heat range or the spark plug gap is too large. The higher you rev the engine, the greater the voltage needed to arc across the spark plug's electrode and ground arm. Also whenever the load on the engine is too great (hill climbing) the cylinder pressure increases, thereby raising the required voltage for spark. Electrical components fail with time, but here is a simple way to eliminate the spark plug as the cause of your bike's problem. Use this spark plug and gap; NGK B8ES gapped at .020 inches. Use a feeler gauge to set the gap accurately. If your bike still has problems, you should have a Kawasaki service technician perform an electrical test on the bike. Sometimes it's as simple as a bad kill switch, or it may just need a thorough cleaning and reseal the wire connectors. If the problem is a defective electrical component, such as a black-box or stator coils, then performing an electrical test with the Kawasaki Factory igniter box simulator and a multimeter is the only way to test your bike's electrical system. Proper testing will save you money on trial-and-error replacement of expensive electrical components.

Kawasaki FAQs

kits with excellent materials and stiffer springs. Barnett plates have wider tabs on the fiber plates, so they resist grooving the clutch basket.

Cylinder Mods

The weakness of the 1990 and 1991 cylinders, is the timing of the exhaust and transfer ports. There isn't enough time for the exhaust gasses to depressurize the cylinder before unburnt mixture gasses flow from the transfer ports. The machining procedure that cures this problem is to turn down 0.5mm from the cylinder base, raise the exhaust port to 26mm from the top of the cylinder, and install a #046 head gasket from Kawasaki.

Crankcase Mods

The 1990 and 1991 models suffered from casting flaws in the front corners of the crankcase ports. The casting holes can be plugged by applying epoxy to areas affected. Also, take care when tightening the oil drain plug. The casting on the crankcase, for the drain bolt hole, is very thin. It's easy to crack the plug hole from over tightening the bolt.

Clutch and Shifting Problems 1990–96 (all models)

The following are some ways to improve the clutch performance and ease of shifting.

1. Drill two small-diameter holes into the female splines of the clutch hub, then chamfer the holes with a triangular file. This will improve the oil flow to the metal clutch plates and reduce the galling to the clutch hub. This mod also gives you a better feel when fanning the clutch through the turns.
2. The stamped-steel plates attached to the shift shaft should be thoroughly chamfered and polished. This reduces the friction on the plates so they can slide together easier, making for quicker shifts.
3. File and polish the edges of the shift star that is bolted to the end of the shift drum. The shift star relies on a spring-loaded roller to keep the transmission in gear.

1985–89 Kawasaki KX125

Flaws: lack of low-end power, clutch problems
Fixes: Boyesen reeds, lap crankcases, Barnett plates and springs

The late-1980s KX125s were great bikes, real work horses. Sure they had some problems but what bike doesn't? Here are some tips for improving the longevity of these bikes.

Best Value Mods

Engine: Boyesen reeds, carb jetting
Suspension: Race-Tech Emulator Valve, Excel rims

Air Leaks

Like all Kawasakis they had characteristic air leaks at the crankcases because Kaws don't use center gaskets; instead, they use a nondrying sealer. Lapping the crankcases makes a big difference in low-end power and engine longevity.

Cylinder Mods

The 1986 model was the slowest 125 of that year. Best mods included turning down one millimeter from the cylinder base and machining the head 1mm at the squish band.

Silencer

The silencer core from the 1985 model should also be used on the 1986 model (order Kawasaki part # 49099-1113).

Soft Rims

The 1986 and 1987 models had problems with the front rims cracking at the weld. Replace the stock piece with a Tallon or Excel rim.

1988–89 Kawasaki KX125

The 1988 and 1989 models had a new engine design that featured the concave piston design and multiple transfer ports, along with a new triple-exhaust valve system. This was a great engine design with loads of potential! The 1988 and 1989 models can be improved in the following ways:

Carburetor

The carb's needle-jet primary hood (the half-cylinder-shaped piece sticking up into the venturi) should be filed down 1.5mms. This will make the engine run leaner in the midrange.

All the KX60s and most of the KX models made before 1993 have three oval-shaped casting plugs positioned around the main-bearing housings of the crankcase. Kawasaki recommends applying epoxy (as shown) to the outside of these plugs as a precaution. In rare circumstances, the plugs can leak, causing either an air or oil leak into the pressurized side of the crankcases.

Head Gasket Leaks

The cylinder head on the 1988 model had chronic head-gasket leaks that would eventually cause the piston to crack off at the top ring groove. The solution is to fit the head and cylinder with alignment pins, which came standard on the 1989 model. Another way to fix the head-gasket problem is to drill out the head stay bolt hole larger and install a Nylok nut and two large-diameter washers. The Nylok nut allows you to tighten the head stay bolt to a lower torque value without the bolt falling out. This enables the bolt to flex from the top shock mount forces but not affect the cylinder head.

1993-96 Kawasaki KX250

Flaws: frame breakage, poor low-end power, weak front brake

Fixes: gusset frame, cylinder porting, braking front disc

The 1993 KX was the first year of the new engine. The main difference was the KIPS valve system. A more efficient wedge valve design was adapted because the old system was prone to mechanical failure and excess noise. The new KIPS system would have problems of its own, but it is still the best exhaust valve design for two-stroke engines. The new chassis was narrower and the top shock mount was made integral to the frame. In 1994, Kawasaki changed the steering head angle of the KX250. They changed the rake angle so the bike would turn better at slow speeds. The rear shock valving is generally stiff while the spring is soft for riders over 175 pounds. Here are some of the mods that I recommend for the KX.

Best Value Mods

Engine: cylinder porting, Boyesen RAD valve

Suspension: Braking oversize front disc kit

Cylinder

I recommend raising the sub-exhaust ports to 40mm from the top of the cylinder and transfer port heights to 58mm. The rear transfers will need to be narrowed with epoxy (4mms) and re-angled so they are aimed toward each other. If you are really after the maximum power, consider having the cylin-

Braking USA makes oversize disc brake kits for the front and rear of most Japanese dirt bikes from 1988 to current year models. These kits work especially well on Kawasaki KX250 and 500 models.

der plated to a tighter piston to cylinder wall clearance of 0.0025 inch. The stock clearance runs between 0.004–0.006 inch. The cylinders for the different years of KXs won't interchange. The 1993 and 1994 are similar and the 1995 and newer models are similar. The intake tract is shorter on the 1995 cylinder. The exhaust duct is a smaller diameter and won't fit with the earlier model pipes.

The 1995 cylinder is great for enduro and Supercross but the small exhaust duct limits its top-end potential.

All of these cylinders have casting slag in the Boyesen ports (located between the intake and transfer ports). You can use a rasp file to remove the slag and enlarge the port to the standard casting lines. Enlarging the port too much doesn't benefit performance.

The best option for an oversized piston is the Wiseco 74mm kit which increases engine displacement to 310cc. The kit fits the 1933–96 KX250s and requires modifications to the exhaust valves and cylinder head. Cometic makes a special fiber gasket for this kit.

Cylinder Head

There is no need to turn down the cylinder head of the 1994 model for more compression. Now you can just use the optional thinner head gasket available from Kawasaki (part #11004-1240).

KIPS Valves

Previous model KX250s had a two-piece KIPS actuating rod. The fit between the two pieces was loose and that caused a variance in the KIPS valve range of movement. In 1994, Kawasaki redesigned the rod as one piece. Kawasaki recalled early production models in the United States and installed an upgraded rod. This part fits KX250s 1992 and 1993. Because the KX250 uses a relatively stiff power valve governor spring, the link-plate tends to crack. If your older KX has sluggish performance, check the link-plate. It is located under the right side engine. Another common problem with the KIPS wedge valve was burred corners. The exposed corners of the wedge valve, get heated from the exhaust gasses while striking the flapper plate. This causes the ends of the wedge valve to develop burrs. The burrs limit the travel of the wedge valve. The wedge valve is prevented from closing to the stop so the powerband feels weak on the low end. At high rpm, the wedge valve is prevented from opening fully. That makes the engine run flat at high rpm because the flapper is hanging out in the exhaust gas stream. The wedge valve should be checked when servicing the top end. Grasp the KIPS rack and move it through its travel, opening and closing the exhaust valves.

Frame Breakage

The 1994 model had characteristic frame breakage on the gusset plate for the rear shock mount. That is due to the too stiff high-speed compression valving in the shock. Too much energy is absorbed by the frame instead of the shock. The valving on the 1995 model was softened to fix this problem. To improve the frame, I suggest adding gusset plates to key areas such as the footpeg brackets and the top shock mount.

Chain Roller Problem

The 1994 KX250 has a design flaw in the placement of the upper chain roller. The roller is mounted too close to the air boot. The roller doesn't even free-wheel and when the chain contacts the roller it spins it, causing it to wear away the air boot. Eventually the air boot develops a hole and debris is drawn into the engine causing a seizure. The solution is to turn down the chain roller's outer diameter on a lathe so it can free-wheel.

Big Brakes

Braking offers a special front brake kit for the KXs. This kit was developed for Mike Kiedrowski and Mike LaRocco when they were team mates for Kawasaki. Many other factory race teams use oversize front and rear Braking discs kits. The KX disc is 20mm larger, making it 260mm in diameter. The kit includes a caliper mounting bracket, the disc, and a set of pads. Braking discs are laser cut from stainless steel and textured for a consistent finish.

If you want to improve the front braking power of your old KX and don't want to spend much money, try a WP replacement brake line. These hard plastic lines don't expand like the stock brake line so the brakes feel less spongy and more like a Honda's brakes. Another simple mod to the brakes are stainless steel hex bolt pins for the brake pads. Moose Racing and WER offer these aftermarket brake pins. These items resist forming divots as the brake pads are engaged and released. Stock Kawasaki brake pins tend to form divots that prevent the brake pads from sliding away from the disc. Typical symptoms of this problem are stuck brakes.

Gearing

Switch to a 50-tooth rear sprocket and this bike will pull stronger through the loamy bends and steep uphills. This works on KX250s 1990–95.

Rear Suspension

The rear shock spring is too soft for riders who weigh more than 170 pounds. A 5.2-kilogram spring is the best choice. The compression valving should be changed for softer high-speed compression when you switch to the stiffer spring.

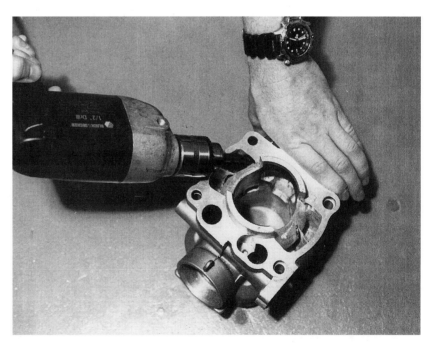

For the 1991 model year, Kawasaki didn't license Eyvind Boyesen's patent on his boost ports, but you can install them in the cylinder. This mod boosts the low- and midrange power. The proper technique for drilling the holes is to start by drilling a pilot hole (1/4-inch diameter), by positioning the drill at a 45-degree angle to the cylinder base and the center line of the cylinder. The maximum diameter of the two boost ports is 3/8 inch/8mm.

1991–92 Kawasaki KX250

Flaws: cylinder wears fast, front end steers slow

Fixes: re-plate the cylinder, Terry triple clamps

These bikes had much-improved frames but different cylinders. The 1991 cylinder needs Boyesen boost ports added to the intake port, for more midrange power. Both cylinders have large intake ports that caused the piston skirts to wear and crack prematurely. Later models had bridged intake ports that solved the piston wear problem. KXs are noted as bikes that handle well at higher speeds. However this makes the bike steer wide in tight slow turns.

Best Value Mods

Engine: Boyesen RAD Valve, KIPS valve mods

Suspension: revalve shock, Terry triple clamps

Steering

The KX fork rake angle is greater than that of a Honda CR. This makes the bike stable at speed but is difficult to turn tightly. Terry Products developed a triple clamp set for the KX, that has a rake angle 2 degrees less than stock. This product works on 1991–93 KX250s. They even make a kit for 1994–95 models, but Kawasaki reduced the rake angle on these frames in production. The Terry Triple Clamp kit requires you to press out the original stem and press the stem into the Terry bottom clamp. This task requires straight jig fixtures and a 20-ton press. Better to trust this job to a professional who has the tools and knowledge. The Terry clamps sell for $250 and the labor is about $50.

Cylinder

I recommend getting the cylinder nickel silicon-carbide plated (Langcourt, US Chrome, or Aptec). There are some options for oversize piston kits. La Sleeve makes a 295cc piston kit and Klemm makes a 310cc kit that includes a sleeve. The 295cc piston can be used in a plated cylinder but the 310cc requires the use of a special sleeve that can only be installed by Klemm.

1990 Kawasaki KX250

Flaws: abrupt powerband, frame breakage

Fixes: lower compression ratio, use shims on engine and shock mounts

This bike was a hard-hitting screamer with an abrupt powerband. The best way to tame it down and get some traction is to clean up the jetting and install a flywheel weight. This was the first

This is a view of the intake side of the cylinder on a 1990 KX250. Most engines with reed valves mounted to the cylinder, have a pair of ports that connect the intake to the right and left transfer ports. The port on the left has been modified for better flow by using a round file. The stock port on the right has rough casting marks.

model with the upside down forks and the perimeter frame. These frames were notorious for cracking near the top shock mounts and the steering head bearing cup.

Best Value Mods

Engine: carb jetting, flywheel weight
Suspension: gusset frame

Carb Jetting

Install these jets in the carb: 6.0 slide and a N87C jet needle. The Boyesen RAD Valve is designed to improve the low-end and midrange power. The compression ratio of the stock engine is too high. It can be lowered by installing the optional thick head gasket available from Kawasaki, or a Cometic fiber gasket.

KIPS Valves

The power valve governor spring tension can be increased by adding two shims next to the spring, Kawasaki part #92026-1238. This will stall the KIPS valves from opening until a higher rpm. Adding a flywheel weight will reduce wheel spin and soften the hit in the midrange.

Flywheel Weight

Adding weight to the flywheel will reduce the wheel spin and soften the abrupt hit in the powerband. If you use a KX250 for DTX or micro sprint racing, don't use a flywheel weight. Flywheel weight put a greater strain on the main bearings on engines that are overrevved.

Ignition Timing

Try retarding the ignition timing. This will reduce the hit in the powerband and make the engine run cooler. Kawasaki makes it easy to change the timing. They scribed marks in the stator plate and a reference mark on the crankcase. Loosen the stator plate mounting bolts and rotate the stator plate counterclockwise to the far mark (about 1mm).

Frame Breakage

That is a big problem on this bike because the top shock mounts were put under a compression load when the top shock bolt was tightened.

The shock mounting plate can be spaced away from the frame with washers to reduce the compression load on the shock bolt. The frames usually broke at the shock mounting plates, bottom motor mounts, and the top steering race in the neck. Gussets could be added to the frame to strengthen it and a weld-on skid plate actually worked the best to hold the frames together. Refer to the chapter on frames for more information on strengthening frames with gussets.

1985-89 Kawasaki KX250 and KX500

Flaws: frame breakage, KIPS valve wear, shock-absorber wear
Fixes: gusset frame, replace KIPS valves, replace shock bushings

Best Value Mods

Engine: thick head gasket, carb t-vents
Suspension: Braking oversize disc brakes, gusset frame

Frame Breakage

Tabs and mounting brackets tend to break away from the frame tubes because these parts were MIG welded on the assembly line. Always have the parts TIG welded and gusseted. Reinforcing the footpeg brackets, engine mounts, top shock mount, and neck are very important. Welding a sheet of 0.6mm stainless steel to the bottom of the frame will act as both a gusset and a skid plate to strengthen and protect the frame.

Shock Problems

Because of strong demand, companies are making seal and bushing kits for the rear shocks. If the shock body has worn out, the best option is to buy a reconditioned Ohlins shock. These shocks are totally rebuildable and have better damping than stock shocks.

Front Forks

Noncartridge forks can be made to work similarly to modern forks with either of these fork kits: Race-Tech's Emulator Valve or Simons Anti-Cavitation kit. The Simons kit is available from Pro-Racing in England.

Brakes

The bolts that support the brake pads tend to develop divot marks with prolonged use. Replace them with WER stainless steel hex-head bolts. A simple way to eliminate the spongy feel of the brakes is to use a White Power hard-plastic brake hose. If the discs are glazed they will make a squealing noise when the brakes are applied. The discs can be resurfaced on a surface grinding machine. Look to a machine shop for this service. Change the brake fluid every three months for best results. Use Motul 300C brake fluid.

Carburetor

If your KX bogs when riding over whoops or when landing from big jumps, fit double vents to the carb as on the 1995 models. There are aftermarket kits or you can get two 1/8-inch-diameter brass T-fittings and hoses from a pet shop. They sell them for aquariums. Route one set of hoses down and one set up under the fuel tank or into the air box. You can improve the low-end power of the 1990 KX250 by installing an N87C needle and a #6 slide.

KIPS Valves

The two drum valves of the KIPS system tend to wear at the drive channels for the center valve. The center valve is steel and the drum valves are just hard-anodized aluminum, so the drum valves wear quicker. When the drum valves wear too much, the center valve remains in the closed position all the time, and that can reduce top-end power.

Check and clean your exhaust valves frequently (see section on exhaust valves for specific instructions) and replace the drum valves periodically.

Crankcase Main Bearings

If your bike has a lot of vibration, the crankshaft's main bearings may be worn, or worse yet, the crankcase races may be oblong shaped. If you disassemble the engine and the main bearings just fall out of the cases, then the races are worn. The bearing races are made of cast iron, and they tend to wear into an oblong shape. It is possible for a machine shop to fit steel races to the crankcases, and this is usually less expensive than buying new crankcases. This problem is common on KX500s.

Gearbox Problems

KX500s that are raced for two or more seasons tend to develop transmission problems. It is characteristic for them to jump out of third gear. The problem is usually caused by rounded engagement dogs on the third gear drive and bent shift forks.

Piston Cracking

The KX500s have problems with pistons cracking at the intake skirt because the stock cylinders wear quickly. This problem is eliminated when the cylinder is plated with Nikasil.

KX250 Compression Ratio

The KX250s have a very high compression ratio. This can lead to a variety of problems, among them, head gasket leaks. Using two head gaskets is a simple way to reduce the compression ratio and the possibility of head gasket leaks.

Reed Petal Breakage

The big bore KXs tend to chip the stock carbon fiber reed petals at the outer corners. This problem can make the engine hard to start, bog at low rpm, and pop at high rpm. The solution is to replace the stock reeds with Boyesen Dual-Stage or Aktive reed petals. They are more durable and increase low-end power.

Clutch Lurching

Kawasaki clutches need stiffer clutch springs. Look to aftermarket companies such as Barnett or EBC for springs. One way to reduce lurching of the clutch is to radius the edge of the clutch actuator rod with a file. This will make it engage smoother. Switching to automatic-transmission fluid will help the clutch work better because these types of oil are designed to work with fiber-to-steel clutch plates.

1990-95 Kawasaki KX500

Flaws: third gear engagement dogs wear, powerband flattens out
Fixes: replace third gear, install thicker head gasket

How do you improve the perfect open bike? It's tough! The only way to improve this bike is too focus on sus-

This is a view of the exhaust port on the KX100 cylinders. I use a cut-off exhaust pipe manifold to mark the inner diameter of the pipe so I can match the exhaust duct to the pipe size. Notice the gross mismatch of the exhaust duct to the manifold. Every KX100 cylinder is restricted like this. Increasing the diameter of the exhaust duct will improve the top-end performance and reduce the piston crown's maximum operating temperature.

This 1990 KX Perimeter frame broke at the rear shock mounting plate holes because the engine and shock mounting plate were not shimmed correctly. Kawasaki makes shims to reduce the clearance between the engine and frame, and shock mounting plates. If you tighten the bolts to squeeze the frame to fit the engine or shock plates, then you are exerting compression forces on the frame which will cause it to break at the mounts. To repair the frame, take it to a professional welder and have a gusset plate TIG welded to the frame and around the mounting tubes.

pension tuning and regular maintenance. Make sure the fork and shock springs are matched to your weight. Use guidelines for setting race sag and determining the proper spring rates as listed in the chapter titled "Baseline Settings." If you want to make your KX500 turn tighter for tracks with many off-camber turns or for enduro riding, then a Terry Kit triple clamp kit will do the job. This triple clamp kit will reduce the steering head angle 2 degrees. The triple clamp was developed by Ty Davis, 1995 National Enduro champ, Baja 1000 winner, and ISDE Gold Medalist.

Best Value Mods

Engine: thicker head gasket
Suspension: proper springs

Transmission

The KX500s have a characteristic problem of developing worn engagement dogs on third gear. The reason this occurs, is because riders often load the engine the hardest while riding in third gear.

Engine Mods

If you want to get a smoother low-end pulling powerband with more over-rev, install two optional thick head gaskets (Part #11004-1186) and an aftermarket exhaust pipe.

1994-96 Kawasaki KX100

Flaws: mismatched ports, soft forks, undercarbureted
Fixes: port cylinder, stiffer springs and base-valve kit, 28mm carb

The KX100 cylinder can be improved greatly. Kawasaki used the stock 80cc cylinder casting and bored and plated it for a larger piston. The problem is, they use a pipe designed for an 80cc engine, and the ports aren't corrected to suit the flow of a larger piston. One simple mod can be performed to the cylinder for better throttle response. Drill two 6mm holes on each side of the intake port into the transfer ports. These are called Boyesen ports, named after the prolific inventor. The KX80 already has them. Also, use a file to widen each exhaust port to a total of 27mm wide (measured with a thin plastic ruler conformed to the bore). Set the height of the exhaust to 24mm from the

top of the cylinder. A simple bolt-on item that gives smoother power with more top-end is a 28mm carb. Both Mikuni and Keihin have carb kits available.

Best Value Mods

Engine: 28mm carb
Suspension: base valve kit

Ported Piston

A boost port can be added to the intake side of the piston; use a KX80 piston as a model for duplication.

Hot Suspension Mods

The big-wheel KX100, introduced to America in 1994, has upside-down cartridge forks. The compression damping of these forks can be greatly improved by installing the compression base valve from the 1992 Yamaha YZ125. Pro racing makes a tuned aftermarket base valve for the KX big-wheel forks.

1990-96 Kawasaki KX80

Flaws: air leaks, connecting rod bearings, lacks low-end power
Fixes: seal casting plugs and lap crankcases, premix ratio to 20:1, cylinder and head machining

The KX performs consistently, handles well, and is reliable. However, many riders complain that the KX80 can't run with an RM80 from corner to corner. That is because the RM has power valves that give the RM80 more low-end torque. The following are some tips on making the KX more competitive with the RM's engine.

Best Value Mods

Engine: 28mm carb
Suspension: Eibach fork springs

Cylinder and Head Mods

The KX80 can be given more low-end and midrange bursting power by turning down the cylinder base on a lathe. This retards the port timing. The stock port timing is too radical for the loamy technical tracks of the Midwest and eastern United States. Turn 0.028 inch or 0.7mm from the base. The cylinder head must also be turned so the deck height from the gasket surface to the start of the squish band is 1mm. The squish angle should be 10 degrees and 5mm wide.

Carburetor

For more top-end power, install a 28mm Keihin PWK carburetor, available from Carb Parts Warehouse.

Crankcases

The crankcases halves are sealed on Kawasakis with a nondrying sealer rather than a paper gasket. As the bike gets older, forces acting on the frame strain the engine mounts and the crankcases, and the crankcases sometimes begin to leak. I recommend lapping the crankcase halves whenever the main bearings are replaced. Kawasaki dealers sell a nondrying gasket sealer called Three Bond #4. It's the same substance as Yamabond, sold at Yamaha dealers. Apply a thin, even coating of the sealer on both sides of the case halves. A business card is a good tool for spreading the sealer evenly across the gasket surface. Let it air dry at 70 degrees Fahrenheit for 10 minutes before assembling the engine.

Another problem affecting the crankcases of KX80s is that the casting plugs vibrate loose. The plugs are positioned around the outside of the main-bearing race. Spread a thin, even layer of epoxy over the plugs to seal them from leaking. Use Duro Master Mend epoxy.

Connecting Rod Bearings

The connecting rod bearing is prone to failure from lack of lubrication. Run a premix ratio of 20:1 and jet the carb accordingly (richer).

Suspension

The 1990s line of KX80s was steadily improved. The forks use a Travel Control Valve, which is similar to Race-Tech's Emulator Valve so there is no need for any expensive mods. Just spring the bike for the rider and change the suspension fluids every 10 races or 20 running hours.

1985-90 Kawasaki KX80 and KX100

Flaws: crankcase air leaks, cylinder wears quickly
Fixes: epoxy and lap cases, electroplate cylinder

Kawasaki struggled for years developing its KX80 into the excellent bike that it became in 1990. Problems with design and materials plagued this model. Common problems included broken frames, crankcase air leaks, and scored cylinders. The frame can be gusseted with mild steel plates at the bottom motor mounts and the steering head. The crankcases can be lapped on a surface lapping plate. It's best to lap the cylinder base surface and the crankcase mating surface. Use Yamabond as a sealer between the crankcases. The cylinders of the older KX80 had a problem of the rings rotating past the ring centering pins and snagging on the rear transfer port edge. The ring centering pins were positioned incorrectly on the piston, too close to the port edge. Wiseco pistons have the pins centered on the bridge between the ports. The standard Kawasaki electrofusion plating wears out quickly. It's best to re-plate the cylinder with Nikasil or ceramasil. If you're looking for more performance from the engine, Boyesen reeds make a big improvement over the stock fiberglass reeds. Also, there is a big mismatch between the exhaust port and the exhaust pipe. I use an old pipe flange as a guide for the grinding tool. This mod works on all KX80s and KX100s through present-day models.

Best Value Mods

Engine: Boyesen reeds, cylinder plating

Suspension: suspension service

1990-96 Kawasaki KX60

Flaws: cylinder ports vary, crankcase plugs leak, forks too soft

Fixes: adjust cylinder ports, epoxy plugs, install Terry fork kit

All KX60s are not created equal! There exist big differences between the cylinders from bike to bike. For example, some bikes have transfer ports positioned too high in the cylinder, and the engine will run flat at high rpm. If the exhaust port is too high and the transfers are too low, the engine will run flat at low to mid rpm. The only way to determine if the cylinder is matched to your application is to measure the port heights of the exhaust and the transfers. Refer to the following section on cylinder porting for actual port dimensions.

This is a view of the intake sleeve of the KX60 cylinder. These channels are ground into the outside of the intake to enable mixture gases to bypass the crankcase and flow directly into the transfer ports. The arrows indicate the flow path. The mixture gases flow for only about 20 degrees of crankshaft rotation, starting from BDC to the point where the transfers close. This mod helps low- to midrange power.

Best Value Mods

Engine: cylinder porting, Boyesen reeds

Suspension: Terry fork kit and stiffer springs

Reeds

There are some simple things you can do to boost the midrange power. One is to install a set of Boyesen dual-stage reeds to help the low- to mid-throttle response.

Cylinder Porting

The KX60 cylinder can be modified to suit a wide variety of riders. The following are some setups for beginner and expert riders.

If you have a good set of files, you can match the exhaust ports to 0.845 inch or 21.5mms, measured from the top of the cylinder. Each exhaust port should be 21mm wide, measured on the circumference of the bore. To change the heights of the transfer ports, you'll need a right-angle die grinder. Set the transfer port heights to 1.265 inches or 32mms, measured from the top of the cylinder. To make crankcase boost ports, use a round file to grind channels in the intake side of the cylinder sleeve. These ports (5mm wide and 3mm deep) will

enable gasses to flow directly through the transfer ports for more midrange power. This procedure can be done for all model years of KX60s.

The setup for low-end porting is more difficult than for top-end porting. The cylinder base must be turned down 0.010 inch or 0.25mm to retard and reduce the exhaust timing and duration. Also, the transfer ports must be modified for lower time-area. This is accomplished by applying epoxy to the rear transfer ports and narrowing them 3mm, measured on the circumference of the bore.

Cylinder Head Mods

I prefer to remove material from the cylinder rather than the head. The head design is difficult to fixture to a lathe. I use an expanding mandrel to hold the cylinder so I can turn down the head-gasket surface or the base-gasket surface of the cylinder. Cylinders modified for top-end power will have 0.010 inch or 0.25mm removed from the top of the cylinder. Cylinders modified for low-end will have the bases turned to retard the exhaust-port timing. The maximum amount of material removed from the cylinder shouldn't exceed 0.010 inch or 0.25mm; otherwise, the piston-to-head clearance will be reduced to the point

Kickstarter Slips

Question: I have a 1990 KDX200. The kickstarter seems to work occasionally. It will kick a few times with compression then kick straight through. What's wrong?

Answer: When you engage the kickstart lever, a spring pushes on a ratcheting gear. Perhaps the spring is broken, or worse, the splines on the kick-start shaft could be stripped. The only way to determine the problem is to remove the right side engine cover and check the kickstart shaft assembly. The assembly has a spring that hooks into a hole in the right crankcase. Unhook the spring and pull the assembly out of the case. Visually check the thin coil spring and the shaft splines for wear. Those parts will just slide off the backside of the shaft. The ratcheting gear and the shaft have tiny dot marks that align together. Make sure they are aligned when you assemble the kick-start shaft.

KDX Hop-Ups

Question: I am trying to improve the power on my 1995 KDX200. I have installed a FMF pipe and silencer, a Boyesen RAD valve and a Wiseco Prolite piston. I would like to gain some bottom and midrange power and more revs. The bike runs like it has a rev limiter. Could you give me some advise on porting specs? My thoughts were to open up the boost ports. Is it possible to open them to much? I'm also considering modifying the head. How high can I increase the compression ratio and still run the bike on pump gas? How much can I raise the KIPS auxiliary exhaust ports?

Answer: You have the right combination of aftermarket products to give the engine a wider powerband. Regarding the flat top-end problem, check the spark arrestor to make sure the packing hasn't blown out of it. Check the exhaust valves too; make sure they aren't carbon-seized. That problem will prevent the valves from opening and choke off the exhaust flow. As far as cylinder porting is concerned, you can match and polish all the sharp edges in the ports, but don't enlarge the boost ports. That will cause a loss of low-end power. Don't attempt to turn-down the cylinder base on a lathe. That model's exhaust valve system is gear driven, and removing material from the cylinder base will change the gear lash. The KDX cylinder head design will run on super unleaded premium, but the KDX engine is sensitive to overheating when you increase the compression too much. Raising the sub exhaust ports 0.020 inches or 0.5mm will give a slight increase in top-end power without losing any low-end power.

Justifying the 240 Kit on the KDX

Question: I am considering installing a 240cc kit in my 1985 KDX200. Who would you recommend to perform this type of work?

Answer: Regarding the 240cc kit for your 1985 KDX, the 240cc kit makes that engine vibrate badly at high rpm because of the greater reciprocating mass (piston assembly). The carburetion becomes erratic at idle, otherwise it makes awesome low- to midrange power. If that's what you're looking for, then go for it!

As far as the method of installation, steel sleeves are an inefficient liner for cylinders. I prefer the method of overboring and electroplating the cylinder, instead of sleeving. That way there are no heat transfer problems and you don't have to spend extra money porting the cylinder because there is no steel sleeve to match.

Langcourt is a motorcycle cylinder electroplating company that electroplates cylinders with nickel and silicon-carbide (about $175). You can buy the Wiseco piston kit and the head gasket from LA Sleeve (about $100), but don't buy the sleeve. You won't need it with plating. You'll have to do some other mods along with overboring the cylinder. The cylinder head will need to be machined for the larger bore size and the chamber volume will need to be adjusted for the corrected compression ratio. The crankcase will need to be modified to accommodate the larger piston, so figure on that labor and parts too. A 36mm carb makes the engine perform better with the larger displacement, so consider that too.

Increasing the displacement of an engine requires attention to other engine components besides the top end. Consider those factors in the total cost when trying to justify the money on such a project.

where the piston could contact the head when the engine warms up to operating temperature.

Pipes

For more top-end overrev, use a tuned pipe such as those from FMF, Pro-Racing, or R&D Racing.

Piston Port

Drill a 6mm hole in the intake side of the piston, centered between the ring alignment pins and just below the bottom ring groove. This will help the top-end power.

Carburetor

The stock carb is too small for expert riders who need top-end power. The KX80 carb (26mm on 1990–96 models) fits into the intake and air boots of the KX60. This carb needs only minor jetting changes to adapt to the KX60.

Primary Gear Sets

Install the clutch basket and crank gear from a 1985 KX80 (Kawasaki part numbers 13095-1052, 13097-1042). These parts change the primary gear ratio so the engine has quicker response.

Crankcases

The crankcases have three casting plugs positioned around the main bearings. Occasionally, these plugs leak, so it's best to smear some epoxy over the plugs from the outside of the crankcases. Photos in an earlier section demonstrate how the epoxy is applied to the casting plugs.

Forks

If you are a relatively large rider or are aggressive with the front brake, you should switch to the optional stiff fork springs (Kawasaki part number 44026-1175) to reduce front-end diving. Terry Kit makes a long-travel fork kit for the KX60 that increases the travel 1 inch. The kit is a bargain at $80 and makes the KX60 forks more plush and responsive to square-edged bumps.

Aftermarket Shock

Pro-Racing in England makes the best aftermarket rear shock for the KX60. The shock is fully adjustable and comes with a reservoir. There are different spring rates available too.

The 1996 factory Kawasaki KX250 in front of the team's monstrous semi rig. *Joe Bonnello*

1983–96 Kawasaki KDX200
By Jeff Fredette

Author's note: Jeff Fredette is a veteran enduro rider who has raced the ISDE 16 times. He's finished all 16 times and scored 10 Gold medals, 5 Silver medals and 1 Bronze medal. Jeff's company, Fredette Racing Products, specializes in Kawasaki KDX 200 models. Jeff offers a wide range of parts, accessories, and high-performance services. Jeff answers tech questions over the phone, and these are the answers to the most popular topics.

Front Suspension
1983–85

Use the stock fork springs for riders up to 180 pounds. Over that weight use 0.32-kilogram springs with 5-weight oil and a fork oil level of 5.5 inches measured with the springs out and the forks bottomed.

1986–88

The best fork oil weight to run is 7.5 (mix 5 and 10 Wt. 50/50). Run an oil level of between 4.75 to 5.5 inches. The forks are characteristically harsh on small rocks and for the best performance they need to be revalved. The use of progressive rate fork springs is recommended on all models for heavier riders (over 170 pounds). The stock fork springs sag over time. The maximum distance that the forks should sag under the bike's own weight is 3/4 inch.

1989–93

These forks are a little soft. Switching to stiffer springs makes a big improvement. For riders who weigh up to 170 pounds, we recommend 0.33-kilogram springs from the 1988 KDX. For heavier riders we recommend progressive springs 18 to 26 pounds. Try setting the compression adjusters 6 to 11 clickers out. If that still isn't to your liking, I offer revalving for the forks.

1995–96

The stock forks are sprung and valved for a 130-pound rider. For riders between 140 and 190 pounds, switch to 21-pound spring, riders over 200 pounds should use 23-pound springs. Set the oil level to 100mm and the compression adjuster to between 10 and 18 clicks out. The Race-Tech Gold Valve kit works well with my shim placement specs.

Rear Suspension
1983–85 KDX

I use the stock spring and set the damper to position #2 for fast riding such as whoops and position #3 for slower riding over rocks. I set the sag to 1/2 inch unladen (the bike's own weight only) for rider under 175 pounds and 1/4 inch for riders over 175 pounds.

1986–88

I used the stock shock valving with good results. The settings that worked best were: 1/2 inch unladen sag for most riders and no sag for riders over 200 pounds. Compression damping settings were best at 3 clicks out for fast whooped out courses and 12 clicks out for tight woods and slow riding over rocks. Run the rebound adjuster at 2.5 turns out. Have the shock oil changed frequently (every 1,000 miles) to prevent shock shaft wear.

1989–93

The stock spring and shock valving is good if dialed-in properly. Start with a fresh oil change. Set the sag to 3.75 inches (with rider and fuel tank full). Set the compression clicker to 6 for fast terrain and 10 for slow terrain. Set the rebound clicker to 8 for fast terrain and 12 for slow terrain.

1994–96

The stock spring and shock valving work well for riders who weigh 170 to 200 pounds. If you are lighter or heavier than that, you would benefit from a different spring. Lighter riders should use a 4.8-kilogram springs and heavier riders should use a 5.2-kilogram spring. When you ride on fast terrain, set the compression adjuster to 8 clicks out, set it to 16 clicks for slow terrain. Set the rebound adjuster in the same way, more damping at higher speeds.

Engine Performance
1983–85

The stock pipe works best with an Answer products SA silencer. The cylinder ports should be cleaned and matched and the carburetor jetting should be as follows: 1983, 150 main jet; 1984–85, 35 pilot jet and a 280 main jet.

1986–88 KDX

The biggest improvement in performance is had by changing the silencer. The Answer SA Pro works well with an FMF pipe. Cylinder porting (clean casting and match port heights) will tame the hard-hitting powerband and give more low and top end. Carburetor jetting is as follows: 1986–87 models, 30 pilot jet, p-2 needle clip position, 330 main jet; 1988 model, 48 pilot jet, p-3 needle

clip position, 155 main jet. When performing a top-end rebuild, the factory service manual doesn't explain the KIPS valve timing procedure. The dot marks on the drum valves align with the ring mark on the actuator rod (rack). To check your work, when the actuator rod is pulled out to the stop, the valves should be open and when pushed in the valves should be closed.

1989–94

These modifications work best to improve the powerband over the entire rev range: FMF pipe and a straight-through silencer, Boyesen RAD Valve, cylinder porting. Carburetor jetting: 48 pilot jet, 1173 needle in the middle clip position, 158 main jet, and turn the air screw to 1.5 turns out.

1995–96

The 1995 model was the first year for the new KX style exhaust valve system. The new design utilizes a wedge valve for the main exhaust port. This design enables better control of the effective stroke and compression ratio over a wider rpm band. The best mod is a FMF pipe. A silencer would be the next best choice. If you can run a straight-through silencer, use the FMF. If you need to run a spark arrestor, use an FMF or an Acerbis 035. The next mod you consider should be cylinder porting. The cylinder needs the casting marks smoothened and polished for more power throughout the band, especially on top end. A Boyesen RAD valve gives a modest gain in performance. If you are having problems with clutch slippage, switch to stiffer clutch springs—Kawasaki OEM #92144-1484. Run the trans oil level on the high side of the sight window. That will also help reduce the noise from the clutch side of the engine.

General Tips
1983–85

The clutch basket nut and crank gear nut are likely to come loose. It is best to apply a thread locking agent such as Red Loctite to the threads and check them for tightness periodically. Keep the ignition clean and dry. Condensation can cause coil break-down. Shoup Enterprises in Colorado can rewind the Mitsubishi stator plates for the fraction of the cost of a new replacement. Make sure

you Loctite the kickstand bolt! The rock screen on the headlight makes a great headlight lens cover. Just bend the tabs to remount over the lens.

1986–88

The rear brakes need more return spring action. This can be done with a conduit connector attached to the brake cam bolt with the "C" of the conduit connector facing the rear. Take an old inner tube and make some rubber bands from it. Run them toward the swingarm and tap a bolt in the swingarm to anchor the rubber bands. Kawasaki brake shoes last the longest. Disc brake conversion kits can be had for about $400 from Fred-dette Racing.

1989–94

Loctite the left footpeg, kickstand, and kickstarter nuts, and the odometer reset knob screw. These are costly parts to replace if you lose them! To cut the handlebars down, use a pipe cutter. That will enable you to remove the end plugs easier. Flush and replace the brake fluid monthly with Dot 4 brake fluid to prevent brake fade.

1990–96 Suzuki RM125

Flaws: nylon reeds crack, air box leaks
Fixes: carbon fiber reeds, seal the air box

The RM125 went through some big changes in the early 1990s. The 1989–92 models are similar in that they have the same generation engine and chassis. The 1993 model featured the redesigned frame, inspired by the testing done by Donnie Schmit and Stefan Everts when they won world championships in the early 1990s. The 1993 model handled better through whoops sections, and when the Twin Chamber forks were introduced in 1994, it made the Suzuki the best handling 125. The 1993 cylinder featured the new sub-exhaust ports. The port timing on these new style cylinders have too much transfer port time area, so the powerband is flat in the low end and hits hard when the exhaust valves open at 8,000 rpm. Here are some tips on improving the RMs.

All the late model 125cc dirt bikes use case-reed induction, meaning that the intake port is located in the crankcases. These types of designs can benefit from crankcase porting. The intake ports that lead up into the transfer ports should be widened and angled up.

Best Value Mods

Engine: carbon fiber reeds, cylinder mods

Suspension: shock revalving

Suspension

The suspension on the RMs is very good. The rear shock, however, needs more rebound damping. This can be improved with revalving or with an aftermarket piston and valve kit such as one from Pro-Action.

Ignition

The new digital ignition system on the 1994–96 models will fit on the 1991–93 models. It must be used as a set (stator and igniter box). The old style ignition suffers from high rpm misfiring over 12,000 rpm, which builds heat and eventually overheats the igniter box.

Intake System

The old style nylon reeds were prone to cracking. They need to be checked. The new carbon fiber reeds help the top-end overrev. Aftermarket carbon fiber reeds are good replacements for the 1990–93 reed valves. The air box doesn't seal very well at the junction of the boot and the box. Reseal this junction with weatherstrip adhesive.

Cylinder and Head Mods

The engine has a similar powerband to the other 125s. It can be modified for powerband more low end with a hard midrange burst from 3,000 to 9,800 rpm or for a strong-pulling upper midrange with more peak horsepower from 8,800 to 12,500 rpm. The first powerband is ideally suited for Supercross, intermediate motocross, or enduro racing. The second powerband is for top experts only! Here are some guidelines for building each engine.

Clutch Problems with 1993–96 RM125

Heavy clutch action with a low trans oil level will make the clutch cover wear out at the bushing where the actuating lever seats. This allows the actuating lever to wobble, causing poor clutch action. The symptoms of a worn cover are dragging, slipping, and difficulties adjusting the lever play. It's impossible to fit a needle bearing to the cover because there isn't enough cover material to fit the bearing. You just have to replace the cover when it wears out.

Low/Mid Powerband

The cylinder base must be turned down 0.032 inch or 0.8mm on a lathe, to reduce the exhaust port duration. Then the transfer ports must be raised to 42mm from the top of the cylinder. The rear transfer ports should be redirected to oppose each other rather than hooking towards the exhaust port.

Hooked ports waste fuel by short circuiting it out the exhaust port before the engine comes on the pipe. Because the cylinder base was turned down, the cylinder head's squish band must be remachined so the piston doesn't contact the head. The distance from the gasket surface to the squish band should be 1.2mm and the squish-band angle (10 degrees) should be matched. Boyesen reeds or a RAD-Valve will match the intake system to the new powerband. Final mod, set the power valve spring tension to one turn clockwise from zero.

Top-End Powerband

The main exhaust port must be raised to 28mm from the top of the cylinder. The two sub exhaust ports must be widened 1mm each. Turn down the cylinder head 0.5mm at the gasket surface. Install a 38mm PJ Keihin carb and start with these jets: 60 slow jet, 5 slide, 1469 needle-middle position, and a 175 main jet. The Messico GP pipe makes 2 horsepower more than the next best pipe. Messico pipe are made in Italy. All of these mods will help the RM produce an honest 36 horsepower at the rear wheel. That is about 6 horsepower more than original with these mods.

ATEV

The 1995 RM125 has a new generation exhaust valve system that features bypass ports that vent gas pressure waves out the exhaust valve chamber. I recommend installing an automotive PCV check valve to prevent water from being drawn up the vent hose. The vent hose is mounted to the upper left side of the cylinder. Insert the PCV valve halfway up the vent hose. This will prevent any debris from being drawn into the cylinder. These new exhaust valves will interchange with older models but they don't offer any advantage.

A Note on the 1996 RM125

The 1996 model used the bypass ports in the exhaust valves just like the 1995 model. The main difference is in the shape of the exhaust valves. In an

▶ RM Clutch Plate Breakage

Question: My 1990 Suzuki RM250 suffers from chronic clutch-plate breakage. What could the problem be?

Answer: The fiber plates on RM250s break when there is too much radial movement between the clutch basket and shaft. There are two main causes of this excess movement: worn bushing and bearing (located between the clutch basket and main shaft), and a loose primary gear. You can check these parts by trying to wiggle the clutch basket while bolted to the shaft. Excess movement indicates that the bushing or bearing is worn. To check the primary gear, remove the clutch basket and try to twist the gear back and forth. The gear is rubber-mounted so it will move slightly, but if it moves a lot, the rubber bushings are probably worn. The only way to fix this problem is to replace the clutch basket.

▶ RMX Gears in an RM

Question: I trail ride a 1992 RM250. I ride on some fast trails and I need a wider fifth gear. Any suggestions?

Answer: You cannot just swap in a RMX fifth gear, unfortunately; the part numbers are different. You could swap the entire trans, but that would be expensive. A-Loop sells drop-in fifth gear sets for about $100 They make these gears for the CR and the RM.

▶ RMX Rebound Adjusters

Question: I rebuilt the forks of my RMX250 forks and one of the rebound adjusters won't thread down; it just keeps turning. What did I do wrong?

Answer: Don't ride your bike until you fix this problem! It is likely that the piston rod was not threaded completely into the fork cap before the jam nut was tightened. The rebound adjuster screw has nothing to stop against. If the jam nut loosens, the piston rod will unthread from the cap and the loose parts will flop around inside the fork tube, causing major internal damage to the fork. Fix this problem a soon as possible! If you don't trust your mechanical abilities, trust the work to a qualified suspension technician.

effort to improve the low-end power of the RM125 cylinder, the new style exhaust valves are oval in shape and have a flat edge that makes them seal closer to the piston. This lengthens the effective stroke and gives the engine better low- to midrange power with a slight sacrifice of top-end power. The cylinder and head mods listed for the 1995 and earlier models work well on the 1996 model too. However, it isn't possible to interchange the 1996 and later cylinders with the 1995 and earlier models.

1985-89 Suzuki RM125

Flaws: chronic piston seizures, ATEV breaks, linkage seizures

Fixes: thick sleeve and Wiseco piston, use 1990 valves in 1989 RM125s, grease bearings

These bike were plagued with all sorts of problems ranging from chronic piston seizures to broken exhaust valves and corroded swingarm and linkage bearings.

Best Value Mods

Engine: Wiseco piston and cylinder sleeve

Suspension: grease linkage frequently

Top End

The cylinders can't be bored past 0.5mm or 0.020 inch; otherwise, the cylinder sleeve becomes too thin and it can't transfer out the heat properly. You must have the cylinder sleeved if you need to bore beyond 0.5mm. The aftermarket sleeves are much thicker than the one in the stock cylinder. Aftermarket sleeves can be overbored as much as 2mm when using Wiseco pistons. RM125s suffer from exhaust valve problems. The old-style drum valves become carbon-seized, so they must be cleaned often. The 1989 and 1990 models crack at the stems causing them to fall into the cylinder bore and crash into the piston.

Crankshaft Seal

The left-side crankcase seals are prone to failure so they should be replaced every 10 engine running hours.

Swingarm

The swingarm bearings and linkage are prone to corrosion, so grease them often.

1996 Suzuki RM250

Flaws: weak suspension linkage, exhaust valve system problems

Fixes: monitor linkage for cracks and lubrication, polish exhaust valves

The 1996 RM250 was *Motocross Action's* Bike of the Year. It was the most improved bike of its class, but every new generation model has its share of problems. The 1996 RMs were delayed because the top shock mounts were welded on to the frames in the wrong position. Soon after the bikes were released, the shock linkage was recalled. Suzuki replaced the original linkage with a new and improved unit. The new unit still requires frequent maintenance and it should be inspected for cracks near the pivot holes. The 1996 engine is a close copy of the Honda CR250 engine, with a 66.4x72 bore and stroke and a cylinder reed valve. The one thing Suzuki couldn't copy was Honda's excellent exhaust valve system. The RM has a center exhaust valve that causes a shock wave in the exhaust port, when the valve is in the high rpm position. This design is also prone to carbon build-up and erratic operation. Some riders complain that this model doesn't have enough top end power, but woods riders favor the excellent low-end to midrange power. Here are some tips for improving the 1996 RM250.

Best Value Mods

Engine: cylinder porting

Suspension: shock revalving

Suspension

The rear shock can be improved by having a suspension technician revalve it for less low- speed rebound damping and more high-speed compression damping.

Engine

The compression ratio is too high and the exhaust port doesn't have enough port-time-area. The subexhaust ports should be raised to 39mm, measured from the top of the cylinder. That will reduce the compression ratio and increase the time-area of the exhaust for more top-end power.

Exhaust Valve System

The exhaust valve system has a number of problems. The center valve doesn't fully recede into the roof of the port, leaving the flat edge of the valve exposed to the exhaust stream. This causes a shock wave that reduces the top-end power. It is possible to radius the bottom edge of the valve to improve the top-end power but with a sacrifice of low-end power. Another common problem is carbon build-up on the actuating rod that links the side drum valves to the center valve. The rod is exposed the exhaust stream on each side of the center valve. This exhaust valve system requires frequent cleaning. You can polish the sharp edges of the valves, in order to reduce the friction, but take care not to remove the brown colored hard anodized coating that protects the valves. Over time the center valve will become so worn at opposing corners that it will be prone to jamming in one position. Suzuki designed a stiff return spring for this new valve system. The spring, located behind the indexing knob on the right side of the cylinder, should be set to turn clockwise from zero tension.

Clutch

The 1996 RM has chronic clutch problems that can be traced to weak designs of the pressure plate and the clutch plates. FMF makes an aftermarket replacement pressure plate for $200. It's much stronger than the stock plate and reduces the dragging/slipping problem. The best clutch plates are the original 1996 KX250 steel and fiber plates. They are nearly the same dimension as the RM plates, but they are of a superior design.

1993-95 Suzuki RM250

Flaws: rich carb jetting, front end dives, clutch plates break

Fixes: lean jetting, revalve rear shock and shorten, install Barnett or 1996 KX250 clutch plates and FMF aftermarket pressure plate

Suzuki changed the crankcases and added more flywheel weight in an effort to reduce the hard hitting midrange. The cylinder hasn't changed since 1992. This cylinder has such large transfer ports that it can't pull the extra flywheel weight and this makes the bike seem as if it has no low-end power. In 1995 Suzuki redesigned

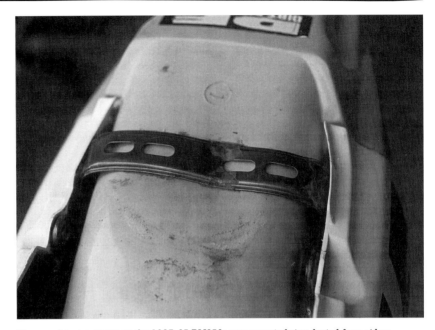

The rear frame support on the 1993-95 RM250s are prone to being dented from riders impacting the rear of the seat. Its best to reinforce this area of the frame support with a flat plate of mild steel with a thickness of 1/8 inch.

The rear shock of the 1993-95 RM250s have too much travel which makes the front end prone to diving in turns. Some tuners insert a 7mm long plastic spacer in between the seal pack and the bottoming washer of the rear shock's damper assembly. This limits the shock travel and changes the weight bias of the bike to be more balanced and less prone to front-end diving.

the exhaust valve system to use bypass ports in an effort to gain low-end power. In 1996 Suzuki changed the entire engine design to one that was very close to the current model Honda CR250. The bore and stroke was changed to 66.4×72mm. The cylinder was changed to the old reed valve in the cylinder design used in 1988. A new exhaust valve system was employed, but it is prone to carbon seizing. Also this exhaust valve design hinders the top-end power potential of this model. Here are some things you can do to tune the RM.

Best Value Mods

Engine: aftermarket silencer, cylinder porting

Suspension: revalve and shorten shock, stiffer fork springs

Intake System

Because of the angle of the stock reed valve, the reed petals tend to flutter badly at about 7,000 rpm. Replacing the petals with ones made of carbon fiber will help. The carb jetting is a bit too rich. I've had the best luck with a Honda CR needle #R1368N with the clip in the middle position, and a 185 main jet. This needle is leaner than stock and the main jet is richer. Combine this with an NGK BP7EV spark plug and your RM will run smoother and crisper through the rev range. The stock air box is prone to water seepage. The air box should be sealed at the seams with duct tape.

Silencer

The original Suzuki silencer is poorly designed. Changing to an aftermarket silencer will dramatically improve the power over the full rev range.

Cylinder Porting

If you want a strong pulling powerband with more low-end and a smoother midrange with loads more top-end over-rev, then the cylinder has to be ported. The exhaust port must be raised to 37mm from the top of the cylinder and widened 2mm on the outer edge of each exhaust port The transfer ports are too large and that makes the stock RM flat at low rpm (under 4,000 rpm). Narrow the set of rear transfers 6mm (each port) at the back corner angles, and direct the ports to flow straight across at each other. This procedure must be done with epoxy since it is nearly impossible to fill the ports with molten aluminum during TIG welding.

Exhaust Valve Precautions

The two most common mistakes made with Suzuki's ATEV exhaust valve system are turning the spring preload knob too far clockwise, which puts too much tension on the valves and then they won't open at all (maximum preload is 1.5 turns clockwise from zero preload), and installing the right-side shaft spring in a crisscross position (that spring is designed so the spring tabs are parallel to each other).

1995 Exhaust Valve System

This system features bypass holes drilled in the exhaust valves. The exhaust gases are allowed to enter the chamber cover and provide resonance. However, there is a serious design flaw. This chamber is vented to the atmosphere, allowing hot exhaust gases to escape out the black rubber vent hose fastened to the left side of the cylinder. The pressure waves present in the exhaust gases travel to the end of the tube and reflect back into the cylinder, drawing cold air and debris into the cylinder. It's best to block the vent tube with a bolt, tapped into the cylinder casting. There is a tube on the right side of the cylinder to vent excess transmission oil gasses and water condensation. I recommend installing an automotive PCV valve. Make sure the PCV valve has hose ends of 1/4 inch. Connect the PCV valve in the middle of the left side vent hose. The PCV valve is a one-way valve. Position the PCV valve so the flow is outward. This will prevent debris from being drawn up the hose and into the engine.

Trans Oil Filling

Suzukis tend to lose trans oil from the countershaft seal or it leaks into the crankcases through the right side crankshaft seal and is combusted in the engine. You can tell when the seal is blown because the exhaust pipe will billow out white smoke, spark plugs will be fouled, and oil will drip from the pipe. Install 1,000cc of oil in the transmission and change it every 10 engine running hours.

Rear Frame Support

The support bar that bridges the rear frame tubes is vulnerable to being dented by the seat base when a rider lands hard from a jump. The frame support bar should be reinforced by welding a piece of steel flat stock on top of the existing support.

Rear Suspension

The rear shock has too much travel and that causes the weight bias to transfer forward. The common solution employed by suspension tuners is to shorten the shock travel. The shock travel can be shortened by inserting shims (8mm in total thickness) between the shock seal assembly and the bottoming plate. Of course, the shock must be disassembled to do this mod and you should entrust this work to a skilled suspension tuner.

Gearing

The rear sprocket should be changed to a 50-tooth. Check the sprocket bolts frequently because they are prone to vibrating loose.

1990-92 Suzuki RM250

Flaws: clutch problems, rich jetting, loose primary gear bolt

Fixes: replace needle bearing, leaner slide, replace bolt

These were fairly reliable bikes in their time. They have good suspension components that can be greatly improved with revalving. The forks need stiffer springs and the compression valving must be softened. The rear shock needs more rebound damping and that has always been a characteristic problem with Suzukis. The engines had some chronic problems such as clutch failures, leaky seals, and piston failures. Suzuki has redesigned these OEM parts for better reliability.

Best Value Mods

Engine: install a 4.5 slide in the carb, Boyesen RAD Valve

Suspension: soften fork compression, install 0.41-kilogram fork springs

Carb Jetting

The carb jetting is too rich. I recommend using a #40 pilot jet, 4.5 slide, position three on the needle, and a 320 main jet. Install a NGK BP7ES spark plug or the equivalent heat range in another brand of plug.

Silencer Mods

Shorten the silencer 50mm to improve the power throughout the rev range. This is easy to do on RMs because it is a straight silencer. Mark 50mmz from the end of the silencer body (not the end cap). With the silencer assembled, use a hacksaw to cut the silencer. Then grind off the rivets from the end cap. Pack the silencer with new packing material

(Silent Sport packing) and put the end cap on the body. Mark the holes for the rivets and drill three new rivet holes in the silencer body. Then install new rivets.

Chronic Clutch Problems

If your RM is having chronic problems of breaking clutch plates the problem might be that the center bushing and needle bearing is worn. This causes the clutch basket to wobble, putting a strain on the steel plates. Barnett clutch kits have wider tabs on the fiber plates and reduce the gouging that occurs in the fingers of the clutch basket.

Cylinder and Head Mods

The main difference between the early and late-model RM250 cylinders is the size of the exhaust port outlet. It is larger on the early models. Suzuki wanted to boost the midrange torque of the later models to they reduced the size of the port, thereby boosting the exhaust gas velocity. That mod is nearly impossible to do on the early model cylinders. However, turning down the cylinder base 1mm will improve power throughout the rev range. The exhaust and transfer ports have the same dimensions as the later model cylinders, so modify the ports as listed in the 1992–95 RM recommendations.

Loose Primary Bolts

The bolt that retains the primary gear on the crankshaft tends to come loose. If the bolt ever comes loose, replace it with one from a 1995 model and apply a thread locking agent to the bolt and torque it to factory specs.

Reed Valve

A Boyesen RAD valve improves the low- to midrange power of the RM250 and is one bolt-on item that is really worth the money.

New Plastic

There is a way to retrofit later model plastic (1993–95) on the first generation of RMs (1989–92). You will have to make a set of brackets to fasten the scoops to the tanks. See the diagram for exact dimensions.

For more top-end performance on the 1987–95 RM250, shorten the rear of the silencer by 2 inches (50mm). I use a piece of tape to mark the saw cut, then carefully use a hacksaw to cut the outer shell evenly around the circumference of the shell. You'll have to file the inner core at the saw cut, then mark and drill the outer shell for new rivet holes. Use rivets to retain the end cap rather than sheet metal screws that are prone to vibrating loose.

1985–89 Suzuki RM250

Flaws: cylinder plating chips, ATEV spring fails, bushings wear

Fixes: electroplate cylinder, replace spring, service bushings

During the late 1980s the RM250 was transformed from a wide, top-heavy trail bike to a sleek racer that carves a tight line. Here are some tips for improving the longevity and performance of the RM250.

The 1987 and 1988 models were very similar and represented a major design change over the 1985 and 1986 models. *Dirt Rider* magazine rated the 1987 RM250 as the best bike of the class. These bikes had conventional cartridge forks and a modern tapered-shim shock-valve design. If you are currently riding a 1987–88 RM250, your bike may have some of these symptoms: front forks rebound too fast, exhaust smoke is excessive, powerband is flat, and spark plugs foul easily.

The 1989 and 1990 models are narrow bikes with low centers of gravity. They featured the original inverted cartridge forks, a case-reed-valve engine, and the new TMX Mikuni carb. These models had a hard-hitting powerband, and the suspension worked well for aggressive riders. Characteristic problems include clutch plate breakage, the transmission pops out of second and third gear, spark plug fouling at low speeds, and rear shock kicking.

Best Value Mods

Engine: cylinder plating
Suspension: Braking oversize disc

Cylinder Plating

The boron-composite cylinder plating material tends to flake on the 1987–89 models. Examine the intake side of the cylinders for wear. The cylinders can be repaired with Nikasil plating from companies such as Langcourt, Nikasil USA, Euro-Tech, or US Chrome.

Exhaust Valve System

The exhaust valves tend to accumulate thick oil deposits that eventually lock the valves in the closed position. When this happens, the engine will run flat at high rpm. Remove the cylinder and clean the valves with oven cleaner, detergent, and water. Manually operate the exhaust valve control lever and make sure the valves move with the lever. There is a spring on the lever, so it can move even if the valves are seized. If the exhaust valve spring tensioner (located on the upper left corner of the cylinder) is turned too far clockwise, then the valves will be sprung in the closed position. If your RM has been overbored and

The Suzuki team used RMs for the motocross, Supercross, and off-road factory racers in 1996. In previous years, highly modified RMXs served the off-road squad. *Joe Bonnello*

has an aftermarket steel sleeve installed in the cylinder, then the exhaust valves must be filed for adequate clearance.

Loose Primary Bolts

The bolt that holds the gear on the right side of the crankshaft tends to vibrate loose. When it backs off the threads, it prevents the exhaust valve governor control from operating the exhaust valves. The best fix is to remove the bolt and clean the bolt and crankshaft threads. Then apply a thread-locking agent such as red Loctite, and torque the bolt to factory specs.

Excessive Spark Plug Fouling

If your RM pumps out exhaust smoke like a mosquito abatement truck and fouls spark plugs, then the right-side crankshaft seal is probably blown. This is a common problem that is cheap and easy to fix. The seal costs about $10. The right-side engine cover and clutch must be removed so you can access the primary gear. The seal is under the primary gear. If you do not have a clutch-holding tool or access to pneumatic impact wrenches, then bring your bike to a mechanic. This is a simple mechanical procedure, but it is dependent on the use of the right tools.

Clutch Plate Breakage

If your RM is breaking clutch plates periodically, then the bushing and needle bearing for the clutch basket may be worn, allowing for excessive axial movement of the clutch. This bushing and bearing should be replaced every two riding seasons. Another cause of clutch-plate breakage is a clutch basket with deep groove marks caused by the fiber plates. When the clutch is disengaged, the plates just stick in the grooves causing the clutch action to be "grabby." Sometimes you can fix the problem by filing down the edges of the grooves in the clutch basket. In most cases you should replace the worn clutch basket as a set with a new bushing and bearing.

Missed Shifts

The 1989–92 RM250s sometimes developed shifting problems from downshifting too often with too great of an engine load. The problem is caused by worn or bent shift forks. The shift forks should be replaced every time the lower end of the engine is rebuilt or every two riding seasons.

Suspension Rebounds Too Quickly

The forks and the shock can slowly develop too fast of rebound damping for the same reason: the bushings are worn out. If the forks make a clanking sound on the upstroke or cause your forearms to pump up severely, then the bushings on the piston rod are so worn that the oil bypasses the piston, thereby reducing the damping effect. The piston-rod seal band and bushing are only available with the repair service from companies such as Pro-Action, White Brothers, Race-Tech, and Scott's.

Bigger Brakes

Oversize brake discs can give a boost in braking power. The front end especially benefits from this mod. A company called Braking makes oversize disc and caliper bracket kits for the front end of the 1989–95 RMs.

Mikuni Carburetor Update

The 1985–88 RM250s had the Mikuni TM carb. Later models had TMX carbs. These carbs do not have an idle adjustment. If you are trail riding and would like the convenience of a bike that idles, then you need a Mikuni TMS carb, available from White Brothers If your RM bogs when landing from big jumps, then add a Boyesen Super Bowl and T-vent kit.

1989–95 Suzuki RMX250 with A-Loop's Pete Dennison

Flaws: weak power, chain guides bend, brakes weak

Fixes: RM top end parts, gusset chain guide tabs, Braking disc

The RMX hasn't changed much over the years. The chassis and suspension have evolved slower than the RM. The main difference between the engine of the RM and RMX is the top end and transmission. The RMX has a superior exhaust valve design but the RM has a better cylinder and head design. The RMX has lower gear ratios for first and second and a higher ratio for fifth gear.

In 1994, Steve Hatch won the AMA National Enduro Championship on an RMX250 modified by A-Loop Racing. Pete Dennison, the president of A-Loop and the founder of Moose Racing, gave the following tips on how to build a championship-winning RMX.

Best Value Mods

Engine: RM cylinder and head, FMF Fat Boy pipe
Suspension: steering damper

Top End

Pete combines the 1994 RM cylinder and head with the RMX exhaust valve system. The RM cylinder has more aggressive port timing and a smaller diameter exhaust port outlet. That boosts the velocity in the exhaust pipe and helps the low-to midrange throttle response. The right side exhaust valve cover from the RM must be used with the RM cylinder. The RM cylinder head seals with O-rings and they are more reliable than the metallic gaskets used on the RMX design. The compression ratio and the turbulence are greater with the RM head. A-Loop modified the cylinder head to compensate for the altitude of the different enduro courses on the national circuit. The coolant system fitting on the RM head is different from the RMX head. A piece of coolant hose, purchased from an auto parts store is all that is needed to adapt the RM head to the RMX radiator.

Carb

A 39.5mm Keihin PWK is the best performing carb for the RMX. It has an idle circuit that makes it more controllable at low throttle openings and the throttle response is smoother.

Pipe

FMF Fat Boy pipe from the RM works well with the RM top-end parts.

Kickstarter

The kickstarter knuckle joint tends to wear prematurely, allowing the kickstarter lever to flop around. Unfortunately there is no aftermarket replacement part. You have to keep the knuckle joint clean and oiled with chain lube.

Brakes

A Braking oversize disc is recommended for the front end. Braking discs are laser cut from stainless steel and offer better longevity and stopping power than OEM discs. Moose Racing hex-head brake pins are more durable than the OEM pins, plus they are easier to remove.

Chain Guide Mods

The chain guide is mounted to the swingarm with straight tabs. There is no support to prevent the tabs from bending inward and guiding the chain off center. Pete recommends butt-welding triangular tabs on the chain guide tabs and the swingarm. Aluminum covers for the guide aren't really effective until the mounting tabs are improved.

1990–96 Suzuki RM80

Flaws: magneto cover leaks, pistons wear fast

Fixes: Boyesen magneto cover, Wiseco Pro-Lite piston

This bike is a great design that suffers from one big problem—poor quality materials used in the engine components. The forks are a little soft, too. Here are some tips on improving the longevity of the RM80.

Best Value Mods

Engine: Boyesen magneto cover
Suspension: Emulator Valve, fork spring preload

Engine

The cylinder bore and the crankshaft bearings wear out quicker than other Japanese dirt bikes. The cylinder uses a steel sleeve that can be rebored to accept oversize piston and rings. Wiseco Pro-Lite forged pistons are much better quality than original cast Suzuki pistons. The connecting rod and main crankshaft bearings need to be changed at least twice per racing season.

Magneto Leaks

Replace the magneto cover with one made of aluminum. This will help seal water out from the generating coils, a common cause of ignition failure. Boyesen Engineering sells aluminum magneto covers for RM80s.

Forks

The forks need stiffer springs but no manufacturer makes springs for the RM80. However, most tuners add 10mm-long aluminum spacers between the fork caps and the springs. Race Tech's Emulator Valve significantly improves the fork damping.

American Bob Moore on his world championship-winning 1994 Chesterfield YZ125.

1994–96 Yamaha YZ125

Flaws: frame tabs crack, chronic coolant leaks,

Fixes: gusset frame, install head alignment pins

This bike is a good design. The exhaust valve system is similar to the RM in that it reduces the volume of the exhaust port and boosts the port velocity at low rpm. This system was refined each model year, to improve performance and reduce the need for maintenance. The 1994 model had some teething problems. Yamaha redesigned the connecting rod and bearing to reduce premature failure. The problem of second gear seizures was remedied in the 1995 model. The frame on the 1995 model was gusseted in several places because the 1994 model developed cracks at the radiator mounts, top shock mount, and foot-pegs. That prob-

lem can be easily corrected with frame gusseting. The YZ cylinder and head need alignment pins because the forces from the head stay can cause chronic coolant leaks. This problem manifests into erosion at the top edge of the cylinder, damaging the Nikasil plating.

The powerband is similar to that of the other 125s, good midrange but falls flat at 10,600 rpm, making 29 horsepower at the rear wheel. Don't believe the exaggerated horsepower claims of some Japanese manufacturers. They all make this same peak power at nearly the same rpm. The YZ has great low to midrange power making it an ideal trail bike. If you want to make your YZ competitive in motocross, you have to do mods to the cylinder and head, plus add a pipe and silencer.

Best Value Mods

Engine: FMF pipe and silencer
Suspension: Eibach fork springs

Shifter Mods

Over the years Yamahas have been criticized as being hard to shift. Polishing the shifting mechanism and drilling oil holes in the clutch hub will help, but the best product on the market is Race Tech's external shifter mechanism. It's fairly expensive but many riders swear by them. This product enhances the leverage ratio of the shift lever.

Forks

The Kayaba forks have great damping but the spring rate is set for a fairly light rider (160 pounds). If you have any problems with headshaking or front-end diving when braking for turns, consider stiffer fork springs.

High-Rpm Powerband

The setup for producing top-end power from the YZ is similar to the other 125s, but much less expensive than the Honda.

Cylinder and Head

The cylinder and head designs of the 1994–96 models are similar, but these specs on the exhaust port and head are applicable to those models. The cylinder transfer ports have the right profile, but the exhaust port needs to be raised and widened for a 12,500 rpm peak. The exhaust port must be raised to 28mm from the top of the cylinder and enlarged 1mm on each side. The head should be machined for a higher compression ratio. If your YZ125 suffers from chronic coolant loss, you should fit alignment pins to the head and cylinder. This will help keep the engine from developing coolant leaks.

Piston Mod

A boost port should be cut out of the intake skirt of the piston. This adds 1 horsepower to the top end. The port should be 10×10mm and centered in the intake skirt, starting 4mm below the ring groove.

Exhaust System

The stock silencer is too restrictive for a high-revving engine. In 1994, World Champ Bob Moore and Motocross Des Nations Champion Paul Malin used FMF pipe and silencers.

Intake System

The intake system is the next component to be modified. You'll need to upgrade to a 38mm carb (Mikuni Jetting: 20 pilot, 4 slide, 63 needle, 360 main jet).

Install carbon fiber reeds (0.5mm thick) or a RAD valve, because the stock reeds start to flutter badly and restrict the intake flow at 11,200 rpm.

Crankcase Porting

This final mod is optional but it makes a significant difference. The crankcases are slightly mismatched to the cylinder, and the transition between the intake port and the crankcase ports can be improved with filing and polishing.

1992–93 Yamaha YZ125

Flaws: flat power, ring pins vibrate out
Fixes: match power valves, Wiseco Pro-Lite
The 1992 and 1993 model cylinders were similar to the 1990 model.

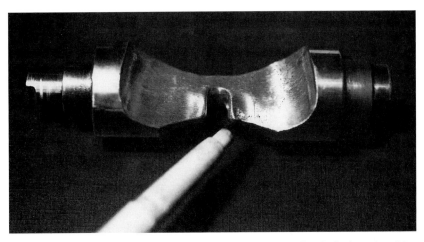

This is a Yamaha power valve. It is critical that this valve be matched to the leading edge of the exhaust port roof when the valve is in the full open position. The degree of mismatch between the valve and port can vary from bike to bike and is based on normal production tolerances.

Best Value Mods

Engine: power valve matching, carb jetting
Suspension: basic servicing

Power Valve Mods

Big gains in performance can be had by matching the power valve to the exhaust port, when the valve is fully open. The power valve governor control is located under the right side engine cover. Installing a ramp-cup and spring from earlier-model YZs can help the midrange power. Yamaha part numbers for these parts are 90501-30742-00 ramp-cup, 3XJ-11912-00 spring.

Piston

A Wiseco piston should be installed because the piston ring alignment pins tend to fall out of the OEM pistons after sustained overrevving of the engine.

Head Mod

The squish band of the cylinder head needs to be narrowed to 6mms, measured from one side of the chamber. This work can be performed on a metal lathe. If you raise the exhaust port, you'll have to reduce the volume of the cylinder head to a total of 9cc.

Cylinder Mods

Recommended cylinder mods include turning down the cylinder base 0.5mm, and raising the exhaust port to 26mm from the top of the cylinder.

The ring locating pin on the YZ125s from 1990-93, tend to vibrate out when the engine is constantly overrevved. Replace the OEM piston with a Wiseco kit for increased longevity.

Apply epoxy to the hook angles of the rear transfer ports. These mods reduce the time-area of the transfer ports and increase the exhaust port. This will help the bike accelerate harder in the midrange with more top-end overrev.

Carb Jetting

Recommended baseline jetting for the 36mm Mikuni carb: 20 pilot jet, 4.5 slide, 56 needle, and a 310 main jet.

Reed Valve

The Boyesen RAD valve works well for overall power gains and Carbontech carbon fiber reeds work well for high-rpm powerbands.

This is the old-style sleeve nut used on the steering stems of YZs made from 1985-94. The sleeve nut is made of aluminum, as is the steering stem. These sleeve nuts tend to fuse to the stems unless you use some type of insulating material on the threads. Use Anti-Seize compound or grease on the threads. If the sleeve nut fuses to the stem, you have to slit it down one side to remove it without damaging the expensive steering stem.

1990-91 Yamaha YZ125

Flaws: weak low-end power (1991 model)

Fixes: change gearing, reeds, and 1990 Power Valve parts

The 1990 top end parts are regarded as the best-tuned components Yamaha ever designed for the YZ125, and the 1991 was notorious as the worst. Where the 1990 engine was great for motocross, the 1991 was had a narrow, hard-to-use powerband (although the 1991 design was the best performing top end for the TZ250 road racer). The weak low-end made 1991 YZ125s slow out of turns. Changing to a lower final drive ratio and installing Boyesen reeds helps a lot. On the 1991 model, it's best to switch to the ramp cup and spring from the 1990 power valve governor. The 1991 model used a two-angle ramp cup that actually works well on the 1992-93 models.

Best Value Mods

Engine: 1991 Model-Boyesen Reeds, 1990 Power Valve Parts, 11-tooth countershaft sprocket

Suspension: basic servicing

Cylinder Interchange

If you have a 1991 model and need to replace the cylinder, consider switching to the 1990 model parts. You'll need to change the cylinder and power valve as a set.

Gearing

Some other simple ways to get more low- to midrange power from either of these models is to use a front sprocket that is one tooth smaller.

Reeds

Boyesen Dual Stage reeds will dramatically improve the YZ's low-end power.

1985-89 Yamaha YZ125

Flaws: weak clutch, engine bogs

Fixes: Barnett clutch, carb jets

The 125s from the late 1980s suffered from drivetrain problems. The clutches didn't get enough oil flow, the clutch springs were too soft, and second gear was prone to breakage. In addition, the Mikuni carb had bogging problems when landing from jumps. The following is an overview of how to fix these bikes.

Best Value Mods

Engine: T-vents for carburetor

Suspension: regular service

Clutch

The clutch is easy to fix. Stiffer clutch springs and better-quality plates such as the ones found in Barnett clutch kits will fix the slipping problem. Polishing the clutch actuating rod helps, too. Yamaha recommends drilling two oil holes (1/16-inch diameter) in each of the female splines of the inner clutch hub. This helps the oil flow, keeping the clutch plates cooler.

Second gear drive and driven gears are prone to breakage. The best precaution is to use the clutch when downshifting and change the transmission oil often. The gear ratios are very wide between first and second gear and these engines don't have much low-end power. If you are having problems bogging the engine out of turns, switch to a 12-tooth countershaft sprocket.

Carburetor

The carb on the 1986-88 models was prone to bogging and starvation problems. Make sure the float level is set parallel to the float bowl base and use these jets as a starting point: 45 pilot, 4 slide, Q-0 needle jet, 290 main jet, and a 3.5 inlet needle and seat. Install the modern T-vent set up.

Reed Valves

The FMF RAM valve works well on YZ125s. Use the short rev plates for more low-end power.

This Devol link has a less progressive linkage ratio and prevents the rear end of the YZs and CRs from chattering while accelerating out of a turn.

1992-96 Yamaha YZ250

Flaws: shock linkage, reeds, detonation, lean jetting (Mikuni carbs)

Fixes: DeVol linkage, Boyesen reeds, #59 Needle and 400 main jet for Mikuni only

This engine and chassis have great potential for improvement. The stock engine has a hard midrange hit but falls flat at high rpm. The stock chassis has a shock linkage system with a high rising rate ratio. This makes the rear end handle harshly when accelerating out of turns. The carb jetting on the models with Mikuni carbs (1994 and earlier) were jetted too lean. The Keihin carb was introduced in 1995 and the standard jetting is very close to optimum. The 1995 model featured an updated exhaust valve system. The new system used a surge chamber for low rpm. This helped soften the midrange hit but the power valve is still susceptible to wearing, as were the earlier models. The 1996 model featured a new chassis with a shock linkage system similar to the DeVol design. The top end was changed too. Yamaha changed the cylinder head design to one with greater piston to head clearance. This mod reduces the need for race gas. Here are some tips on improving the handling and powerband of the YZs.

Best Value Mods

Engine: Boyesen reeds, head mod
Suspension: DeVol linkage

Shock Linkage

DeVol Engineering has developed a rear suspension linkage kit. This kit improves the rear suspension by eliminating the mid-speed damping spiking causes when going in and out of turns. DeVol changed the linkage ratio curve to be more linear. This reduces the shock shaft speed into a range where the stock shock can be adjusted to handle the braking and acceleration bumps that lurk in the bends of a race course!

Intake and Carb

The best products for better engine performance are the Boyesen Superbowl and RAD Valve. The original reed valve peaks and starts to flutter at only about 7,000 rpm. The RAD Valve has a wider flow-range, so it extends the top end. The new float bowl design prevents the fuel from foaming and starving the engine.

Cylinder and Head Mods

The port timing of the original cylinder makes the powerband come on abruptly and fall flat early. Care use of epoxy and a grinding tool could transform the cylinder into a wide, stronger pulling engine, with more top-end potential than any of the other bikes.

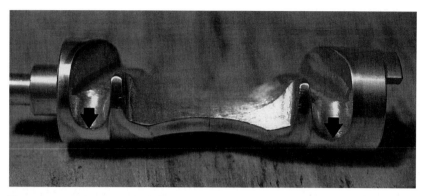

This is a power valve from a YZ/WR250. The arrows on the outer edges denote the modification to the sides of the valve that control the sub exhaust ports. By filing the valve 4mm, you can effectively advance the timing of the sub exhaust ports so they bleed-down the pressure in the cylinder prior to when the main power valve opens. This mod reduces the hit in the midrange of the powerband, and improves traction over slippery surfaces like mud, tree roots, and rocks.

An easy way to extract more top-end from the YZ250 is to grind round the lower side of the oval exhaust port outlet. This will reduce the exhaust gas velocity and improve flow at high rpm. Regarding the porting, the best mod for gaining top end is to raise the sub-exhaust ports to 38mm, measured from the top of the cylinder. The squish velocity rating of the stock head is very high, too high for premium unleaded fuel. The stock engine detonates in the midrange due to the high compression ratio and squish velocity. The solution is to narrow the cylinder head's squish band 9mms, measured from one side of the chamber.

Ignition timing

Set the ignition timing to 0.8mm BTDC. This will eliminate any chance of pinging but unfortunately reduces the midrange hit in the powerband.

Cylinder and Head Mods 1996

The 1996 model cylinder and head have less transfer time area than the previous models. You can adjust the ports to the same specs as the earlier models by raising the transfer ports 1mm. The cylinder head can be turned-down 0.020 inch or 0.5mm on the face.

Power Valve Mod for WR250

Many riders complain that the powerband on the WR is difficult to ride on slippery off-cambers because the power "hits" too hard. Part of the reason is that the power valve snaps open in a narrow rpm band. The power valve timing can be easily changed using a file. To mellow the WR's powerband, you need to file open the subexhaust ports, on the power valve. This will enable those ports to open sooner and slowly bleed-off some of the combustion pressure before the big exhaust port opens. This is the same principle that the 1995 YZ YPVS is based on.

Carb Jetting

The carb jetting for the Mikuni was too lean. The needle and main jet can be richened to a #59 needle and a 400 main jet. This makes the engine rev higher with more power. The Keihin carb used on the 1995 and later models is jetted very close and only needs changes to suit local conditions.

Reeds

The next time you remove the cylinder from your YZ or WR, turn it upside down and look up the rear crankcase boost port. You'll notice that the upper and lower ports are blocked by the reed stop plates. Install a set of Boyesen reeds because they don't require the use of the reed stop plates and that will enable the boost ports to flow as they were intended to.

Clutch Mods

You can make the clutch easier to pull by rounding the edge on the actuating lever. Oil circulation holes can be drilled in each female spline on the clutch hub. I recommend using Cratex rubberized abrasives and an electric drill to polish the splines on the clutch hub. This will make the clutches plates react quicker without generating excess friction. The 1994 Yamaha Wrench Report recommends replacing the thrust washer that fits between the crankcase and the clutch basket with part number 2K7-16154-00-00. This thrust washer is 1mm thinner and will improve the leverage at the handlebar.

Power Valve Governor

In 1994, Yamaha switched to a five-ball ramp from a four-ball ramp in the power valve governor mechanism. This mechanism is located under the right side engine cover. Yamaha recommends switching to the old four-ball ramp because the extra fifth ball makes the power valve open too soon. This effect is beneficial to enduro riders, but motocross riders will notice that the engine is sluggish when shifting from third to fourth gear on uphills. The balls are the same dimension for 1990-94, so all you need to change is the ramp and discard one of the ball bearings. The Yamaha part number is 5X5-11911-01-00 (Retainer).

YZR Long Rod Kit

Yamaha markets a kit that includes a longer connecting rod, a spacer plate for the cylinder, and longer power valve linkage. The long rod yields benefits for engines designed for high rpm. With a longer connecting rod, the piston will accelerate quicker from BDC causing the reeds to open farther. The rod spends more time at TDC, which enables the flame front to spread across the chamber before the piston moves on the down stroke. The spacer plate raises the cylinder to lower the primary compression ratio (increase in the volume of the crankcase) and positions the cylinder for the proper port timing. This kit is intended for expert level motocross and DTX racing. This mod works well with other components such as aggressive porting, 39.5mm carb, and a high-revving pipe.

1991–92 Yamaha YZ250

Flaws: forks rebound fast, rear end kicks, engine pings and detonates

Fixes: replace fork bushings, install DeVol linkage, richen jetting and modify cylinder head

These models don't handle as well as the next generation of YZs but they had good engines with strong low-end power. These bikes are an excellent second-hand bike and can be bought for bargain prices.

The WR250 used engine designs that were a generation behind the YZs (until 1994). Many of the mods and accessory parts recommended for the YZ250 will work well on the WR250.

Best Value Mods

Engine: Boyesen RAD valve
Suspension: stiffer fork springs

Exhaust System

The stock exhaust system doesn't work very well. Pro Circuit makes an excellent pipe and silencer for this bike that improves the power all throughout the rev range.

Intake System

Replace the stock reeds with Boyesen dual-stage reeds and discard the stock reed stops. The reed stops block the rear boost ports.

Forks

Change to a set of 0.41-kilogram Eibach forks springs. If the forks rebound too fast and make a clanking noise, then the piston rod bushings are worn out. That is a common problem. The oil bypasses the rebound piston and flows past the bushing, thereby eliminating most of the damping effect. The bushings must be replaced as a set. They are available from aftermarket companies such as Pro-Action, Race-Tech, and Pro-Circuit.

Rear Suspension

DeVol makes a linkage kit for this bike that will make the older YZs handle almost as well as the 1996 YZ. The rear shock should be revalved in conjunction with the DeVol linkage kit. Check the chrome finish on the shock shaft because they are prone to pealing. Check

This is a view of a YZ/WR head being turned in a lathe. The shiny area shows the modification to the squish band. The squish band is narrowed to 9mm measured from one side of the chamber. The tool angle is set to 25 degrees. This mod reduces the need to run high octane racing fuel and reduces the problem of detonation that can damage the piston and cylinder. This mod works well on the year models of 1990–95 YZ/WR250s.

the bottom of the shock linkage because the links hang so low on a YZ, and they are prone to cracking when the bike is bottomed out.

Cylinder Head Mod

The squish band of the cylinder head is too wide and causes the engine to ping in the midrange. Using a lathe, narrow the squish band to a width of 9mms, measured from one side of the chamber. This mod also helps top-end power and makes it possible for the engine to burn super unleaded premium fuel.

Power Valve Problems

The power valve has a stop-tab on the left side which controls the full open and closed positions of the power valve. The power valve is made of aluminum and the stop plate is made of steel. The aluminum tab wears, allowing the power valve to rotate open and closed too far. When the valve closes too far it contacts the piston and could cause the piston rings to break. Inspect the tab of the power valve; if it has worn more than 1mm, replace it.

Sleeve Nut

The aluminum sleeve nut that retains the top tapered bearing on to the steering stem tends to seize to either the stem or the top clamp. Remove the sleeve nut and apply antiseize or moly paste to the inside and outside of the nut. If the nut is seized on your bike, the best way to remove it is to apply heat with a propane torch and spray penetrating oil on the nut. Caution: Never spray the penetrating oil at the torch because it is a flammable liquid.

1985–90 Yamaha YZ250

Flaws: rod breakage, shift centering gets loose

Fixes: monitor rod clearance, epoxy pin

Yamaha has always had a great 250. Every year the development team focuses their attention on making the bike perform better and last longer. Overall, the YZs are durable bikes. The following is a list of some areas to pay careful attention to.

Best Value Mods

Engine: Boyesen boost ports, Boyesen reeds

Suspension: Emulator Valve, chain buffer

Crankshaft Connecting Rods

Before 1990, the YZ250 had a 130mm-long connecting rod that was prone to breaking 10mm below the small end. This happens when the connecting rod's side clearance is allowed to wear past the manufacturer's service limit. In 1990, Yamaha shortened the rod to 125mm and that fixed the problem. Unfortunately, you can't interchange the rods. Just monitor the rod's side clearance and replace it when it becomes worn.

Boyesen Ports

On the 1985–90 models, there is only one port linking the intake to the transfer ports. On these models, drill an additional hole (1/2 inch diameter) on the opposite side of the existing hole and install Boyesen reeds. The midrange power will be greatly improved.

Shift Centering Pin

On the right side of the crankcase, behind the shift lever, there is a steel pin that is used as a pivot for the shift-shaft spring. The fit of the pin in the cases is loose, and they can fall out, causing the shift lever to flop around. The best fix for this problem is to smear a dab of epoxy on the pin to hold it into the case. Be sure to clean the surfaces first or the epoxy won't adhere.

Noisy Chain Buffers

The chain buffer blocks on the 1988 YZs were made of a hard, durable material. Unfortunately, the chain makes a horrible slapping noise when it hits the buffer block. Switch to the block from the 1989 model. It is made from a softer material.

Clutches

The 1988 YZ had an inferior clutch pressure plate design. Switch to the 1989 part. It has stronger ribs on the backside. The latter part makes it easier to adjust the clutch to prevent dragging and slipping. Stiffer clutch springs will also help.

Some YZ250s have only one boost port on one side of the intake port. On these models you should add another boost port on the opposite side of the intake to balance the flow in the cylinder. These ports affect the low- to midrange power.

Forks

The best mod for the damper rod forks (before 1989) is a Simons Anti-Cavitation kit with vented fork caps or a Race-Tech Emulator valve.

Rear Shock

In the mid-1980s, YZ250s used a component called a B.A.S.S. system. That device was activated by the foot brake through a cable. The cable operated the compression valve of the rear shock. It was designed to adjust the shock damping when riding through whooped-out straights while dragging the rear brake. The B.A.S.S. system required constant adjusting, cleaning, and servicing, and the cable adjuster was prone to corrosion failure. Most suspension technicians disable the B.A.S.S. system when servicing these shocks. Another characteristic problem with the YZ shocks is shock-shaft corrosion. This problem is aggravated by lack of oil-changing service. The shaft starts to turn blue and the chrome peels off the shaft, eventually causing seal failure. Change your shock oil often.

Transmission Problems

Put your YZ up on a stand. With the engine off and the trans in neutral, try to rotate the rear wheel. If it is very difficult and there is a lot of drag, it could be a sign that the bearing that supports the left side of the clutch shaft could be working its way out of the crankcases and rubbing up against second-gear drive. Eventually, the bronze bushing inside the gear will seize to the shaft. Whenever you have the engine apart for new bearings, replace the left-side clutch-shaft bearing and use a sharp drift-rod to stake it to the cases. This will prevent it from sliding out toward the gear.

Electrical Problems

The biggest cause of hard starting is a poor ground at the secondary coil (top coil under fuel tank). Remove the coil and file the frame tabs where the coil mounts. Another common problem is high resistance in the generating coils (coils behind flywheel). The coils can be repaired for half the price of a new stator plate assembly.

1993-96 Yamaha YZ80

Flaws: poor low-end power, non-adjustable forks

Fixes: cylinder and head mods, adjustable base valve

Although the YZ80 is a good bike for expert mini-riders due to an abundance of high-rpm power and good suspension, it has too little low-end and midrange for most riders. The problem is a combination of radical port timing and high gearing. Like most of the minis, the YZ doesn't have the quick response to keep up with the RMs out of turns.

Best Value Mods

Engine: cylinder and head mods
Suspension: base valve kit

Cylinder Mods

Here is a way to get more midrange from the YZ80. Turn down the base of the cylinder 0.028 inch or 0.7mm and remove the same amount from the squish band of the cylinder head. This retards the port timing and reduces the port duration, plus increases the compression ratio.

Intake

Install a set of Boyesen dual-stage reeds.

Gearing

The stock gearing is too high and should be changed to 13/52, for quicker acceleration. Expert riders prefer changing to a larger carb (28mm) for more overrev.

Clutch

Yamaha recommends switching to stiffer clutch springs. The part number is 90501-216A6-00.

Forks

The forks can be improved greatly by installing an adjustable base valve kit. This makes the forks more plush. There are two options for base valves: 1992 YZ125 OEM base valve or a tuned valve from Pro-Racing. The stock fork and shock springs are too soft for most riders. The way to check the spring rate is to set the race sag to 75mm in the rear and check the unladen sag (bike's own weight without rider). If the unladen sag is under 10mm, then you need to install a stiffer shock spring. The front fork sag should be between 20 and 30mm. If the forks sag more than 30mm then you need to install stiffer springs.

1993-96 Yamaha YZ100 Conversion

If you want to convert into a YZ80 into a big wheel 100, it is possible with a combination of aftermarket engine and wheel parts.

Engine Mods

L.A. Sleeve makes a big bore kit for the YZ80. It is sold as a kit that includes the piston, ring, pin, and clips. L.A. Sleeve offers steel sleeves and a range of oversize pistons. The YZ 108cc piston kit is a modified 1987 CR125 piston. You can order the piston kit and base plate then have the cylinder electroplated. That way there is better heat transfer and no additional porting labor is needed. The port time areas of the stock 80cc cylinder are well suited for a 108cc displacement. The cylinder head must be enlarged to 54mm, duplicating the original 10 degree squish angle. The crankcases must also be modified to accept the 54mm piston. On the front side of the cases there are two small V-shaped tabs. They must be ground off so the piston can reach the bottom of the stroke. The part numbers for the L.A. Sleeve piston kit and base plate are W5183PS and BSP-5183. In England, Stan Stephens makes a big bore kit and a billet clutch basket for the late-model YZ80s.

Chassis and Suspension

Tallon Engineering in England makes big wheel kits for the YZ80. The kit includes rims and spokes. The front forks can be made adjustable by installing a base valve from a 1992 YZ125.

◗ Top End Clicking Noise

Question: My 1989 WR250 Yamaha makes a clicking noise from the top end, until about half throttle. Any ideas?

Answer: The powervalve stop tab get worn, from slamming closed thousands of times. This enables the power valve to rotate further closed at low rpm. The clicking noise is probably from the piston rings striking the power valve. Disassemble the top end and look for shiny spots on corresponding areas of the power valve and the piston. You can use a file to relieve the power valve at the shinny area. This will provide a clearance gap so the powervalve does not contact the piston. This same procedure should be performed to YZ and WR cylinders that use steel sleeves, and are overbored for larger pistons.

◗ 1988 YZ Clutch Drags

Question: I have a 1988 YZ250 and the clutch drags badly. There is no happy medium in clutch adjustment. The clutch plates and springs measured up within spec. Can you give me a clue?

Answer: Your bike has a simple problem that is common only to the 1988 model. The clutch's pressure plate is a poor design. The plate is too thin and it is prone to work hardening and cracking. Yamaha redesigned the pressure plate for the 1989 model. So just buy a new pressure plate for the 1989 YZ250 and install it in your bike.

◗ Brown-Stained Tank

Question: The fuel tank on my YZ125 is stained brown. What can I do?

Answer: The problem you describe is fuel fumes that seep through the plastic and out to the surface. Using octane booster will make it worse. In really bad cases, you can wet sand the tank with 400 grit wet-dry sanding paper. Try scrubbing the fuel tank with Soft-Scrub Kitchen Tile Cleaner and a clean white nylon brush. That cleaner leaves a fine white residue. Regarding the finish, forget painting it, that won't stick. Instead, consider a radiator guard and tank graphics kits.

RESOURCES

Resource Guide for the United States

Advanced Sleeve Corp.
8717 East Ave.
Mentor, OH 44060
216-974-0032
Manufacturer of OEM and aftermarket cylinder sleeves for two- and four-stroke engines.

AC Racing
12145 Slauson Ave.
Santa Fe Springs, CA 90670
310-945-2591
Races stands, skid plates, specialty parts for KTM 50 SXR, and more.

Acerbis USA
9402 Wheatlands Ct, #A
Santee, CA 92701
Plastic handguards, SIDI boot distributors, more.

A-Loop Racing
3911 Norwood Dr.
Littleton, CO 80125
303-791-3104
Manufacturer and distributor of weld-on flywheel weights, lighting kits, and off-road accessories. Suspension tuning for off-road and high-altitude engine tuning specialists.

Amp Research
1855 Laguna Canyon Rd.
Laguna Beach, CA 92651
714-497-7525
Design engineering for motorcycle and bicycle suspension products.

A-Ride
1059 E. Gartner Rd.
Naperville, IL 60540
708-369-5592
A suspension tuning specialist.

Andrews Motorsports
251 Goodman RD.
Concord, NC 28027
704-782-6134
Curt Andrews is an engine and suspension tuning specialist. His brother, Mike, runs a series of off-road riding schools.

Applied Racing Products
1115 Industrial Ave.
Escondido, CA 92029
619-743-8190
Manufacturer of specialty hard parts such as clamps for Answer Prolite handle bars, aluminum and titainium bolts, and trick parts for 50cc MX bikes.

Aircone, Inc.
240 Elliott Rd.
Henderson, NV 89015
702-566-1077
Manufacturer of exhaust system parts. Will roll expansion chamber cones based on TSR layout specs.

Barnett
9920 Freeman Ave.
Santa Fe Springs, CA 90670
310-941-1284
Manufacturer/distributor of aftermarket clutch parts.

Bill's Pipes
Norco, CA
909-371-1329
Exhaust system manufacturer.

Bley Usa, Inc.
712 Chase Ave.
Elk Grove, IL 60007
630-437-0671
This company specializes in reconditioning vintage motorcycle for AHRMA racing. Best design and machining facility in the motorcycle industry.

Borelli Dirt Bikes
Mendota, IL 61342
815-539-5091
Garry Borelli offers high-quality low-cost repairs for dirt bikes. Suspension and engine rebuilding are his specialties.

Boyesen Engineering
1555 Krumsville Rd.
Lenhartsville, PA 19534
A manufacturer of reed valves, reed petals, magneto covers, float bowls, and Twin-Air filters. Responsible for many engine and suspension innovations used on modern dirt bikes.

Braking
820 Manhattan Ave.
Manhattan Beach, CA 90266
310-798-4830
A manufacturer and distributor of high-performance brake parts such as stainless steel discs, oversize kits, and Kevlar pads.

Brush Research
213-261-2193
The manufacturer and distributor for Flex-Hones. A product used for cylinder bore deglazing.

Bumpsticks
2450 Johnson Rd.
Huntington, MD 20639
410-535-0625
Repair and modification of engine and suspension components for dirt bikes.

CC Specialty
6035 CC Lane
Lawrenceburg, TN 38464
615-762-6995
Distributes tools for modifying four-stroke cylinder heads and two-stroke cylinders.

Carb Parts Warehouse
7777 Wall St.
Valley View, OH 44125
216-524-1599
Mail-order distributor of Mikuni and Kehin carburetors and parts. Specializes in prejetted oversized carbs for dirt bikes.

Carbontech
61 Capay Circle
San Fransisco, CA 94080
Manufacturer of carbon fiber reed petals and exhaust silencers.

Carrolton Kawasaki
2655 E. Beltline Rd.
Carrolton, TX 75006
214-418-0093
Tim Dreyer is a race mechanic skilled in engine and suspension tuning, plus general dirt bike repairs.

CEET
1220 Liberty Way
Vista, CA 92803
619-599-0115
Manufacturer of seat covers, seat foam, and more.

Cernic Cycle
500 Cooper Ave.
Johnstown, PA 15906
814-539-4114 or 800-ERNIC5
Mail-order retailer of Honda and Suzuki OEM parts. Also sells engines, salvage parts, and riding gear.

Chaparral
555 S. H St.
San Bernadino, CA 92410
909-884-3183
Mail-order company offering discounts on name brand accessories and aftermarket products.

Clean Racing
2980 Mclintock Way, Unit C
Costa Mesa, CA 92628
714-957-3920
Suspension tuning and rebuilding specialists.

Cometic Gasket
8732 East Ave.
Mentor, OH 44060
216-974-1077
Manufacturer of aftermarket engine gasket kits. Also offers small runs of custom gaskets.

CRE Imports
54 Spectacle Pond Terr.
E. Wareham, MA 02538
508-295-0812
Distributor of Italian-made accessories for Honda enduro bikes. Lighting kits, exhaust systems, and big-bore kits for Hondas.

Cycle Gear
303 43rd St.
Richmond, CA 94805
510-412-4327
Mail-order company; aftermarket products.

Cycle Suspension Service
12 Davidson Rd.
Colchester, CT 06415
860-537-4306
Manufacturer of aftermarket suspension accessories.

DeVol Racing
741-D Stevenson
Enumclaw, WA 98022
360-825-2106
Manufacturer of frame guards, glide plates, radiator gaurds, and linkage kits for Hondas and Yamahas.

DG Specialty
1230 La Loma Cir.
Anahiem, CA 92806
Manufacturer of aftermarket performance parts. Offers hop-up parts for vintage MX bikes.

Dirt Bike Specialties
12665 Stephenson Levey Rd.
Burleson, TX 76028
817-478-5680
Kevin Stillwell offers suspension tuning services (see reference in the chapter on revalving).

Dirt Cycles Salvage
508-478-5700
Salvage parts for dirt bikes, available by mail-order.

Dyno Port
1896 Townline Rd.
Union Springs, NY 13160
315-258-5618
Manufacturer of aftermarket exhaust systems. Also offers engine performance services.

E&K Cycle Sales
205 E. Jefferson
Sweet Springs, MO 65351
816-335-4481
Salvage and new parts for Hodaka motorcycles.

Enco
5000 W. Bloomindale Rd.
Chicago, IL 60639
800-860-3400
Mail-order retailer of measuring and machine tools.

Enduro Experts
459-J Pole Bridge Rd.
Cardiff, NJ 08232
Experts in the preparation of enduro bikes.

Engine Trix
260 S. Alma School Rd.
Mesa, AZ 85210
602-964-6270
Repair and stroking of two-stroke crankshafts.

Enzo Racing
17658 San Candelo
Fountain Springs, CA 92708
714-964-8010
Mail-order service and parts for Kayaba suspension.

FMF
25933 Belle Porte
Harbor City, CA 90710
310-539-6884
Manufacturer of exhaust systems, reed valves, and suspension components. Mail-order service for two-stroke cylinders and suspension components.

Factory Connection
10 Crossroads Ind. Pk.
Rochester, NH 03867
603-335-7023
Suspension repair and tuning services.

Factory Pipe
150 Parducci Rd.
Ukiah, CA 95482
707-463-1322
Manufacturer of aftermarket exhaust systems.

Falicon
1115 Old Coahman Rd
Clearwater, FL 34625
813-797-2468
Repair and stroking of crankshafts.

Forward Motion Inc.
639 E. Lincoln Hwy.
Dekalb, IL 60115
815-758-7290
Author Eric Gorr's company, specializing in technical videos, computer design and machining services for motorsports racing engines.

Fox Enterprises
3650 N. 17th St.
St. Charles, IL 60174-1126
630-513-9010
A distributor for Mikuni carbs and parts.

Fox Racing
15850 Concord Circle
Morgan Hill, CA 95037
408-776-8800
Off-road riding gear and apparel, videos, more.

Fredette Racing Products
31745 Dixie Highway
Beecher, IL 60401
708-946-0999
Repair and tuning of Kawasaki KDX and KLX.

Gilbert Engineering
7699 Hilltop
New Tripoli, PA 18066
610-298-3383
Wes Gilbert offers engine-building services to the owners of motorsports vehicles.

Graydon Proline
15935 Minnesota
Paramount, CA 90723
(310) 531-7142
Aluminum sub-frames, more.

H&H Cycle Center
Rd1 Bx568
Osceloa Mills, PA 16666
814-339-6424
Repair and machine shop, parts and accessories, for new and vintage motorcycles.

H&H Worldwide
8820 Bright Star
Douglasville, GA 30134
770-920-1371
Franchised dealer for European motorcycles.

Harbor Freight Tools
3491 Mission Oaks Blvd.
Camarillo, CA 93011-6010
Mail-order company specializing in low-cost measuring and machine tools.

Ico Racing
504-882-3107
Manufacturer of off-road computers.

IMS
6240 Box Spring Blvd.
Riverside, CA 92507
909-653-7720
Hot Rods connecting rod kits, large fuel tanks.

JN Innovations
2415 Radley Ct. #3
Hayward, CA 94545
510-783-5332
Suspension service.

JR Electronics
206-823-4440
OPTAK exhaust gas temp/tachometer gauge.

JT Motorsports
5708 Urbana Pike
Frederick, MD 21701
301-846-4318
Kawasaki and Suzuki dealer.

Japan Motors
741 Yarmouth Rd.
Hyannis, MA 02601
508-778-7211
Specialists in big bore kits for two-stroke dirt bikes.

Klotz
P.O. Box 11343
Fort Wayne, IN 46857
800-242-0489
A refiner of performance fuels and lubricants.

Kustom Kraft
886 Bluff City Blvd.
Elgin, IL 60120
847-697-4343
Cylinder sleeve repair and installation.

L.A. Sleeve
12051 Rivera Rd.
Los Angeles, CA 90670
310-945-7578
A manufacturer and distributor of cylinder sleeves.

Langcourt Ltd.
2080 McMillen
Auburn, AL 36830
334-887-9633
Repair services for electroplated cylinders.

Lightweight Products
144 North Alta Vista Ave.
Monrovia, CA 91016
818-357-2722
Titanium and aluminum fasteners and axles.

Lockhart Racing
991 Calle Negocio
San Clemente, CA 92672
714-498-9090
Oil coolers and carrier racks for dual-sport bikes.

MB Racing
P.O. Box 238
111 S. Main
Orangeville, IL 61060
815-789-4747
Billet triple clamps and other CNC machined parts.

McC. Inc.
518 W. St. Charles Rd.
Villa Park, IL 60181
630-782-2010
Chicago area's finest European motorcycle shop.

MMF Racing
12145 Slauson Ave.
Santa Fe Springs, CA 90670
310-693-9096
A manufacturer of aluminum guards for dirt bikes.

MX Tech
4136 W. 6940 N. Rd.
Bourbonnais, IL 60194
815-939-2196
A suspension repair and tuning specialist.

Mansson Technologies
Pleasanton, CA
510-426-1040
Titanium bolts, nuts, washers, and axles.

Megacycle Cams
90 Mitchell Blvd.
San Rafael, CA 94903
415-472-3195
Manufacturer of camshafts.

Mikuni
8910 Mikuni Ave.
Northridge, CA 91324-3496
West Coast distributor of Mikuni carbs and parts.

Mossbarger Racing
138 S. Cherry St.
Marysville, OH 43040
513-642-2027
A manufacturer of aftermarket reed valves.

Motion Pro
119 Independence Drive
Menlo Park, CA 94025
415-329-0427
Manufacturer of special tools for engine repair.

Moto Italia
123 Water St.
Randolphe ME 04346
207-582-8851
Importer for Italian-made aftermarket products.

Moto Pro
19916 Old Owen Rd.
Monroe, WA 98272
360-793-1398
A Race-Tech franchise specializing in enduro bikes.

Motorcycle Mechanics Institute
2844 W. Deer Valley Rd.
Phoenix, AZ 85027
800-528-7995
Technical school that teaches motorcycle repair.

Motorwerks
128 E. Woodruff
Port Washington, WI 53074
414-284-9661
Custom pipe builder.

Moto Worx
74 Garden St.
Feeding Hills, MA 01030
413-786-0141
Specialist in carb modifications.

Myler's
8414 McDowell Ct.
West Jordan, UT 84088
800-367-7699
Aluminum radiator repair.

NCY
1315 Las Villas Way
Escondido, CA 92606
619-432-9501
Specializes in Yamaha YZ dirt bikes.

Nikasil USA
7932 Armour St.
San Diego, CA 92111
619-560-7139
Repair services for electroplated cylinders.

NIKS
12051 Rivera Rd.
Santa Fe Springs, CA 90670
800-487-6457
NIKS brand connecting rod kits, PRO-X piston kits.

Nine One One MX Shop
13680 N. Redbud Tr.
Buchanan, MI 49107
616-695-4050
Accessory shop located at the Red Bud MX track.

Noleen Racing
16276 Koala Rd.
Adelanto, CA 92301
619-246-5000
Specializing in the tuning of Yamaha YZ dirt bikes.

Northwest Sleeve, Inc.
150-B NE Victory
Gresham, OR 97030
503-666-8430
Repair service for resleeving cylinders.

Onology Engineering Inc.
7917 Silverton Ave.
San Diego, CA 92126
619-578-4688
Manufacturers of aftermarket electrical parts.

PC-1 Racing
Box 730
Orange, CA 92666
Manufacturers of Filter Skins air filter protectors,
Plastic Renew, and Pro Vent carb vent kits.

PPS
4065 Lapalma Unit G
Anaheim, CA 92807
714-630-4777
Suspension tuning. Imports Marzocci and Ohlins.

PVL Ignitions
1115 Milan Ave.
Amherst, OH 44001
216-988-4474
Manufacturer of electrical parts like complete ignition
systems, internal and external rotor flywheels.

PAX Racing
9724 Nagle Ave.
Arieta, CA 91331
818-897-0373
An aftermarket accessory stockist for 50cc autos
and PW50s. Also engine and suspension tuning.

Penske Racing
Box 301
Reading, PA 19603
610-375-6180
Manufacturer of shock absorbers.

Performance Engineering
1333 Pine Ave. Suite B
Orlando, FL 32824
407-856-8545
Specializing in engine and suspension tuning.

Perma-Flex
614-252-8034
Makes blue silicon molding for port modeling.

Powermist
67 Stickles Pond Rd.
Newton, NJ 07860
201-383-1061
Refiner of specialty fuels for two-stroke racing engines.

Pro-Action
3201 6th Ave.
Beaver Falls, PA 15010
412-846-9055 World Headquarters
Specialists in suspension repair and tuning services.

Pro Circuit
4214 E. Lapalma
Anaheim, CA 92807
714-993-5400
Exhaust systems, engine and suspension tuning.

Pro Concept
286 S. Overlook Dr.
San Ramon, CA 94583
510-735-8258
Manufacturer of the Magnum Bottoming System.

Pro Design
11611 Salinaz #C
Garden Grove, CA 92643
714-534-0620
Cylinder heads with interchangable chambers.

Pro Pilot
25 Squire Terrace
Colts Neck, NJ 07722
908-946-8365
An accessory and service shop devoted to dirt bikers.

Pro Source
33W672 Roosevelt Rd.
West Chicago, IL 60185
630-208-7925
Accessory and service shop; sells used bikes.

Pro Spec
411 Riverview Dr.
Walnutport, PA 15088
610-760-9568
Aktive reeds; engine and suspension tuning.

R&D Racing
11419 Bombardier Ave.
Norwalk, CA 90650
310-864-8218
Exhaust systems, engine and suspension tuning.

RPM
24 Woodland Heights
Wales, MA 01081
413-245-3830
Bearing race repair service.

Race Tech
3227 Producer Way
Pomona, CA 91768
909-594-7755
Manufacturer of suspension parts and accessories.
Has over 50 franchised service shops in North
America.

Race Tools
1356 Buffalo Rd.
Rochester, NY 14624
716-529-3750
Manufacturer of special tools for suspension
servicing and tuning.

Radiator Works
17635 Arrow Blvd.
Fontana, CA 92335
800-430-7234
Radiator repair service by mailorder.

Red Cedar Engineering
8304 Holly Drive
Canton, MI 48187
313-416-9498
The most advanced dyno test cell for two-stroke
engine design. Manufacturers of a unique
crankshaft assembly jig.

Rick Peterson Motor Sports
1011 San Bernardino Rd.
Covina, CA 91722
818-967-3052
A specialist in over-boring cylinders and stroking
cranks, for late model dirt bikes.

Ritter Cycle Racing
11202 Ellis Rd.
St. Jacob, IL 62281
618-644-3211
Engine rebuilding services.

Rocket Rex Racing
10001 Choiceana Ave.
Heperia, CA 92345
619-949-4193
Performance tuning services.

Rossini Racing Products
RD#1 Box 106a
Washington, NJ 07882
908-454-8730
Engine and suspension tuning, large accessory
store for dirt bikes.

SAE Society of Automotive Engineers
400 Commonwealth
Warrendale, PA 15096-0001
412-772-7129
Books and research papers on engines.

Scott's Performance
2625 Honolulu Ave.
Montrose, CA 91020
818-248-2453
High-performance services for dirt bike engine and
suspension components. Manufacturer of special
tools for cartridge fork repair. Importer of UNIC
steering dampers.

Shock Therapy
227 N. Brea Blvd.
Brea, CA 92621
714-255-9485
Suspension repair company.

Shoup Enterprises
3172 Glendam Dr.
Grand Junction, CO 81504
303-434-0906
Specialists in rewinding Mitsubishi stator coils.

Sloan's Honda Yamaha
2233 NW Broad St.
Murfreesboro, TN 37129
800-342-1681 ext. 22
A franchised Yamaha and Honda dealer with a
racing support program that includes discounts on
parts, engine rebuilding, and suspension tuning
services. Ask for Jerry Link.

Spectro
Rt. 7
Brookfield, CT 06804
800-243-8645
Petroleum refiners, offers products ranging from
suspension to premix oils.

Stator Pros
12 First St.
Bridgewater, MA 02324
508-285-9652
Specialists in the repair of electrical components.

Steahly Products
9950 SE Bullrun Rd.
Corbett, OR 97019
800-800-2363 U.S. & Canada
503-695-2417 Others
Manufacturer of thread-on flywheel weights, other
off-road accessories.

Stoughton's Cycle Ranch
4406 W. Washington St.
Indianapolis, IN 46241
Mail order accessories from a huge retailer store
featuring AXO, Oakley, Pro-Circuit. They also have a
White Brothers franchise for suspension service.

Supertrapp
4540 W. 160th
Cleveland, OH 44135
216-265-8400
A manufacturer of aftermarket exhaust systems for
four-stroke dirt bikes.

Sudco
3014 Tanager Ave.
Commerce, CA 90040
800-998-3529
A distributor for Nikuni and Kehin carbs and parts.

Swain Tech
35 Amin St.
Scottsville, NY 14546
716-889-2786
A company that applies performance coatings to
engine parts such as pistons, valves, header pipes.

Suspension By Jake
1732 Border Ave.
Torrence, CA 90501
310-787-7818
Showa suspension repair and tuning specialist.
Stockist and retailer of Showa replacement parts.

TSR
8052 E. Rosecrans
Paramount, CA 90723
A two-stroke tuner who developed computer
programs to aid engine tuners in developing precise
changes in engine components.

Tech Care
7754 M-59
Waterford, MI 48327
810-666-4651
A complete dirt bike shop offering parts,
accessories, and suspension and engine service.

Tech Products
201-848-0668
Solid foam tire inserts for off-road bikes.

Terry Cable
17376 Eucalyptus St.
Hesperia, CA 92345
619-244-9351
Manufacturer of products for Kawasaki KX models. Products such as offset triple clamps, double-pumper fork kits, and KX60 long fork rods, as well as cables for all dirt bikes.

Throttle Jockey
4728 E. 100 N.
Kokomo, IN 46902
317-457-5784
A manufacturer of graphics, numbers, and stickers.

Thumper Racing
3441 US Highway 259
Marshall, TX 75670
800-259-5186
A company that offers complete machining services for four-stroke dirt bike engines.

Too Tech Racing
19333 Sturgess Dr.
Torrance, CA 90505
310-371-3887
Rick Johnson, the author of the chapter on suspension forces, offers repair and tuning services to the owners of MX racing bikes.

Torque Center
14666 W. National Ave.
New Berlin, WI 53151
414-786-4420
A large retail and mail-order accessories shop located near Milwaukee.

Trackside Racing
26480 France Ave.
Elko, MN 55020
612-461-2350
A dirt bike accessory and repair shop that offers custom pipe-building and tuning services.

TUF Racing
2727 Sycamore Rd.
Dekalb, IL 60115
815-756-3588
A mail-order OEM parts retailer, UFO and Factory Concepts graphics specialists.

US Chrome
650 Oak Park Ave.
Fondulac, WI 54936-1536
414-922-5066
Specializing in the repair of cylinders with electroplating.

Ultimate Suspension
317 W. Erie
Spring Valley, IL 61362
815-663-1200
Walt Spayer is a suspension tuner who specializes in working interactively with racers on revalving.

UNI Filter
1541 S. Harris Ct.
Anaheim, CA 92806
714-939-6300
Manufacturer of foam air filters.

Upstate Cycle
100 Laurens Rd.
Greenville, SC 29607
864-232-7223
A Husky and ATK shop specializing in performance mods.

VP Engineering
2921 Patricia Ave.
Des Moines, IA 50322
515-276-0701
A manufacturer for Hot Rods connecting rod kits and the publisher of the Dynomation computer design programs.

Velo Rossa Engineering
406-3 S. Rockford Dr.
Tempe, AZ 85281
602-397-4735
A manufacturer of special tools such as a tubing vise that works well for drilling lubrication holes and ports in pistons.

WER
Box 279-A
Great Meadows, NJ 07838
908-637-6385
A manufacturer of steering dampers, specialists in suspension revalving for enduro racing.

Wheel Works
12787 Nutwood
Garden Grove, CA 92640
714-530-6681
Specialists in rims, spokes, tires, and bearings.

White Brothers
24845 Corbit Place
Yorba Linda, CA 92687
714-692-3404
http://www.whitebros.com
A large scale catalog company specializing in off-road parts and accessories.

Wiseco
7201 Industrial Prkwy.
Mentor, OH 44060
216-951-6600
A manufacturer of forged piston kits for all motorsports racing vehicles.

Works Connection
6070 Enterprise Drive
Diamond Springs, CA 95619
916-642-9488
Skid plates, frame guards, and more.

Works Performance
21045 Osborne St.
Canoga Park, CA 91304
818-701-1010
Handcrafted shock absorbers.

XR's Only
6944 E. Santa Fe Ave.
Hesperia, CA 92345
619-244-2626
A specialist in parts and accessories for Honda XR motorcycles.

Z Racing
2350 Orangethorpe
Anaheim, CA 92806
714-449-1374
A specialist in tuning and repair of KTM motorcycles.

United Kingdom Parts Manufacturers and Suppliers

Apico/Vesty Uk
Unit 2c Merrow Business Centre
Merrow Lane
Guildford, Surrey GU4 7WA
01483-450560
Distributors for a line of titanium bolts, frame gaurds, RADZ graphics, and drivetrain kits.

Aptec
Southbrook Road
Gloucester GL4 7DN
0452-300800
Cylinder reconditioning specialists.

B&C Express
Station Rd., Potterhanworth,
Lincoln, LN4 2DX
01522 791369
A parts distributor for many products including Moto-Air filters and PJ-1 products.

Bert Harkins Racing
Unit 6, Townsend Centre, Oughton Regis,
Dunstable, Beds., LU5 5JP
01582-472374
Importer for Acerbis plastic products and Scott goggles.

Bill Brown
High St.
Whitehaven, Cumbria CA28 7PY
01846-692697
Importer for Maico motorcycles and the distributor for Wulfsport riding gear.

Bryan Goss
8 Yeo Valley Business Centre
Newton Road
Stoford, Yeovil BA22 9US
01935-72424
A large scale trade-only parts and accessory distributor.

CDI's 'R' Us
Frances House, 11-15 Frances Ave.
Wallisdown, Bournemouth, BH11-8NX
01202-576699
Specializing in the diagnostic and repair of ignition components.

Cgh Imports Ltd.
88 Mosley St.
Burton - Upon - Trent, Staffordshire DE14 1DT
01283-500450
Importers for Pro-Circuit products and Splitfire spark plugs.

Corby Kawasaki
Courier Rd. Phoenix Pkwy.
Corby, Northants
NN17 5BA
01536-401010
Mail-order Kawasaki parts.

Cradley Kawasaki
St. Annes Rd., Cradley Heath
W. Midlands
01384 633455
Mail-order Kawasaki parts.

Cpk Moto
Gladiator Way, Glebe Farm Estates,
Rugby, CV21 1PX
01788 540606
A distributor for Pirelli tyres, Regina chain, and
Vemar helmets.

DAVE CLARK RACING
HEATH HOUSE, NEW LONGTON, LANCS.
PR4 4YS
01772-612118
Importer of Husaberg motorcycles.

Dep Sport
Buckland Hill
Maidstone, Kent ME16 0SQ
01622-765353
A manufacturer of exhaust systems, bike stands,
and various hardware for dirt bikes. Also offers a
barrel tuning service.

Dirt Wheels
London Road (A45) Ryton On Dunsmore
Coventry, West Midlands CV8 3FW
01203-301852
This company specializes in highly modified KX60
and 80s. They offer custom frame kits, suspension
service, and engine tuning.

Edmondson Racing
Acorn Unit 2, Ring Road
Chasetown Industrial Estate
Chasetown, Nr Walsall, Staffs
WS7 8JQ
0543-677088
Derrick Edmonson offers his expertise in engine
and suspension tuning, and features a powder
coating service for the frames of dirt bikes.

Elbe Moto-X
524 Stoney Stanton Rd.
Coventry
01203 687049
Main stockists for Fox, Renthal, D.I.D., Premier,
Arai. Look for their support vehicle at the British
Championships.

Electrex
Unit44 Vanalloys Bus. Pk.
Stoke Row, Oxfordshire, RG9 5QB
01491-682369
Stator coil repair.

Eurotek
Ripon Business Park
16 Campbell Close
Dailamires Lane
Ripon, North Yorkshire HG4 1QY
01765-608209
Importer for MSR riding gear and a KTM dealer.

Eric Gorr's Forward Motion Racing
639 E. Lincoln Hwy., Dekalb,
Illinois, USA 60115
01018157587290
Barrel tuning, reconditioning with Nikasil, and big
bore kits for two-stroke dirt bikes.

Falcon Shocks
Unit 5 Ryans Bus. Pk.,Stanford Ln.
Wareham, Dorset, BH20 4DY
01929-554545
Twin shock manufacturer and repair specialist.

Gas Gas
Stable Lane
Off Leek Road
Buxton, Derbyshire SK17 6UG
01298-25460
The importer for Gas Gas motorcycles.

Husky Sport
35 Longshot Lane Industrial Estate
Bracknell, Berkshire RG12 1RL
01344-56860
The importer for Husqvarna motorcycles.

Julian Dobb's Performance Workshop
01623 451334
This former pro rider and veteran GP mechanic
makes his experience available to you in the form of
performance tuning services for engine and
suspension components. Julian also offers complete
bike prep and general dirt bike repairs.

Kais Motorcycles
Punchbowl Garage, Atherton,
Manchester, M46 0LT
01942-896366
Mail-order parts and Ohlins service. KTM, Suzuki,
GasGas, RTX, TM dealer.

MD Racing
Unit 3-6, 10 Armourly Rd.
Lufton Trading Est., Yeovil, SOM., BA22 8RL
01935-29646
Importer for FMF exhaust systems and CEET covers
and graphics.

Merlin Books
Po Box 153 Horsham,
Sussex, RH12 2YG
01403 257626
merlinbooks@dial.pipex.com
Free catalog featuring technical information
products like books and videos on all motorcycles.

MH Racing Services
Unit C1 Fiveways Industrial Estate
Westwells Rd., Hawthorn, Wilts. SN13 9RG
01225-811583
This former GP mechanic specializes in Ohlins, WP,
Showa, and Kayaba suspension service. Importer
for Messico and Race-Tech. Specialty services such
as barrel tuning, crank and engine rebuilding/
blueprinting, and titanium nitriding for fork tubes.

Mick Berrill
1-3 Henry St.
Northampton, NN1 4JD
01604-36760
Mail-order accessories.

Mito Uk
105 North Rd.
Parkstone, Poole
01202 741580
A specialy product importer for Fresco exhaust
systems, Tecnosel seats and stickers, and Pro-Grip.

MXB
Wonastow
West Industrial Estate
Monmouth, Gwent,
South Wales NP5 3AH
0600-772211
Specializing in reconditioned salvage parts for dirt
bikes.

Moto Cross Services
148-150 Preston Road
Yeovil, SOMERSET
01935-26481
Stocks of accessories from America and Europe.

Motocross World
19 Arches Business Centre
Mill Road, Rugby CV21 1QW
01788-535207
This company sponsored the winningest schoolboy
team in 1995 and specializes in CR80 and CR100
performance kits.

Moto Vision
P.O. Box 257
Horsham, West Sussex
01403-257984
A video chronicle of the sport of motocross and
stockist of the GP yearbook *MX The Book*.

Moto-X Rivara
29 Hero Walk
Rochester, Kent ME1 2UZ
01634-839764
Parts and accessory stockists for auto 50cc bikes.

Moto-Extreme
High Street, Warmly
Bristol, Avon
01179-600627
A stockist of accessories and tools for dirt bikes.

Multitek Sports
Lancaster Way, Earls Colne Ind. Pk.
Colchester, Essex, CO6 2NS
01787-223228
Importers for SoCal sports wear.

Off-Road Only
Crossgates, Llandrindod, Wells
Powys. LD1 6RB
01597-851273
Mail-order accessories.

Phil Ayliff Products LTD.
25 Alliance Close
Nuneaton, CV11 6SD
01203-641247
Trade distributor for Dunlopads.

Plymouth Off-Road
36-38 Molesworth Rd.
Plymouth, Devon, PL1 5NA
01752-606888
Importer for JD Performance pipes for KTM LC4.
Rally bike preparation specialist. KTM and TM
dealer.

PM Tuning
7 Beech Grove, Hestbank Lane
Nr. Lancaster
Lancs LA2 6JH
0374-160266
Specialists in cylinder repair and tuning. Also
operates a Dynojet dynomometer testing center.

Proline Racing Products
Unit 2 The Cottage
Ullingswick, Hereford HR1 3JG
01432-820179
The trade distributor for MXA seat covers, seat
foam, and graphics.

Pro-Racing
15 Gresley Close Drayton Fields
Daventry, Northants. NN1 5RZ
01327-301322
A full service mail-order shop specializing in engine
and suspension tuning services. Also stocks
accessories like lighting kits, factory pipes, and
Denicol petroleum products.

Pro-Tech
4 Greenslate Ave., Apply Bridge
Nr. Wigan, Lancs., WN6 9LG
01257-254760
Suspension tuning and repair services.

Putoline
Unit 4, Arena Bus. Pk., Roman Bank
Bourne, Lincs., PE10 9LG
01778-394909

Race Spec
Yauncos Cottage Tillers Green
Dymock, Gloucestershire GL 18 2AP
01281-890250
GP racing veteran Dave Watson operates this shop
with services ranging from riding lessons to
suspension service for motorcycles and push bikes,
engine tuning services and accessories, and the
importer for Marzocci forks.

Ray Hockey Motorcycles
The Old Smithy, Lianvapley
Abergavenny, Gwent NP7 8SN
01600-85535
A Yamaha dealer and mail-order accessory
specialist.

Ron Humphreys
12 Eden Way Pages Industrial Park
Leighton Buzzard, Bedfordshire LU7 8TP
01525-384829
A Honda dealer and mail-order accessory specialist.

Rsr Sport
The Mill Queen Street
Barnard Casstle, Co. Durham DL12 8EG
01833-631524
Manufacturers of high-quality riding gear.

RTX
Pinewood Lodge
High St.
South Ferriby, South Humberside DN18 5HY
01469-541983
Manufacturers of inexpensive dirt bikes and
importers of Russian made motorcycle products.

Sammy Miller
Gore Road
New Milton, Hampshire BH25 6TF
01425-616446
A specialist in vintage racing motorcycles; bikes,
parts, and rebuilding services.

Serval Marketing
Icon House, Iceni Ct., Ickfield Way,
Letchworth, Herts. SG6 1TN
Trade distributor or AXO and Boyesen products.

Silkolene
Derby Rd., Belper, Derby, DE56 1WF
Manufacturer and distributor of petroleum products.

Stan Stephens
6 Portobello Parade
West Kingsdown, Kent TN15 6JP
01474-853540
An engine rebuilding and tuning specialist that also
imports products for all forms of motorcycles from
trials to sidecar and road race.

Sylvesters Yamaha
Spring Lane Mills, Woodhead Rd.
Holmfirth, Huddersfield
01484-683665
Yamaha dealer offering mail-order parts service.

Tallon Eninggeering
44 Lynx Trading Estate
Yeovil, Somerset BA20 2NZ
01935-71508
A manufacturer of high-quality wheel and drive-train
products.

Taylor's Racing
23-25 Station Hill Rd.
Chippenham, Wilts. SN15 1EG
01249-444193
A motorcycle shop specializing in Suzuki and
Honda parts and Feroce riding gear.

Terry Rudd Motorcycles
Fen Road Holbeach
Spalding, Lincs. PE12 8QD
01406-422430
Honda dealer specializing in custom-built CRs.

Trick Racing
Toftwood, Stoke, Poges,
Bucks
01753-645087
Importer for Terry Products triple clamps and
Double-Pumper fork kit.

Walker Engineering
P.O. Box 100, Halifax,
West Yorkshire
01422-345568
Motorcycle trailers and racks.

Watkins Radiators
80 Woodruff Close, Robinswood
Gloucester, GL4 6YN
01452-527135
Radiator repair services.

West Country Windings
Unit 71, City Bus. Pk.
Somerset Plc., Stoke, Plymouth
01752-560906
Stator plate rewinding service.

INDEX